Getting Ready for the Big Event

Six to Twelve Months Before the Wedding

1. Discuss with your fiancé what you both want most from this day.
2. Set your wedding date.
3. Talk with a bridal consultant.
4. Get organized. Find what works best for you to keep yourself organized.
5. Use the "Cost Comparison Worksheet" in Chapter 3 to determine your estimated wedding budget.
6. Gather all the players who might or will contribute financially and decide on a realistic budget.
7. Talk to the officiant and reserve your ceremony site.
8. Reserve your reception site.
9. Reserve your caterer.
10. Investigate the different types of wedding photography and book a photographer.
11. Check out using a videographer and hire one.
12. Select a florist.
13. Celebrate the news with your friends and ask them to be in your wedding party.
14. Book both ceremony and reception musicians.
15. Shop for your gown.

Five Months Before the Wedding

1. Order your wedding apparel, including bridesmaids' gowns, and reserve the tuxes.
2. Make your reservations for your honeymoon.

Four Months Before the Wedding

1. Order your invitations, other wedding stationery, and paper supplies.

Three Months Before the Wedding

1. Order your wedding cake and the groom's cake.

Two Months Before the Wedding

1. Meet with the florist to begin planning your floral décor.

Six Weeks Before the Wedding

1. Plan the menu for the rehearsal dinner.
2. Arrange for any special transportation.

Five Weeks Before the Wedding

1. Mail the invitations.

alpha
books

tear here

Top Ten Wedding Survival Tips

1. Sit down with your fiancé and talk about what you want this wedding to be. The wedding needs to reflect your personalities and your priorities. It is *your* wedding, so you need to make sure it's the type of wedding you both want to have.

2. Allow plenty of time to plan. Weddings are detail-oriented events. The more time you have on your side, the wiser you will spend those wedding dollars.

3. Find a system that will help keep you organized. There are all kinds of systems out there, from CD-ROMs to three-ring binders. The catch is actually *using* the system. All the details concerning your wedding need to be kept in one place.

4. Get everyone together who has a part in paying for this event and discuss the type of wedding you two want. The "What's Important to Us Worksheet" and "Cost Comparison Worksheet" in Chapter 3 can help you determine your budget. Then, work within that budget. Do your homework and become an intelligent wedding consumer.

5. Keep the lines of communications open with all parties as much as possible. This isn't always easy to do with our scattered society and blended families, but the more you share about what is being planned and ask for advice from family members, the more they will feel included and less stressed about the plans you are making.

6. Learn to compromise. Some compromise will be necessary to keep costs under control. Be prepared to know what is most important to you, and then let go of some of the smaller, less-important items.

7. Keep your sense of humor. If you get into an argument over plans, take a deep breath and start over. Wedding planning is extremely stressful, so try to keep things in perspective.

8. Only take one friend or relative with you to help shop for your gown. The more opinions you are offered, the more difficult it will be for you to make a decision.

9. Exercise and recreation you enjoy can do wonders for stress relief. Schedule times for recreation and exercise into your calendar just like you would an appointment with the caterer. Also, eat right and get enough sleep!

10. Take time to savor this time in your life. Sure, there are lots of details to worry about, but take time to relax and enjoy this time with your fiancé and your families. It should be fun!

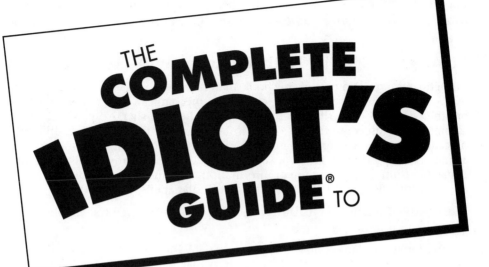

THE COMPLETE IDIOT'S GUIDE® TO

The Perfect Wedding

Third Edition

by Teddy Lenderman

alpha books

Macmillan USA, Inc.
201 West 103rd Street
Indianapolis, IN 46290

A Pearson Education Company

For my wonderful sons, Andy and Ben—the men in my life. I'll love you forever! And in loving memory of Dorothy Penner, my mentor and dear friend.

Copyright © 2000 by Teddy Lenderman

International Standard Book Number: 0-02-863894-8
Library of Congress Catalog Card Number: Available upon request.

02   01   00   8   7   6   5   4   3   2   1

Interpretation of the printing code: The rightmost number of the first series of numbers is the year of the book's printing; the rightmost number of the second series of numbers is the number of the book's printing. For example, a printing code of 00-1 shows that the first printing occurred in 2000.

Printed in the United States of America

Publisher
Marie Butler-Knight

Product Manager
Phil Kitchel

Managing Editor
Cari Luna

Acquisitions Editor
Amy Zavatto

Development Editor
Amy Gordon

Production Editor
Christy Wagner

Copy Editor
Krista Hansing

Illustrator
Jody P. Schaeffer

Cover Designers
Mike Freeland
Kevin Spear

Book Designers
Scott Cook and Amy Adams of DesignLab

Indexer
Tonya Heard

Layout/Proofreading
Angela Calvert
Svetlana Dominguez
Betsy Smith

Contents at a Glance

Appendixes

Contents

Foreword

The good only gets better.

When Teddy Lenderman wrote the first edition of *The Complete Idiot's Guide to the Perfect Wedding,* she drew on years of experience and tapped into the resources of the Association of Bridal Consultants to gather examples from around the world. Now, in this third edition, she has kept the best from the first two editions and added new material. This book reflects the best knowledge, wit, and wisdom of one of the world's best wedding professionals. More than a "how-to" book, it combines practical advice with realistic suggestions on why you should do some things and what you can eliminate to maintain both your budget and your sanity.

Your wedding is a milestone in your life. There are three major rites of passage in everyone's life—birth, marriage, and death. Your wedding is the only one you can control. And that is a key. It is the day you can control. It is your special day, not your mother's ... or your sister's ... or your aunt's ... or your wedding consultant's. Keep it in perspective, though. We often hear marketing pitches that this is "the most important day of your life." Well, if that's true, then everything else that follows—including your wedding night and the birth of your first child—is of lesser importance. Yes, it is an important day, hopefully one that will never be repeated.

Keep in mind, too, the importance of the various elements of the day. Too many brides place too much emphasis on the reception. The key to the day is the ceremony. You are pledging your life to someone else, someone with whom you plan to spend your life. That is what is important. The reception, in reality, is just a party. Probably the biggest party you will ever throw, but still just a party! Teddy helps you keep all the elements in their proper places. She does this with her own brand of humor. She is, to use one of her favorite descriptive words, a "hoot"—and she writes as she speaks. But she also writes from experience. Teddy is a Master Bridal Consultant, the highest educational designation the Association of Bridal Consultants awards. With almost 2,300 members worldwide, there are only 19 Master Bridal Consultants. Laugh with her; learn from her.

There is no such thing as a perfect wedding. If yours is perfect, then you and your guests will have nothing to look back on and laugh about. Beyond major challenges, laugh off the minor "disasters" and have a blast! If your wedding works well, there will be minor glitches that you can laugh about, but your guests will talk about the good things for years to come.

If you are going to plan your own wedding, this book will be an invaluable guide; you should be able to plan easily, efficiently, and with little stress. If you plan to use a bridal consultant, then use this book to help you develop the intelligent questions to help you work better with the consultant. Above all, enjoy the planning and the wedding itself. And enjoy this book. It is one of the best investments you can make.

Gerard J. Monaghan
President, Association of Bridal Consultants
New Milford, Connecticut

Introduction

We are here, the new millennium, the year 2000. Today's wedding couples are more mature, have their careers fairly well in place, and are eager to get the planning process started. Many times the couple pays for the wedding and reception themselves. There are all kinds of options out there for the engaged couple; from having a weekend wedding to flying off to a exotic destination wedding site, to the traditional wedding at home. Whatever your plans or ideas, it sometimes seems that you have to be a genius to pull off a successful wedding.

Thousands of complex questions are just lurking out there, waiting to be answered. It's hard to know where to go or whom to turn to for help. You start thinking, "I must be an idiot. I don't have the faintest idea where to begin."

Well, you're not an idiot—not even close. You are, however, about to become a wedding consumer. You will have lots of questions, and you will need many, many answers.

You deserve honest answers to your questions and some guidance from someone who knows this industry inside and out. You also deserve to be treated with respect by vendors. This book tries to answer your questions and provide you with the information you need to gain the respect of vendors. It also attempts to guide you through the months of planning that lie ahead.

Weddings, although one of life's most traditional events, have changed over the past few years. And this book has also changed, too. While it still focuses on traditional wedding ceremonies and receptions and gives you a general overview of the process, it keeps you current with new trends and new ideas. It emphasizes to use your uniqueness to its fullest to make this wedding yours. There are many, many choices out there. Mom may not be in the picture to help. And Mom might not be paying for this wedding. There are changes, but with a little help from this book, you will be able to glide through this process without much friction.

This book is the result of the experience and satisfaction I have gained in helping more than 310 couples enjoy the wedding of their dreams. In 1985, I began my wedding consulting business, Bearable Weddings by Teddy. In the ensuing 15 years, I have shared ideas with and learned from dozens of other wedding professionals through countless seminars and conferences. I have learned the hard way how to choose competent and professional vendors and how to avoid potential nightmares. I have also broadened my horizons through the give-and-take of teaching a noncredit course, "How to Plan and Enjoy Your Wedding," for Indiana State University in Terre Haute, Indiana.

I've always been a believer in continuing education, and in 1993 I obtained the highest level of recognition that the Association of Bridal Consultants awards: Master Bridal Consultant. It took me seven years to achieve that, but my learning never stops. I learn so much from the brides and grooms I've had the pleasure of working with—that alone could fill a book.

I've been where you are right now about 310 times. I know the frustration you are feeling, the intimidation, and the feelings of being overwhelmed at the same time that you're so happy you could just burst.

Well, slow down. Take a deep breath and get ready for some major work on understanding the wedding industry. That knowledge will help you gain an insight into a field you probably know nothing about. Once you have some understanding and knowledge of what is out there as far as the wedding industry goes, you will be better equipped to be an intelligent wedding consumer.

You wouldn't rush right out and buy a new car without first studying the car industry and trying to figure out what is best for your particular needs and value. No, you'd pick up brochures, talk to friends and family, go into the car dealership and look around, ask questions, and get a feel. Right? So what's so different about shopping in the wedding industry?

Nothing—absolutely nothing.

That's what this book is all about. You—the bride and groom—will learn what can help make your life and the lives of your family and friends so much easier. It's really not difficult, but it will require some time and energy on your part. The sole purpose of this book is to take the overwhelmingly complicated task of planning a wedding and make it E–A–S–Y.

How to Use This Book

Before you spend that first dime, I suggest that you read this book from cover to cover. Try not to get so carried away with the romance and the newness of being engaged that you lose your sense of perspective.

Use a highlighter to mark the points you need to understand more fully. Take notes on possible vendors you want to contact. Really use this book! The book's unique design will give you all the help you need. The more you use it, the easier your planning will be. Do not rush right out and reserve a catering hall, for example, before you read this book. Let me help you determine what to look for in a facility that's going to be a big part of your wedding day and your wedding dollars.

Become an intelligent wedding consumer, and spend your dollars wisely. Understand your responsibilities, and figure out the best way to approach them. Most of all, enjoy! This should be one of the most pleasant, fun-filled, exciting times in a couple's life. This book can help with that. It won't make the process of planning perfect, but it can help take the bumps out of the road to a very bearable wedding.

Included in this book are worksheets associated with particular chapters. For example, the chapter on photography contains a worksheet to help you select your photographer. Record your discussions with the photographer on the worksheet, and make notes on anything else you feel is important. Within each chapter, you will be given questions to ask the professionals. Read those sections very carefully so that you can ask intelligent questions.

In the front of this book is a tear-out card containing the key survival tips for planning your wedding. While this card can't possibly sum up what this book covers, it does offer some key points for you to consider. Tear out this card and carry it with you over the months of planning.

To help you get the most out of this book, you will see the following special information boxes scattered throughout:

Nuptial Notes

Terms and definitions that might come in handy.

Teddy's Tips

Tips or timesavers that can help you be more efficient.

Wedding Woes

Warnings and solutions to common problems you might encounter.

Bouquet Toss

Wedding trivia provided just for comic relief.

Acknowledgments

Wow! The third edition of this book. Whoever would have thought that a bridal consultant from the Midwest (Indiana, of all places) would be asked to write a book on weddings. The first edition went well, the second edition did well for the short amount of time it was on the market, and now I am putting on the finishing touches to the third edition. My thanks to Macmillan for having the confidence and trust in me to write this edition. To my Acquisitions Editor, Amy Zavatto, your support, humor, and patience have meant a great deal to me. Thank you very much. And to all the other "behind-the-scenes folks" at Macmillan, thank you, too. You are the ones who make my job easy.

The photography in this book comes from five great photographers. They cover weddings from coast to coast. A big thanks to them for donating their pictures for this edition:

Classic Contemporary Photography by Geno
Indianapolis, Indiana
317-255-9000

Colter Photography
Rushville, Indiana
765-629-2044

Gregeiger Company Unlimited, Inc.
Orange, Connecticut
203-795-8651

Stephanie Hogue Photography
Oxnard, California
805-985-6022

Wyant Photography, Inc.
Zionsville, Indiana
317-873-2282

Trademarks

All terms mentioned in this book that are known to be or are suspected of being trademarks or service marks have been appropriately capitalized. Alpha Books and Macmillan USA, Inc. cannot attest to the accuracy of this information. Use of a term in this book should not be regarded as affecting the validity of any trademark or service mark.

Part 1

Don't Spend a Dime Yet!

You're engaged to a wonderful person. You've been floating on cloud nine since the proposal. You've announced the good news to your family and friends, and now you can't wait to get started on the wedding plans.

Catch your breath, let your feet touch down for a moment, and ready yourself to read Part 1. This part introduces you to some of the things you should know before you write that first check. You'll find advice on how to start your planning, which questions to ask, and where to go for help. You'll learn how to determine the type of wedding you want to have and how that decision affects your wedding budget.

Planning a wedding is a big deal, and the wedding business is big business. The more you know about the industry and how to use it to your advantage, the better your planning will be and the more relaxed you'll be when you finally walk down that aisle.

Chapter 1

Your First Step Toward the Altar—Getting Started

> **In This Chapter**
>
> ➤ Getting organized
>
> ➤ Investigating bridal shows
>
> ➤ Utilizing the Internet
>
> ➤ Tapping into other helpful resources

As I mentioned in the introduction to this book, you wouldn't go out and buy the first car you saw without doing some research on its qualities or gas mileage; you might even consult *Consumer Reports* for expert tips. Likewise, you wouldn't have brain surgery without first consulting and interviewing several doctors. And you wouldn't go looking for the perfect home without the help of a reputable real-estate agent. The same is true for the wedding industry. You need to understand what's out there and what's available before you start spending those precious dollars.

So, before you make that first purchase, you need to understand what the wedding industry is all about and how to get yourself organized. I'll also provide you with other resources that can help you along your path to wedding bliss.

Understanding the Wedding Industry

The first thing you need to know about weddings in this country is that the wedding industry is big business. In 1999, the wedding industry grossed between $38 to $42 billion dollars, second only to the Christmas season in retail. Now, that figure just doesn't cover the wedding itself. It also covers things like setting up your new home, the honeymoon, and your rings. But the big day is still a significant piece of the cake. That's also something that many first-time wedding couples fail to understand. Just knowing how big the industry is might give you some perspective on why you don't want to rush right out and reserve the first reception site you see. This wedding process will cost you some money—you don't have to mortgage the house to have the wedding of your dreams, but you do have to plan wisely.

Finding a System to Keep Yourself Organized

The number-one suggestion I make to the brides I work with is to find and use some kind of organizational system. It doesn't matter what this is, whether it's a three-ring binder, a CD-ROM program, or a folder with pockets. (Obviously, this book will be a big part of your system, and it should be.) The type of system you choose to use really doesn't matter. What matters is that you use it. Keep everything that relates to your wedding in this system: receipts, contracts, material swatches, a calendar with appointments marked, phone numbers of all your vendors, and reminder lists. Make sure you have this system with you whenever you visit a vendor. Even if you're not an organized person, force yourself to become more so. Your system should be so much a part of your being that when you are without it, you feel like you are missing something. Let me explain why this is so important.

Usually, I pick up my client's bridal gown the day of her wedding and take it to the ceremony site for her. On one routine run to a bridal shop to get the gown for a bride, I told the shop owner who I was and what I was there for. She then informed me that the bride still owed $350 on the gown. Now, during the years, I have purchased small, last-minute items for brides when the situation warranted it, and then we settle later.

However, $350 was a bit beyond a small item. I called the bride and explained the problem—she not only told me that the shop was in error, but she also produced the receipt for the gown marked "Paid in Full." So, I drove to her home, picked up the receipt, and drove back to the shop. The owner grudgingly admitted that the mistake was hers, and I left the shop with the gown. Moral of the story: Had the bride not been organized and able to produce the receipt (a mere three hours before the wedding), she would have handed over another $350 to get the gown out of hock. Keep yourself organized, even if it's not something that comes naturally to you. It will pay off in the end.

Teddy's Tips

Be patient with yourself! Taking some time now to read and understand what you need to do will pay off later. Keep every receipt, and keep them together in one place! You never know when you might have to produce one quickly.

Investigating Bridal Shows

So, you've figured out a system you're comfortable with and one that you will use. Now what? Depending on how much time you have, you may want to attend a bridal show in your area.

What to Expect

Bridal shows are great ways to meet the vendors from your area whose services you will be using. These shows are usually promoted by area merchants to let the community know what wedding services are available in the area. Merchants rent booth space to display the products or services they can offer the customer. Interested customers visit with these merchants at their booths.

The usual format for such events might include time to talk with individual vendors, a fashion show by area bridal shops, and sometimes drawings for door prizes the vendors provide. One bride I know attended a show two years ago and won the grand prize: two round-trip tickets to Hawaii! Not a bad deal for giving up a Sunday afternoon.

The whole idea behind bridal shows is twofold: You get to see what's available in your area, and the vendor gets your name and address for possible contact. The bride and groom, or the parents of a bride or groom, can browse the different vendors and get a feel for what they have to offer. Sometimes, you will be able to tell whether a vendor can provide what you need by just looking at the booth setup. If crepe-paper streamers and balloons decorate the booth and you're thinking more in terms of satin ribbon and crystal, then you should look at other displays.

Bouquet Toss

One reason the diamond is a popular stone for engagement rings is because the ancients believed that its sparkle arose from the flames of love. Ancient people also believed that the bride should wear a diamond on the third finger of the left hand because that finger is said to have the only vein that runs directly to the heart.

How to Get the Most from a Bridal Show

Okay, so you're walking around the floor of the local civic center trying to take in all this wedding stuff, with your arms getting longer by the moment as your little tote bags get weighted down with brochures, pamphlets, and other promotional items. To get the most from your visit, you need to talk to the folks behind the booths, although the better vendors will never be behind their booths—they will be out in the aisle, meeting and greeting prospective clients. Hear what they have to say. Is it a hard-sell? Does the product look like something you would want to have at your wedding? Are the vendors personable? Do they seem to know what customer service means? Pick up any handouts or brochures they offer, and make notes on items you particularly like. When you get home, you can spread out your notes and brochures and see what's available. This can give you a good starting point.

Teddy's Tips

Watch for professional behavior from vendors: appearance, mannerisms (gum chewing—yuck), good grammar, eye contact, and so on. How do they present themselves? Do they act bored or interested?

The real reason the vendors at a bridal show agree to give up an entire Sunday is that they receive a list of all attendees at the show. You probably will receive some flyers or direct-mail pieces from some of the vendors following the show. Many times, you will receive additional coupons or discounts from these vendors after the show.

Now, remember: Not all wedding vendors use the medium of the bridal show to advertise. Many bridal shows are very expensive for participants. You may find that several of the more established vendors choose not to participate in shows. Every wedding professional has a preferred method of advertising, and bridal shows are only one of those methods. What bridal shows will do is give you a feel for the services offered in your area.

Using the Internet

The Internet has grown so much since I last updated this book in 1997 that the changes are hard to keep up with. The Web sites you can choose from are endless, and the mass of information can easily rattle the most patient person's sanity.

Michael Connor of WdWEB.Company—Wedding Detail—Party Detail, in Williamsburg, Michigan, has been helping people with Web sites for years. He knows the wedding sites you should know about like the back of his hand. The following sections contain his advice to you on what the Internet is, how to get hooked up to the Internet, and the best sites available to help with those wedding plans. His Web site is www.wdweb.com. Happy hunting.

Becoming Intimate with the Internet

As the Internet age continues to grow, staying in touch with the right sources can be a daily job. The Web site changed, you can't get hooked up right, or your computer goes out—then what? While using the Internet can be overwhelming, it is a very valuable tool in today's society when it comes time to plan your wedding. The Internet is a place where you can browse information files, exchange information with other people, use e-mail (I love e-mail, and so do most of my clients), and actually buy products or services. You just have to know how to use it.

Beam Me Up, Scottie

Your computer doesn't come already connected to the Internet, although you could find software and programs that help you connect to the Internet on a PC (personal computer) you have purchased. To access the Internet from your PC you need a modem, phone line, software for connecting, and software for e-mail and browsing the World Wide Web (WWW). It would also be very handy to get an Internet Service Provider (ISP) that connects you to the Internet. Here's the equation: PC to phone line to ISP to Internet to WWW. Lucky for you that nowadays most PCs come with a modem already in them, and frequently you can get all your software in one package offered by your ISP.

Teddy's Tips

Check with a friend or local computer store about ISPs that offer local access to the Internet from your community. While the big players—America Online, CompuServe, and AT&T—offer Internet access, ISPs are everywhere and can offer connectivity without long-distance dialing fees. Monthly connectivity fees go from $9.95 on up.

The Web vs. Newsgroups

Once connected to the Internet, you can browse the Web for wedding information or use online bulletin boards, commonly known as newsgroups.

The Web is a collection of hundreds of millions of pages that you can access by using your Web browser software. Two popular Web browsers are Microsoft Internet Explorer and Netscape Navigator. Every page on the Web has an address; by entering either a page address or a site address into your browser, you will be connected to that resource almost instantly. Finding your way around the Internet is often as easy as using links, easy-to-use buttons on a Web page that take you to other Web pages.

Newsgroups are electronic forums where people can ask questions or offer advice and opinions. Questions and answers are posted to the newsgroup for all to see. Two newsgroups that focus on wedding planning are alt.wedding and soc.couples. wedding. Both are valuable sources of great information and ideas to help you plan your wedding.

Show Me Your Sites

In the following sections, Michael Connor tells you which are the most popular sites to browse and then offers "must-see sites" for each item of the planning process I discuss.

Wedding Shows

Two main sites that feature wedding shows are www.bridalfashionshows.com and www.bspishows.com. The Bridal Fashion Show site will send you an e-mail reminder one month and one week before the scheduled live show in your area. It's a great service since bridal shows are a great place to meet local wedding professionals, taste cakes, and view floral displays, dresses, invitations, and items for your new home. Leave the nieces and nephews at home for these shows. There's too much to see to be watching Timmy. An additional site is www.afwpi.com.

Wedding Portals/Directories

Wedding portals/directories are the easiest way to find information on weddings. A portal is like a mall, but everyone in the mall or "portal" is in the same type of business ... the one-stop shopping for weddings. Caterers, bridal shops, coordinators, clergy, and so on, from your area are all located in the same place. This allows you to stop searching the Web and start concentrating on viewing products and contacting professionals. Michael's must-see sites are ...

➤ www.weddingdetails.com

➤ www.weddingchannel.com

➤ www.theknot.com

➤ www.weddingnetwork.com

Honeymoons on the Web

The Internet has opened the door to finding fun and exotic places for your honeymoon. Many locations you may have never heard of before. The Internet also puts pictures, videos, and detailed information right at your fingertips, making your choice much easier.

If you do a general search for "honeymoons," for example, using AltaVista (www.altavista.com), 113,080 sites and 27 different directories come up. That's a lot of pages to visit. If you try to be more specific in your search, for example, typing "Tahiti honeymoon," your search yields fewer sites. The easiest method is to use a honeymoon planning Web site or travel agency Web site to locate specific information. Some sites to visit are ...

➤ www.honeymoon-information.com

➤ www.honeymoons.com

➤ www.afterido.com

➤ www.weddingbells.com

➤ www.cruisingtoparadise.com

Wedding Stores Online

There are several sites that have thousands of products, from favors to centerpieces and everything in between. By checking out these sites, you will come up with a multitude of ideas, products, and options to fit your budget and taste. Once you decide on your wedding theme and colors, it will be very easy to visit these online stores and order without having to drive around the state. To make good use of these sites, make a list of products you want to order, their prices, and the Web site; then make another notation on this list that shows when you ordered an item and a phone number for that order. Sites to see are …

➤ www.theweddingshopper.com

➤ www.modernbride.com

➤ www.weddingsuperstore.com

➤ www.bridallink.com/store2

Personal Bridal Pages

Should you have a Web page? The answer is YES! It will save you time and money and will help you communicate better with your family and friends. Imagine your page with a picture of the two of you and a little background information. Then add a brief synopsis of your jobs, hobbies, and heritage so that friends and family can get better acquainted with you. Post your wedding date, time location, and reception information and include a map. What a blessing for out-of-town guests. Also, include where you are registered for gifts. Many national chain stores are online and linked with their stores all over the world. Two Web sites that allow you to set up your own personal Web page for your wedding free of charge are …

➤ www.weddingdetails.com

➤ www.theknot.com

Wedding Advice on the Web

Right now (because the Web changes so much), there is only one site that will allow you to ask a question and get a personal answer back via e-mail: Wedding Details (www.weddingdetails.com).

Wedding Details has a variety of experts and professionals ready to assist you in every way. From questions about etiquette, to dancing pointers (that first dance with Dad), to tradition and cultural advice, this site has the experts to answer your questions.

Online Bridal Registry

It has never been easier to register online. With thousands of items to choose from and all those extra ones you want to register for, you can't miss. Online registry offers you the convenience of registering where you like without having to worry about whether or not a certain store is in your area. Perhaps you would like to add a glass vase from Macy's in New York to your list, but most of your friends and family are in Idaho. Online registry is the answer, allowing friends to order conveniently and safely over the Internet. The Della Weddings online registry (www.dellaweddings.com) is linked to a number of stores, including Dillards, Neiman Marcus, Williams Sonoma, Crate & Barrell, and Gumps. Other sites to see are ...

➤ www.theknot.com

➤ www.weddingnetwork.com

Finding a Wedding Consultant Online

The largest organization for bridal consultants in the world is the Association of Bridal Consultants (ABC) with over 2,400 members. ABC has made it easy to find a consultant in your area by allowing you to send in an e-mail request. They will locate a consultant near you and send you his or her information. (More about bridal consultants in Chapter 2, "Wake Me When It's over—Hiring a Bridal Consultant.") Two sites that will help are ...

➤ www.bridalassn.com

➤ www.weddingdetails.com

Using the Library

Although using the library isn't as fast as using the Web, it can be a dependable source when getting started with your wedding plans. Libraries contain many resources, the most obvious being magazines you can browse through for inspiration and ideas. Libraries also may have a resource guide to either wedding vendors in your area or a other wedding-related materials. For example, a local library might list possible wedding sites and the contacts for those facilities in one of its resource guides. It never hurts to check with your local librarian.

Asking Friends for Suggestions

Friends, both well-meaning and otherwise, are another source of information during the early stages of wedding planning. Friends who have married recently can be especially helpful. Find out who they used for the various service providers and what they thought of the vendors. Find out where they held the reception, whether they were pleased with the facility, and what it offered. Ask which caterer they used and which florist. Find out if they were pleased with the wedding photography, and ask how and when photographs were taken. What would they do differently now?

Find out how the wedding day went and what they could have done to make it better. Ask about any problems they had and what they could have done to prevent them. Pick their brains; most newly married brides and grooms are pretty talkative about their wedding day. Try to pin them down. If Mary Ann tells you that her wedding day was one of the most embarrassing days of her life, find out why. Did the wrong flowers arrive at the church? Did the cake really fall over into the punch bowl?

If the couple had to do it over again, what would they change, or what would they do the same? Get specifics! Generalities in this area don't offer you much insight. "The flowers were pretty" may be a nice sentiment, but it's more helpful to know whether the florist followed the color scheme, had a professional business manner, and delivered the flowers on time. In other words, was this florist a vendor that you should consider contracting? Ask to view wedding photographs and wedding video. Get all the details you can.

Bouquet Toss

You think you have problems? How would you like to select a new wedding ring every year? That's what the primitive brides had to do. Their rings were circles of hemp or rushes woven together into the shape of a circle. Because the fibers disintegrated over a period of time, women had to replace their rings every year.

Taking a Class to Learn More

Many colleges (community or otherwise) offer adult-education classes, many of which are offered solely for enjoyment and cover a wide range of topics. If there's a college or university in your area, check out the resources there.

Since 1988, I've taught a noncredit course for Indiana State University called "Enjoy Your Wedding." It runs for five weeks every spring, and sometimes also in the fall. I've had good comments from the students, and I've learned so much from them, too. I know they are learning the information they will need to wade through the countless hours, days, and weeks of wedding planning.

So if you're trying to figure out where to begin with this monumental task, or if you need some direction in finding and dealing with vendors, see if you can take a class in your area that can provide you with some guidance and some answers.

The Least You Need to Know

➤ Take your time to become informed. Read this book thoroughly, take notes, and browse wedding magazines. Determine what you want your wedding to be.

➤ Use a system of organization—a CD-ROM program, a notebook, or a folder—to hold your receipts, brochures, fabric swatches, appointment calendar, and so on.

➤ Check out the Internet for information regarding anything and everything to do with your wedding.

➤ Ask recently married couples for advice. Get all the specifics you can. Find out what they would do differently and what they were happy with. Find out the details of why they liked or disliked particular vendors.

➤ Look for adult-education classes that can help you get started and that can provide some guidance on how to deal with vendors.

Chapter 2

Wake Me When It's over—Hiring a Bridal Consultant

> ## In This Chapter
>
> ➤ Understanding what a bridal consultant is
>
> ➤ Determining whether you need a bridal consultant
>
> ➤ Choosing and using a bridal consultant
>
> ➤ Finding out what a bridal consultant can do for you

I've often wondered just how the business of bridal consulting or wedding coordinators came about. I think it has always been a part of the wedding stages, but either Mom or Aunt Tilly, who were experts in strategic planning, military combat, and details upon details, probably took over that role. We don't have moms with that much time anymore. We are a much more scattered society, and we are a society that uses specialists in almost every field. The wedding industry is no different.

This chapter will help clear your thinking on what exactly bridal consultants can and can't do for you, and it will give you an idea of the role they can play in your wedding. They're not for every wedding, but a good consultant can make your life so much easier and less stressfull. Read on and discover the world of consultants.

So Who Are These People, Anyway?

First of all, let's define some terms. A *bridal consultant* is someone who consults with brides and grooms (and often with members of their families) about planning, coordinating, or arranging for a wedding. An *independent bridal consultant* is a consultant who does not work with another vendor, such as a florist or caterer, but instead has a self-contained bridal consulting business. A *wedding coordinator* is someone who helps coordinate or conduct the wedding activities. A *wedding day coordinator* works onsite for the rehearsal and for the day of the wedding to ensure that the wedding flows smoothly.

A *wedding director* is similar to a wedding day coordinator; the term is relatively common in the South. A *church wedding coordinator* is someone on the staff of a church or in a church's women's group. Usually, she's not a true wedding consultant or coordinator, but rather someone who makes sure the church's rules are followed. There's also the *wedding professional,* which describes anyone in the wedding business but doesn't specifically mean that the person is a consultant or a coordinator.

Sounds pretty confusing, doesn't it? The independent bridal consultant and wedding coordinator are the focus of this chapter. For simplicity's sake, the term *bridal consultant* is used to cover both consultants and coordinators, unless specifically stated otherwise. Although these people sometimes have different responsibilities, many of their functions overlap. Some bridal consultants, for example, do not coordinate the activities on the actual wedding day (but most do).

The Evolution of the Bridal Consultant

One of the rapidly changing areas of the wedding industry today is the increase in the number of bridal consultants being hired by couples. Out of simple necessity, these professionals are becoming an integral part of the wedding industry. In today's society, the boy next door seldom marries the girl next door. Families often live in various parts of the country, and there's a need for someone local to be available as a home base.

The development of bridal consulting parallels—and, in some ways, has helped create—the development of the wedding industry. Before 1980, there was usually little coordination among vendors. In some cases, for example, the photographer might not even know what the gown looked like before the wedding day. The consultant helps ensure that all the vendors communicate with each other and that the wedding industry pulls together to make each wedding a coordinated affair, as close to perfection as possible.

I often help out-of-town brides who want someone to coordinate the details with the folks at home. For

Teddy's Tips

In 1982, the Association of Bridal Consultants had two members in the entire world. As of November, 1999, it has a world-wide membership of more than 2,500.

example, the local newspaper called a couple years ago to interview me for an article on the business of weddings. They wanted to follow one bride through the last month of her wedding-planning stages. They wanted to go to all the final consultations, have a photographer capture the moment on film, and see just how that last month of planning ticked off. Of the five weddings I had scheduled for that June, only one had a local bride. All the others were out-of-town brides who had hired me to make sure someone on the home turf knew what was happening and to take care of the details. This is one of the prime reasons you may want to include a bridal consultant on your vendor list.

Timing Is Everything

Another major reason the bridal consultant has become so popular is that so many women are working full-time—often in time-consuming, fast-track careers—and simply don't have the time or energy to take on the monumental task of planning a wedding. Gone are the days when the mom was at home and had time for such large projects as planning her daughter's wedding. Most of the mothers I work with are also career women. Time is a valuable commodity, and career women understand that.

The bridal consultant also serves other purposes. Even if the couple and both sets of parents are local, they will have little experience dealing with wedding vendors, unless they plan weddings for a living. That's why Chapter 1, "Your First Step Toward the Altar—Getting Started," emphasized just how big the industry is. When you choose a bridal consultant who has planned many weddings in your area, she knows which vendors to steer you to for the budget you have in mind. She also knows which vendors to avoid and why. She's a combination counselor, financial adviser, etiquette expert, organizer, referee, and, at times, a good friend. She can make your life so much easier. It's still your wedding; it's not the consultant's wedding, your mother's wedding, or your fiancé's mother's wedding. It's the wedding that you and your fiancé want it to be. The bridal consultant's only purposes are to make your plans come true, to make your day run smoothly, and to help make both of you look your best.

As an example of how a bridal consultant can help you, let me tell you a story. For the second wedding that I coordinated back in 1985, I was brought in to make the long-awaited day a reality. The mother of the bride and the bride had done most of the legwork and brought me in during the last month to pull things together.

On the big day, the bride and the bridesmaids were busy getting dressed when the bride's mother came up to me outside the dressing room. She had that panicked look on her face that I have now come to know and understand. She said, "Okay, now what?" I explained that everything was running on time and smoothly (so I thought, at the time), and said she should go back into the dressing room and savor this time with her daughter. With a huge sigh of relief, she returned to the dressing room, thrilled that she didn't have to perform any other task at that moment.

Meanwhile, back in the church lobby, I discovered that the florist had forgotten all three grandmothers' corsages, so I called the florist to have them delivered. Then the trumpet player called the church and informed me that he'd had too much to drink at the rehearsal dinner and couldn't play for the wedding. I immediately inquired whether he needed help dressing and driving to the church or whether he could manage that himself. He was so taken aback that I didn't excuse him that he muttered something about not needing any help. He showed up a little green, but he played a fine trumpet—and that's all I cared about.

Then the flower girl (ah, children in weddings, now that could be an entire chapter in itself—see Chapter 6, "The Wedding Party—a Circle of Friends," for more on flower girls, as well as other participants in the ceremony) caught the flounce of her dress on a nail and ripped off the entire thing, except for four inches. I thought, "Geez, what else?" and then found out how handy a stapler could be. I was able to staple the dress and flounce together, and no one was the wiser. Neither the mother, nor the bride, nor anyone in the family knew a thing about all this turmoil taking place just an hour before the wedding.

It just so happened that this particular mother of the bride was a writer for the local paper. Two weeks after the wedding, the mother's column, titled "The Wedding Day," appeared in the paper. It was about being in that dressing room helping her daughter prepare for her wedding and having her daughter's life flash before her eyes: bringing her home from the hospital, surviving her tomboyish stages, going off on her first date and the proms—all those wonderful things that mothers and fathers store away in their memory banks.

Hiring a bridal consultant to attend to all the last-minute crises and details gave that mother and daughter time together at a very special moment in their lives. Had the mother been out arguing with the florist and the trumpeter or trying to coax a four-year-old into holding still long enough to have her dress stapled, she would have missed that time with her daughter.

Wedding Woes

Read the Yellow Pages carefully! Don't be fooled by the heading you find a vendor's name under. Make sure that vendor's expertise and experience match the qualifications you're looking for.

Obviously, there's another benefit the professional bridal consultant offers: quality time. Keep that in mind when you look for a bridal consultant. You want someone who is going to give you peace of mind and quality time on your wedding day.

What You See Is Not Always What You Get

Along the path leading up to your wedding, you're likely to run into wedding professionals who refer to themselves as bridal consultants. The florist who works with the bride is consulting the bride about the flower needs for her special day. The salesperson in the bridal shop also might refer to herself as a bridal consultant because she works directly with brides concerning gowns and accessories. The photographer, the catering manager, and the reception site coordinator all might refer to themselves as bridal consultants as well.

Most of the time, however, their expertise is in a particular area of the wedding business, such as a *floral bridal consultant.* Don't confuse these specialized consultants with a bridal consultant who deals with the entire wedding process. Use your Yellow Pages wisely. Just because the DJ is listed under "Wedding Consultants" does not mean that he or she knows the first thing about planning a wedding.

What Is the Consultant's Role?

Working one-on-one with the bride and her family from the engagement to the honeymoon, the bridal consultant can ensure that all aspects of your wonderful day happen as you had planned. Some couples hire consultants as soon as they announce their engagement. I've actually had mothers call me for advice and counsel before their daughters even have a ring, much less have a date chosen. Other couples choose to hire a consultant near the end of the process—six weeks or so from the actual day—to pull together those loose ends and to oversee the rehearsal and wedding day activities. The bottom line here is that you should decide just how much you want to involve the bridal consultant. You're the boss; the final choice always should be yours.

Bouquet Toss

The rules of traditional American wedding etiquette haven't changed since the early twentieth century, when Emily Post and Amy Vanderbilt wrote their now famous treatises. While some traditions remain intact, other customs have relaxed over the years. At the turn of the century, for example, proper wedding etiquette dictated that the receiver of a wedding invitation must respond formally, in writing, to the sender. No response cards were enclosed back then. While that idea is still "proper etiquette," that practice is all but forgotten, and the enclosure response card is a standard part of wedding invitations today.

There are no "wedding police" out there. If you truly want to do something at your wedding or during the planning stages that may not be proper etiquette, get some impartial advice. Try to determine whether the custom truly is not in good taste or whether it simply wasn't a custom practiced at the turn of the century. It may be one no one would bat an eye at in the year 2000 and beyond.

You might decide that you just want to bend a consultant's ear for a couple hours to help you get started. I've had several brides who were getting married away from my area make an appointment to get some advice about how to begin. That's fine. If that's all the help you think you'll need, then definitely take that route.

How to Find the Right Consultant for Your Wedding

As mentioned earlier, you can check out the Yellow Pages as a first step in locating a competent bridal consultant, as long as you review the listings carefully. The best method, however, is to ask friends and family for names of consultants they have used. Many vendors will also recommend bridal consultants in their area they have worked with and whom they feel comfortable with. In addition, the church may have worked with bridal consultants they felt especially good about having at the wedding. You also can get the names of consultants in your area by contacting certain trade associations, such as the Association of Bridal Consultants. This association is located in Connecticut (860-355-0464; fax 860-354-1404) and will be happy to give you names of members in your area.

Asking the Right Questions

Start by making an appointment with the bridal consultant. Telephone interviews leave a lot to the imagination; you'll understand whom you're dealing with if you sit down face to face. Sometimes there's a charge for this meeting, so ask about charges when you call for the appointment. Ask for references of other brides with whom the consultant has worked. Ask how she charges—is it by the hour, a flat fee, or a percentage? Make sure you completely understand costs.

Ask about what she can do for you, and also ask if there are things she will not take care of for you. Does she use a contract or a letter of agreement? A contract should protect both you and the consultant from problems caused by misunderstandings. Make sure it spells out, in reasonable detail, who—including you and Aunt Tilly—will do what, when, and for how much. Does the bridal consultant require a deposit or a retainer?

Get a feel for who this person is. She should put you first. You should feel as though you're her only client and that she will bend over backward to make your wedding as special and stress-free as possible. Check out the "Bridal Consultant/Wedding Coordinator Worksheet" at the end of this chapter to help you ask the right questions.

As I said earlier, this is your wedding, not the bridal consultant's, and you need to know and understand just what role the bridal consultant will play in your wedding. Ask if she takes commissions from vendors. Although it's perfectly acceptable for her to do so, you still should decide which vendors you will use.

On occasion, I have had prospective clients ask if they can observe me at a wedding before they make the decision to hire me. I have absolutely no problem with that, as long as they dress appropriately and let me do my work, and as long as I have my client's approval. They can see me in action, doing what I'm good at and what I love. And, so far, they have always decided to hire me.

Be aware that, just as with other service providers, there are bad apples in the bridal consultant barrel as well. Analyze the conversation in your first meeting with the consultant. If she uses the word "I" lots in the conversation with you, hear what she's really saying: "I want to have candy for your favors." "I want the flowers to be in shades of pink." "I see your wedding as a very formal affair." "I hope you'll use engraved invitations." "I'm sure you'll want a seated dinner instead of just hors d'oeuvres." Hey, whose wedding is this anyway? Listen carefully to what she says and how much pressure she asserts.

Many people call themselves bridal consultants simply because they have assisted with a family or friend's wedding. These individuals most likely do not have the experience and resources you will find with a professional bridal consultant who has been in the business for a while and whose very livelihood depends on maintaining a good reputation.

Wedding Woes

Any time you ask for a reference and the vendor won't provide it, look elsewhere.

Deciding Whether a Consultant Can Help You

When the wedding professionals have a wedding in the family, you might think they would cross over boundaries and try to do it all. Not so, according to Cele Lalli, retired editor-in-chief of *Modern Bride* magazine, and certainly one of the leading wedding experts in the country. When her daughter, Erica, was married three years ago, Cele didn't hesitate to call in the pros.

She hired a bridal consultant to oversee the entire event and offer overall guidance, and she hired other association members for the rest of the wedding. No conflict arose between her roles of editor/wedding expert and mother of the bride because, she says, "I followed my own advice, called in the pros, and never forgot that the wedding had to reflect what the bride and groom wanted." Her satisfaction in working with experts "who took

Teddy's Tips

I refer to bridal consultants as female because the majority of them are. However, there are competent, professional male bridal consultants out in the trenches, too. According to the Association of Bridal Consultants, 2 percent of all consultants are male.

enormous professional pride in … surpassing our highest expectations" made me feel proud to be a part of this industry.

Teddy's Tips

Look for a bridal consultant who is a member of an organization of wedding professionals. This generally indicates that the consultant is continually learning, growing, and keeping aware of changes and trends in the wedding industry.

Okay, you've met with a bridal consultant. You've found out what she charges, and you like what you're hearing. This consultant has lots of experience, and her credentials are great. Her references check out, but you're just not quite convinced.

Let's get practical here. The bridal consultant can save you time, money, and energy. Because of her repeat buying power, she sometimes can negotiate prices with vendors that the individual cannot. Many times, the bridal consultant will receive a discounted price for suggesting a particular vendor and will pass that savings on to you, the client. Say you want to contract a certain reception facility that rents for $400. You might be able to contract it for less—maybe as much as half—through your experienced bridal consultant. The vendor knows that if his work is good, the consultant will return with other clients. That's what I mean by repeat buying power.

Aside from the repeat buying power issue, you might find that some vendors may not do business with individual couples. One facility I occasionally use will not rent for wedding receptions unless the couple is my client. This facility knows that I will do all that is possible to make sure that the facility is not harmed.

One bride was on a tight budget but felt that she needed the extra guidance and help to get the most for her dollars. We met with the florist and worked out a flower plan. The bride wanted huge bouquets of mixed spring flowers, including irises, roses, orchids, lilies, snapdragons, and tulips. When the estimate came back, it was three times what was in the budget. The bride called, very upset, and asked what to do. Because of the good working relationship I had with the florist, he wanted to work with us and make the bride happy. For less money, we were able to create the same look with less-expensive flowers. (The first thing we did was replace the orchids—at $15 apiece, that seemed like a good place to start.)

Here, the consultant's relationship with the florist helped the bride to save some time and money.

What's It Going to Cost?

The consultant's fee should be included in the overall budget, not considered an add-on. It doesn't matter whether you have $100,000 to spend or $2,000—this cost should be treated the same as your other wedding costs (flowers, reception site, favors). For example, let's say you have $10,000 to spend on the wedding. If the consultant's fee is $1,000, then she should be able to give you a $10,000 wedding for $9,000. Most times, if you engage a bridal consultant, you will stay at or under budget and get more for your money.

Your best friend who offers to coordinate your wedding does not have that repeat buying power, nor the resources or experience to make your day bearable. You need someone impartial. If your best friend is afraid to tell you that your idea stinks because she doesn't want to hurt your feelings, how does that help you? While the bridal consultant doesn't want to hurt your feelings either, she also does not want you to be embarrassed. She will find a tactful way to tell you the truth, and you will thank her for that honesty.

A bridal consultant or wedding coordinator isn't for every bride. However, you should at least be aware that these professionals are one option you can choose in your wedding planning. And they're not just for the big-budget weddings, either. A good consultant can be a valuable asset in putting together the wedding of your dreams.

The Least You Need to Know

➤ Bridal consultants and wedding coordinators can help you with the smallest details of your wedding, from the engagement to the honeymoon, or just the wedding day itself.

➤ Ask friends, check the Yellow Pages, or call the Association of Bridal Consultants to find one in your area.

➤ Interview the potential bridal consultant and ask many questions. Find out about her fee structure and whether she requires a contract. Ask what she's willing to do and what she will not do.

➤ Listen carefully to her presentation in your initial meeting. Is she focused on making this the wedding you want? And don't forget to check her references.

Bridal Consultant/Wedding Coordinator Worksheet

Name: _____

Address: _____

_____

Telephone: _____

Referred by: _____

Other references: _____

_____

_____

_____

Fee: _____

How to be paid (installments? retainer?): _____

Contract required?   Yes _____   No _____

Questions to ask:

> How long in business?

> How many weddings has she coordinated?

> Professional associations?

> How does she view her role?

> Professional education?

> Describe a typical wedding day.

> What can she do and what will she do?

Other questions you may want to ask:

> What are the consultant's background and credentials?

> How does she keep up with changes in the industry?

Chapter 3

Simple or Extravagant— Setting Your Budget

In This Chapter

➤ Deciding how formal you want your wedding to be

➤ Understanding how the level of formality affects your budget

➤ Realizing that money does matter

➤ Using cost comparison

➤ Determining a budget

➤ Determining whom to involve with the finances

This chapter talks about the financial part of the wedding. Ugh! I know it's not a popular topic, but it's necessary. Without a realistic budget in mind, you'll be overspending long before you know it. Before you set a budget, you need to understand several factors to make your wedding dollars count. Read on carefully.

Blue Jeans or Black Tie?

Determining how formal you want your wedding to be will help you establish the basis for your overall wedding strategy. The level of formality you choose determines, to a great extent, the overall cost of your wedding. It's a good idea for all players— the bride, the groom, the in-laws, and anyone else with a financial interest in this wedding—to sit down together and figure out just how fancy you want this affair to be. Essentially, you can choose from the following four levels of formality:

➤ Ultraformal

➤ Formal

➤ Semiformal

➤ Informal

Ultraformal: Glamorous and Glitzy

The fanciest type of wedding you can have is *ultraformal*. This is the kind of wedding a movie star, royalty, or the President's daughter would have. An ultraformal wedding is always very large, both in the number in the wedding party and in the number of guests invited. For an ultraformal wedding, you can expect to have 6 to 12 bridesmaids and more than 350 guests.

Decorations at the ceremony site are extensive, complete with large floral arrangements, many candles, garlands of greens, and tulle and ribbons everywhere. The attire for the wedding party is formal as well. The bridal gown is elaborate and may include beading, pearls, sequins, or a combination of all three. The gown usually has a cathedral-length train and also may have a floor-length veil. The bride's attendants dress similarly, with either tea-length or full-length dresses to complement the bride's gown. The men dress in tails, complete with white tie.

Bouquet Toss

A large factor in determining how formal your wedding will be is deciding how many guests you want to invite. Start with a number you can comfortably entertain at the reception, and divide that number by four. This process can vary depending on your personal family situation, but normally the bride's parents, the groom's parents, the bride, and the groom all submit guest lists. There may be duplicates on the lists, so check for that. If that number is too high, begin eliminating names by whatever means you can determine. Many families invite only those friends who know the bride or groom well, leaving out business associates. Many couples want those in attendance to be only people who are special to them.

Ultraformal weddings are always conducted after 6 P.M. The reception almost always includes a sit-down dinner and dancing, and a band or orchestra usually performs a variety of music for the guests' dancing pleasure. The determining factor that marks a wedding as ultraformal is that most of the guests also dress in formal attire. The men usually wear tuxedos and the women formal dresses, either cocktail or full-length. Favors are often a big part of the ultraformal wedding, and guests may leave the reception with elaborate gifts, such as silver picture frames; individual, monogrammed boxes of candy; or a set of crystal candlesticks.

Formal: Elegant and Graceful

The *formal* wedding currently is a typical type of wedding in the United States. A formal wedding normally includes three to eight bridesmaids and from 150 to 350 guests. The bridal gown still might be elaborate, but it may include a chapel-length rather than cathedral-length train. The attendants' dresses complement the bride's gown, and the men are dressed in formal wear, but usually not white tie.

A formal wedding generally is conducted in the late afternoon or early evening and usually offers a buffet, a sit-down dinner, or very elaborate hors d'oeuvres. As with the ultraformal wedding, dancing usually is part of the reception, with band music or a DJ. Decorations both at the ceremony site and the reception may be extensive and usually include flowers and candles. While not quite as grand as those found at an ultraformal reception, table decorations still may include elaborate centerpieces. The guests most likely will receive mementos, although not as high-end as the favors at an ultraformal reception.

Teddy's Tips

Weddings tend to grow in size and complexity. Think carefully now about your options and what you want to include. As you start adding to your must-have list, the complexity and costs can begin snowballing.

Semiformal: Tasteful and Dignified

The *semiformal* wedding generally includes one to four attendants and 100 to 150 guests. Decorations are less extensive, both at the ceremony site and the reception. The bride's gown may be full length or tea length, and she may or may not wear a veil; she may opt for fresh flowers in her hair. Likewise, her attendants are dressed more simply.

Semiformal weddings are often conducted in the late morning or the early afternoon, and the food at the reception is much less elaborate. You might choose to serve finger sandwiches, cake, and punch or champagne. Frequently, both the ceremony and the reception are in the same facility for a semiformal wedding. There may be dancing—usually to the tunes of a DJ—or you may opt for background music.

Informal: Casual and Comfortable

An *informal* wedding usually is conducted either in a judge's chambers or in a home setting. Generally, an informal wedding includes fewer than 50 guests, and the bride and groom each have one attendant. The bride may choose to wear a suit or a fancy street-length dress, and the groom may wear a suit. The honor attendants dress appropriately.

The reception for an informal wedding may consist of cake and punch, and perhaps champagne for the toast. Decorations may simply be flowers for the wedding party and a cake top. Dancing is not appropriate at an informal reception, but you can have a reception at a later time to which you invite more guests and include dancing in the festivities. Technically, this would not be a reception, but rather a party in honor of the couple.

How the Level of Formality Affects Your Budget

The type of wedding you decide to have—ultraformal, formal, semiformal, or informal—plays a huge part in determining the overall cost of your wedding. The standards that determine the level of formality, however, are not carved in stone, and there are no hard-and-fast rules. Your wedding may cross over into a couple formality levels, but you do need a starting point. Choose the level of formality with which you are most comfortable and which seems to fit best within your budget.

Teddy's Tips

The average cost of a formal wedding in the United States—including a dinner for 200, engagement and wedding rings, a gown, menswear, a band, a photographer, a florist, invitations, and all the extras—costs approximately $15,000 to $18,000.

If dancing is very important to both of you and the budget will allow it, then by all means include that aspect in your reception plans. If you want a small, intimate wedding, attended by only a few friends and family members, then you may want to go with an informal wedding. If you want a full-blown affair complete with dancing, lots of flowers and candles, and a cathedral-length train on a dress full of pearls and beading, then just be sure you understand that you will pay much more than you would for an informal wedding in the judge's chambers. Use the "What's Important to Us Worksheet" at the end of this chapter to determine the elements you believe are important to include in your special day.

Setting a Realistic Budget

The budget! This probably is the biggest area of turmoil for most couples. No one—I repeat, no one—wants to talk about the cost of the wedding. But ultimately, you do have to broach the subject, and the earlier you begin talking about it the better.

Now comes the real issue. Just how much is this whole affair going to cost? Well, it's not going to be cheap, but I firmly believe that you don't have to mortgage the farm for your wedding. Let's define what we mean by a wedding budget. A wedding budget is what you can realistically expect to spend on the wedding and reception, and it includes an estimate of all your other wedding expenses.

Cost Comparison

Turn to the end of this chapter and glance at the "Cost Comparison Worksheet." This worksheet lists all possible wedding expenses. The purpose of this worksheet is to find the norm for your market area and to determine what sets each estimate apart. It won't help you one bit if I quote you the cost of hiring a photographer in Indiana if you live in Boston. You have some homework to do here, but it will pay off in the end (literally).

Now is the time to begin reviewing those names of possible vendors you have gathered from bridal shows, your family, your friends, and maybe from your bridal consultant. Call at least three vendors under each entry to determine where their prices fall.

To give you an idea of how to use this worksheet, let's take the photography section as an example. Suppose that Photographer A charges $1,000 for 36 8×10 photos and three hours of his time; Photographer B charges $1,500 for 30 8×10 photos and four hours of her time; and Photographer C charges $500 for 30 5×7 photos and four hours of his time. Now determine what's important to you and your fiancé, and what appears to be the best deal. Are 8×10 photos really important to you? What about the amount of time spent at the wedding by the photographer? What is Photographer A's overtime fee? If it's $150 an hour (which it can be) and you go over by two hours (which can happen), then you're right in the ballpark with Photographer B. It takes time to do a cost comparison, but it can be a valuable tool.

Putting Your Budget on Paper

When you've finished the "Cost Comparison Worksheet," you can turn to the "Wedding Budget Worksheet" at the end of this chapter. Using your completed "Cost Comparison Worksheet" (hint: use a pencil), run down the list of service providers. If you decided that either Photographer A or B would be okay price-wise, write down both fee estimates on the budget worksheet. This is only a starting point, but it will get you moving in the right direction. Continue to do the same with each entry on the budget worksheet, and then add everything up and see what ballpark you're in. You may be way, way out of the park, or you could be right on target.

Many times, couples don't have any idea what a wedding will or should cost in their area. The president and vice president of the Association of Bridal Consultants—who know what weddings cost—said even they were in sticker shock when their elder daughter married in January 1994. By using the "Cost Comparison Worksheet" and then putting those figures down on paper, you know what kind of money you're going to be spending.

The next step is compromise. If you want a dinner reception for 650 of your closest friends but you just can't figure out how you can afford it, see where else you can cut costs to make up the difference. Maybe you can serve less elaborate food for the reception, have fewer flowers, or cut your guest list a little. You have to be willing to give and take. Unless you have unlimited resources or Uncle Ralph died and left you a huge inheritance, you have to be cost-conscious in your thinking. If you want that number-one-rated photographer in your area who costs $2,000 just to book him, then think about ways to decrease your flower bill, or go with a DJ rather than a band. Give and take—that's the name of the game.

Teddy's Tips

The more open you are to compromising with the budget, the less stress over money matters you are likely to have later. You're also less likely to be disappointed because your budget cannot accommodate your dreams.

Let's say you have $12,000 to spend on this wedding. Your parents are contributing $4,000; the groom's parents are adding another $4,000. That leaves $4,000 for you and the groom to come up with. And remember, you have to cover everything with that amount— *everything.*

Included in that everything are the rings, the honeymoon, the reception, the photographer, the bride's gown, the veil, the accessories, and so on. That's why it's so important to determine early what kind of dollars you're willing to spend on this wedding. I've seen too many couples and parents get so stressed out over the cost of the wedding that they lose sight of what this special time is all about—it should be exciting and joyful. Don't let the almighty dollar sign ruin your day—set a budget and follow it closely.

Whom to Involve

When determining your wedding budget, be sure to include all members of the wedding finance committee. That may include the bride and groom, all parents, grandparents, and others. Sit down in a relaxed atmosphere, and talk about the expenses of this wedding. Most of all, think positive and be willing to give and take.

The groom does have a responsibility for some parts of the wedding costs. Traditionally, the groom and his family cover the bride's bouquet, the flowers for the groomsmen, the rehearsal dinner, and the flowers for the mothers. Sometimes, the groom's parents also may offer to pay for part of the cost of the reception, the photography, or the floral bill. Etiquette dictates that the bride or her parents cannot ask the groom's parents to help with the expenses. If they offer, however, the bride's parents may choose to take them up on it. After all, it's their son's wedding, too, and they may want to feel as though they're contributing a part.

Who Pays for What?

Weddings are considered traditional ceremonies of a life passage. As customs and traditions have changed during the years, so have the rules for who pays for what. Traditionally, the bride's family has paid for the majority of the wedding costs. However, that is changing, and more couples are coming up with creative ways to meet their financial obligations. Today, it's not uncommon for the couple to pay all their expenses or for a combination of contributors to give funds for the wedding, including both sets of parents, grandparents, and even close friends.

The "Who Pays for What Worksheet" at the end of this chapter gives you an idea of the traditional items in a wedding budget. But this worksheet is only a guide. This is the twenty-first century, and there are many ways to divide wedding expenses. Find the way that works best for you.

Wedding Woes

Never leave key players out of the budget discussion. If you don't have the financial resources to spring for this wedding on your own, you need backing from family. Play it smart.

The Least You Need to Know

➤ Determining the level of formality early on lets you decide what's important. It also enables you to establish a realistic budget.

➤ There are no hard-and-fast rules concerning the levels of formality. These are suggestions. Find a starting point, even if the wedding you want seems to cross a couple formality levels.

➤ Use cost comparison to determine prices in your area. You can't begin putting together a budget if you don't have an idea of the going rate for services in your area.

➤ Sit down in a relaxed atmosphere with everyone who needs to be involved with the wedding finances. Be realistic in what you want and what you can afford. When you have established your budget, do your best to work within it.

➤ Think positive, and be willing to give and take!

What's Important to Us Worksheet

Number of guests: _150 - 200_

Number of attendants: _____

Time of day: _3:00 -_____

Time of year: _____ summer_____

Other: Limousine, photography, ~~videography~~, special items (hot air balloon, vintage cars), decorations (balloons, flowers), flowers (~~silk vs.~~ fresh), and attire · formal

- candles   - roses - yellow

- chair covers   - rose petals

- yankee candle wedding gifts

Reception:

- ☒ Cake and ~~punch~~
- ☒ Hors d'oeuvres
- ☐ Buffet
- ☒ Sit-down dinner
- ☒ Open bar
- ☐ Limited bar
- ☐ Cash bar
- ☒ Champagne toast
- ☒ Music - DJ
- ☒ Dancing
- ☒ Favors - DJ

Other ideas: _toys, glow necklaces, electric slide, train_

_____

_____

_____

_____

Cost Comparison Worksheet

Item	Vendor Name and Contact	Cost Estimate
Jewelry store Engagement and wedding rings		
Bridal consultant		
Ceremony site rental	St. Margaret Mary's	
Reception site		
Caterer		
Bridal shop Gown, veil, attendants' dresses		
Wedding stationery Invitations, announcements, enclosures, other paper		
Photographer	Kresge	
Videographer		
Florist	Maria's	
Musicians— Ceremony		
Musicians— Reception	Heidi Lynn Phantom Shadow Bob Foltz	
Wedding cake	Dingledeins Shanks	

31

Item	Vendor Name and Contact	Cost Estimate
Groom's cake		
Attendants' gifts		
Men's formal wear		
Party rental equipment		
Limousine		
Favors		
Programs		
Honeymoon Hotel, travel, tours, wardrobe, gifts		

Wedding Budget Worksheet

Item	Estimate	Actual
Rings		
~~Engagement ring~~	$_____	$_____
Bride's wedding ring	$_____	$_____
Groom's wedding ring	$_____	$_____
Other	$_____	$_____
~~Bridal consultant~~	$_____	$_____
_____	$_____	$_____
Other	$_____	$_____
Ceremony		
Site rental fee	$_____	$_____
Officiant's fee	$_____	$_____
Ceremony assistants' fee	$_____	$_____
Other	$_____	$_____
Reception		
Site rental fee	$_____	$_____
Food	$_____	$_____
Beverages	$_____	$_____
Service personnel	$_____	$_____
Party rentals (chairs, tables, linens, etc.)	$_____	$_____
Other	$_____	$_____
Wedding cake *by slice*		
Charge for cake	$_____	$_____
Delivery fee *Bob Miller*	$_____	$_____
Groom's cake	$_____	$_____
Other	$_____	$_____
Reception		
~~Napkins~~	$_____	$_____
~~Personalized matches~~	$_____	$_____
Favors	$_____	$_____
Toasting goblets	$_____	$_____
Cake knife	$_____	$_____
Scrolls	$_____	$_____
Other	$_____	$_____

Item	Estimate	Actual
Bride's clothing		
Gown	$_____	$_____
Headpiece and veil	$_____	$_____
Alterations	$_____	$_____
Shoes	$_____	$_____
~~Gloves~~	$_____	$_____
Hose	$_____	$_____
Jewelry	$_____	$_____
Garter	$_____	$_____
Lingerie	$_____	$_____
Other	$_____	$_____
Photography		
Engagement announcement photo	$_____	$_____
Wedding portrait	$_____	$_____
Wedding photographs	$_____	$_____
Wedding albums	$_____	$_____
Other	$_____	$_____
Videography		
One camera	$_____	$_____
Two cameras	$_____	$_____
Three or more cameras	$_____	$_____
Fee for extra tape	$_____	$_____
Editing charge	$_____	$_____
Other	$_____	$_____
Flowers		
Ceremony flowers	$_____	$_____
Reception flowers	$_____	$_____
Personal flowers	$_____	$_____
Other	$_____	$_____
Wedding stationery		
Invitations	$_____	$_____
Announcements	$_____	$_____
Reception cards	$_____	$_____
Response cards	$_____	$_____
Thank-you notes	$_____	$_____
Informals	$_____	$_____

Item	Estimate	Actual
Maps	$_____	$_____
Newsletters	$_____	$_____
Other	$_____	$_____
Music		
Ceremony		
Soloist	$_____	$_____
Organist/pianist	$_____	$_____
Reception	$_____	$_____
Other	$_____	$_____
Groom's clothing		
Tuxedo or suit	$_____	$_____
Shirt	$_____	$_____
Tie	$_____	$_____
Vest or cummerbund	$_____	$_____
Shoes	$_____	$_____
Accessories	$_____	$_____
Other	$_____	$_____
Gifts		
Attendants	$_____	$_____
Gifts to each other	$_____	$_____
Parents' thank-you gifts	$_____	$_____
Other	$_____	$_____
Transportation		
Limousine	$_____	$_____
Parking	$_____	$_____
Other	$_____	$_____
Rehearsal dinner (included, even though traditionally paid for by groom's family)		
Food	$_____	$_____
Beverages	$_____	$_____
Service personnel	$_____	$_____
Room rental charge	$_____	$_____
Flowers/decorations	$_____	$_____
Other	$_____	$_____
Honeymoon		
Hotel accommodations	$_____	$_____
Transportation	$_____	$_____

Handwritten notes in margin: 50 (near Vest or cummerbund), 500 (near Parking), 50 per person (near Service personnel)

35

Item	Estimate	Actual
Tours	$_____	$_____
Meals	$_____	$_____
Passports	$_____	$_____
Traveler's checks	$_____	$_____
Other	$_____	$_____
Additional expenses 35-		
Marriage license 40	$_____	$_____
Postage for invitations	$_____	$_____
Gratuities	$_____	$_____
Blood tests/physicals	$_____	$_____
Hair stylist 50	$_____	$_____
Makeup artist 35	$_____	$_____
Birdseed or petals $/person	$_____	$_____

Who Pays for What Worksheet

The Bride and Her Family

- ➤ Wedding dress, headpiece, and accessories
- ➤ Ceremony site rental
- ➤ Bridal consultant
- ➤ Reception site rental
- ➤ Reception food and drink
- ➤ Flowers for the ceremony
- ➤ Flowers for the reception
- ➤ Groom's wedding ring
- ➤ Invitations, announcements, enclosures
- ➤ Gift for the groom
- ➤ Gifts for the bridesmaids

The Groom and His Family

- ➤ Bride's engagement and wedding rings
- ➤ Gift for the bride
- ➤ Rental of formal wear
- ➤ Marriage license
- ➤ Officiant's fee
- ➤ Boutonnieres for the men in the wedding party
- ➤ Bride's bouquet

The Wedding Party

- ➤ Their wedding attire
- ➤ Accessories to go with the attire (shoes, headpieces)
- ➤ Gift for the bride and groom
- ➤ Transportation to the city (if out-of-town)

Part 2

First Things First

This part of the book talks about what you need to reserve first and how far before the big day you need to make the reservations. Although it might not seem like it now, there is a method to all this madness. The chapters that follow explain the order in which you need to do things and take you step by step through what you need to do next. For example, you don't want to rush right out and order your invitations. You have several major items to pin down first. Read through all of Part 2 before you even begin to think about going out to meet the vendors. The information here should give you a fundamental understanding of what you should do before you put down that first deposit or order that first corsage.

A "Planning Check-Off List" is provided at the end of Part 2 to help you keep things organized and to prevent you from forgetting any important details. This list shows you exactly what you need to be doing from six months before the wedding right up to the big day. Keep this list with you during these planning months, and you'll feel more relaxed and confident as you plan.

Chapter 4

Get Me a Church on Time!

In This Chapter

➤ Choosing a date

➤ Selecting the ceremony site

➤ Working with the officiant

Probably some of the most obvious duties to cover at the beginning of your wedding planning are setting a date, finding a place, and making the arrangements for someone to perform the service. These tasks are not as time-consuming as meeting with the caterer or visiting the reception facility, and they need to be done first. I fondly refer to these as the "biggies." After all, if you don't have a date, how can you plan anything else? Read on!

Setting the Date

Before you can reserve one of the biggies, you need to determine a date for the occasion. When choosing a date for your wedding, keep in mind family commitments (birthdays and other anniversaries), holidays, how far guests will have to travel, special events and tourist activities taking place in the area, and weather conditions.

Plan Around Big Events

Planning a May wedding in Indianapolis around the time of the Indianapolis 500 race is probably not a wise move. In fact, it would likely be a very expensive proposition. Hotels and motels double their room prices, crowds swell the city beyond imagination, and many of the ideal reception spots are booked years in advance for race activities. If you waited until June or moved the date up to April, you would be in much better shape to deal with the rest of the stress that comes with planning a wedding.

Likewise, a wedding in New Orleans during Mardi Gras is not a wise idea. Again, you would have to deal with loads of tourists and inflated prices, in addition to the difficulty of booking a reception site. Save yourself a lot of planning nightmares by checking out the tourist trends in your area. Then try your best to avoid scheduling your wedding at the same time as a popular special event.

Teddy's Tips

Be sure to refer to the "Planning Check-Off List" at the end of Part 2, "First Things First," to help you remember what to do in the months before your wedding day.

Other dates that you should try to avoid—mainly because of floral difficulties—are Mother's Day weekend and Valentine's Day weekend. Both of these times are very, very busy for florists; some florists will not even accept a Mother's Day weekend wedding because they find it too difficult to handle the pressures of a wedding along with holiday floral orders. Just as important for you, flowers almost triple in price during these holidays. The professionals will be much more accommodating at other times and can give you the service and products you deserve.

You also can check with the local convention and visitors bureau to make sure there are no really big conventions in town that will take up many hotel rooms and reception sites.

Holidays: Pressure Cookers or Money Savers?

Holiday weddings, especially during the Christmas season, can be stressful given the very hectic nature of the season, but they also can be money savers. Most facilities are already decked out for the holidays, which means you can save big bucks on decorations. The cost savings doesn't come without a price, however. We all know the kind of stress that can accompany the holidays in everyday life; add the task of planning a wedding, and you compound that stress many times over. However, if you love Christmas and can handle the added pressure, you can save substantially on your decorating costs.

One of the prettiest Christmas weddings I can remember included 500 white poinsettias, candles on every aisle, red ribbons and fresh greenery at the entrance, and a large Christmas tree in the lobby area. The church congregation had already decorated for the season, and it was breathtaking. The best part was that the couple didn't spend a dime on any of it.

Waltzing with the Weather

Be sure to take the area's weather into consideration for the time of year you're planning your wedding. For my own January wedding in 1971, I never even considered the weather as a factor. Now, because I'm from Indiana, I should have known better. It snowed eight inches on the day of the wedding. Lucky for us, the snow came straight down, it didn't really drift much, and everyone was able to drive to the church.

When I coordinated a January wedding a few years ago, however, I drove 35 miles on solid ice to get to the church the morning of the wedding. Everyone, including the groom, was late. You can't control the weather (although, at times, I sure wish I could), so if you live in an area where bad weather conditions may be a problem, try to take the weather into consideration when you set the date.

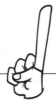

Bouquet Toss

One simple thing that can easily sneak up on you is remembering to apply for the marriage license. Each state has different requirements and policies, including the length of the waiting period, the ages of both parties, blood tests (or other medical examination), identification requirements, and how much the license costs.

Within each state, each county may have its own set of rules. Your first step should be to call the office of the marriage clerk or county clerk in your county seat and ask how to proceed. You should investigate the requirements several months before your wedding date. Many counties now make allowances for long-distance couples, but you should find out well in advance of your wedding day.

Consider Other Commitments

Family commitments also make a difference in setting a date. Make a list of those commitments before you pick a day. You can say to Aunt Martha, "We're thinking about sometime next May for our wedding. Can you think of any dates that you and Uncle Fred may not be able to attend?" You don't have to do this with all your relatives—and unless you have a very small family, you can't—but try to consider the schedules of those people whose presence is especially important to you.

Teddy's Tips

Set your date with the church and the reception site early. Sometimes you have to juggle the date to coordinate both facilities.

If you and your groom have school commitments or careers that are affected by the time of year, take those commitments into account as well. The main reason I was married in January was because my husband is a farmer, and January is his off-season. Likewise, if you're an accountant, then a wedding date before April 15 is probably not wise planning.

If you take some time now to plan around other family commitments, your local traditions (festivals, large sporting events, and so on), the holiday schedule, your own work or school schedules, and your local weather conditions, you will please more of your guests in the long run and make life a little easier. In the end, though, you and your fiancé need to be happy with the date.

Selecting the Ceremony Site

Okay, you have a date in mind. After you determine when and how formal you want this wedding to be, you need a place for the ceremony.

The place you choose for your wedding ceremony can be as unique as you, the couple. The obvious choices are those with a religious tone. You can have the ceremony in a church, cathedral, chapel, or temple. You also can choose a hall, private club, hotel, restaurant, garden or other outdoor setting, your home, or a judge's chambers. Or, you might choose a truly unique setting. Couples have married in hot-air balloons, at the top of roller coasters, on horseback, on the beach, and even underwater.

Choose a ceremony site with some special significance for the two of you. For example, if you met each other at church or maybe in a park, then those sites might be appropriate for your wedding. Most couples who choose a religious setting are married in their home church or temple. If you're not a member of a church, or if your home church isn't large enough to accommodate your guests, consider renting church space. Several denominations rent to nonmembers, but tracking down these organizations sometimes can be difficult.

Examine the Facility Firsthand

Whether it's your home church or a rented space, look at the physical side of the facility. How many guests can it comfortably hold? I coordinated a wedding several years ago at a church with a capacity of 300. The couple, however, expected 450 guests. We had to bring in 150 folding chairs to have on hand in case we needed them. We did. It was not an ideal situation, but at that point, we had no choice.

Check the musical equipment that comes with the facility. Does it have an organ or piano? What are the restrictions? Can any organist play the available equipment? Also check the sound system and availability of microphones for soloists, if appropriate.

Check parking availability. Is it ample to meet the needs of your guests? Will the guests have to walk far? What about lighting and safety considerations outside if the service is at night? I once coordinated a wedding in which the couple hired four off-duty police officers to guard the guests' cars during a service in a part of town that was considered risky.

If you plan to get dressed at the ceremony site, ask to see where the bride traditionally dresses. In the Midwest, most brides dress at the ceremony facility; check out the dressing rooms for mirrors, restrooms, and electrical outlets. A dressing room that doesn't have an outlet for hair dryers or curling irons is a pretty frightening possibility if it must accommodate eight women. What about the lighting in the dressing room? Is it adequate? Do you need to bring a lighted makeup mirror?

Ask to see the sanctuary or the room in which the ceremony will be held. If you have 40 attendants, make sure the facility can handle that number. I once coordinated a very large wedding party in a church with an altar area that was so tiny we literally had to stack the attendants in sideways just to get them situated. At the end of the ceremony, the bridesmaid on the end turned too quickly, and her bouquet stabbed the next bridesmaid in the nose. Not exactly the finale of your dreams!

Understand the Fees and Policies

Be sure to ask about fees. Yes, a church is a business, and many churches charge for the use of the facility, and some of these fees can be quite steep. Ask what the fee includes. Churches that charge a single fee that includes all the necessary services (musicians, janitor, officiant, and rent) probably offer the best deal. You're going to have to pay for those services anyway, so if you can line them all up with one stop, that's not a bad option.

Ask if there are any wedding policies for the facility. Many churches and other sites where weddings occur regularly provide a wedding policy booklet that explains the rules—what you can and cannot do in the facility. Get a copy of this booklet for yourself—and for your bridal consultant, if you

Teddy's Tips

Make sure you read and fully understand the church wedding policies before your wedding day. If you can't work with its rules, look elsewhere. If there are restrictions on certain parts of the church rental, be sure to inform those who will be affected, such as your vendors or attendants.

have hired one—and review the policies with her. Be sure to abide by these rules; they were written for a reason. If there are any restrictions on decorations, music, or photography, be sure to let your vendors know. You don't want surprises on your wedding day when the florist is told he can't use the lovely pew bows because the church has a rule against it, or when you find out that the videographer cannot work in the sanctuary during the service.

Use the "Ceremony Site Worksheet" at the end of this chapter to ensure that you've asked all the right questions and have thoroughly investigated a facility before you actually write the check to reserve it.

Working with the Officiant

Someone has to perform your service—that's a given. Whether that person is a justice of the peace, a judge, a priest, a rabbi, or a minister, someone with the legal authority allowed by the state must preside at your marriage. My best advice when working with this person is to make him or her your friend, not your enemy. After all, he's going to perform a very important ceremony in your life, and you want fond memories of this event.

Susan, a bridal consultant in a western metropolitan city, shared one experience with me that emphasizes the importance of working with your officiant. Some years ago, Susan coordinated a wedding in which the mother of the bride got into a power struggle with the priest. This mother called the priest all hours of the night to ask silly questions that could have been answered during normal working hours. If the priest suggested something, the mother always had a reason not to do it his way. She wouldn't budge. Susan said you could tell, as the wedding plans progressed, how stressed the mother was making the priest, almost as if this task had become her avocation. The day of the wedding arrived, and all systems were go. Susan had everyone lined up ready to make their grand entrance, when all of a sudden, the priest appeared in front of the church and launched into a stand-up comedy routine. Whether he had always wanted to be on *The Tonight Show* and had never been asked, no one will ever know. What we do know is that he proved to the mother who was really in charge—it was payback time.

Within the first 35 minutes of the wedding, the priest rearranged the entire wedding plan. First of all, he asked the bride's guests to get up and trade places with the groom's guests. He said he wanted everyone to get to know each other. Then he started telling jokes: "Did you hear the one about the priest ...." After 35 minutes of joke-telling and musical chairs, he proceeded with the ceremony.

The mother was beside herself. Her daughter's wedding had turned into something far different than what she had imagined. The priest not only had the best lines, but he also had the last laugh. Some of the guests found the situation humorous; some left the church for a smoke; others wandered down to the corner bar. On top of everything, the bride was crying. Susan, who normally is completely composed and in charge, was also rapidly losing her grip on reality. (This is why bridal consultants usually have gray hair.) All this chaos occurred because, instead of working with the priest, the mother created an adversarial relationship.

The officiant is your link to the legal aspects of your wedding. Without his consent and cooperation, the wedding may take place, but if the officiant doesn't complete the legal paperwork to validate the marriage in the state, the union won't be legal. So, although you may have different ideas about what you want to include in your service, it's wise to approach the officiant cautiously. Meet with him. Ask for opinions and advice. Get the officiant on your side first, and then talk about the particulars of your service. It helps to have an amiable relationship with your officiant.

I actually have coordinated a wedding in which the officiant refused to marry the couple just two weeks before the wedding. It wasn't that the officiant was concerned about the marriage itself—he just didn't like the way in which the couple answered a question he posed to them. He called the mother two weeks before the wedding (invitations had been out for weeks at that time, the reception was arranged, and all systems were go) and told her to find another officiant. This was not an easy task, given the particulars of that wedding. And it's certainly something that you would not want to go through two weeks before your big day.

These stories aren't meant to frighten you, although they certainly may have that effect. Certainly, most officiants are pleasant and friendly and want to help make your wedding day memorable. The reason I mention these true tales of uncooperative officiants is so that you understand that a little common respect and courtesy can go a long way toward making the officiant a friend.

Teddy's Tips

It's always a good idea to befriend your officiant. Besides helping the ceremony proceed smoothly, the officiant must properly complete all legal paperwork in order for your marriage to be valid.

When I was married, we met with the officiant, and what he said was the rule; you didn't ask questions. We don't have that type of society anymore. People ask questions. They want things done their way and no other way, and everyone, from the officiant to the couple, can be disrespectful of each other's feelings. The bottom line here is that you most assuredly need the officiant to be your friend. Do your best to work with him, and he will do his best to make your wedding ceremony a very pleasant experience.

The Least You Need to Know

➤ Consider weather conditions, family commitments, and local special events and celebrations when you select your wedding date.

➤ Select a ceremony site that best suits your needs. Check out the number of guests it will hold, its location, the size of its altar area, and parking.

➤ Treat the officiant with respect. Try your best to work with your officiant to ensure a smooth road both to the church and down the aisle.

Ceremony Site Worksheet

Name of facility: _St Margaret Marys_

Address: _____

Telephone: _____

Contact: _____

Fee: _____

Includes:

Organist _____   Officiant _____   Janitor _____

Kneeler _____   Aisle cloths _____   Candelabra _____

Meeting with contact: _____

Number of guests facility can accommodate: _____

Musical equipment provided: _____

Dressing room facilities: _____

Parking areas: _____

Wedding policy booklets: _____

Facility restrictions: _____

_____

_____

Added fees for rental items (such as candelabra, kneeler, aisle cloth):

_____

_____

Special accommodations for people with disabilities (parking, access, restrooms, and so on): _____

_____

Notes: _____

_____

_____

_____

_____

Chapter 5

Seeking Your Soirée

In This Chapter

➤ Making sure you get what you pay for in your reception facility

➤ Reserving the reception site

➤ Finding a good caterer

➤ Understanding your responsibilities when serving liquor

Okay, folks, it's time to talk about the reception, the biggest party you will ever throw. It takes careful, timely planning and lots of research to get the party you want. I'm going to hit this chapter hard because the reception can be the most costly item in your wedding budget. You need to know what to look for in a good catering facility and in the caterer himself, and you need to make the big decision: to serve or not to serve liquor. Party on!

The Reception Site—Getting What You Pay For

The reception (facility rental and catering costs) will account for about 35 percent of your total wedding bill. When planning your wedding reception, make sure you pay close attention to all the details so that you get your money's worth. Remember to book early; the prime reception sites will be reserved as far as 18 to 24 months in advance in larger cities. (Be sure to turn to the "Reception Site Worksheet" at the end of this chapter.)

One Size Doesn't Fit All

Your biggest consideration is whether the facility is large enough to accommodate your guests. There's nothing worse than being cramped in a facility that is too small with far more guests than you imagined. Make sure that it can hold your guests comfortably with the activities you want. Check the number of people the facility will hold and figure on the maximum number of guests you could expect. Are you including dancing in your reception plans? Is there room for the wedding party to stand and be introduced, or to enter from an outside area as they are introduced to the guests? Will you be having a receiving line at the reception? How does the traffic flow pattern of guests usually work?

Deal with the Details

Make doubly sure that you get what the facility will and will not provide *in writing*. The little things, such as linens, table skirting, microphone hookups (or the microphone itself), napkins, and dance floors are items you need to know about before the day of the wedding. Most reception sites provide those items as part of their contract, but that is not always the case. Just know what you're getting when you pay your deposit.

Ask questions of the manager. If the manager's only comment is "We can't do that," see if you can find another facility that is more accommodating. The manager works for you, not the other way around.

Reserving the Reception Site

Many reception sites—whether a private club, a hall, the church's social hall, a restaurant, or the civic center—will accept early reservations. You can reserve many of the prime reception sites at least a year in advance; you can book some sites in the larger cities as much as 18 to 24 months in advance. Hopefully, you will have some choices in your locale. If possible, visit potential sites while weddings are being set up. This will give you a better feeling of what to expect than if you're looking at an empty room.

Teddy's Tips

Book the reception site early! Get the details in writing of the items that the facility provides, and make sure that you feel comfortable with the manager.

Ask friends, family members, and certainly recently married couples where they had their reception. That's a good starting point. Also, check in the Yellow Pages (under headings such as "Banquet Facilities," "Halls and Auditoriums," and "Party Centers") for sites you might not have thought about. Many times, private clubs will rent facilities as well. I know of a beautiful old Victorian house that has been turned into a women's club that can be rented for wedding receptions. Look at the local university or college, too; possibly, there are sites on those campuses. Of course, many hotels and country clubs have banquet facilities you can use for receptions as well.

If you don't have many choices for a reception site and the weather in your area will permit, consider having an outdoor reception, either at your home or in a park or garden. (See the "Outdoor and Garden Weddings" section in Chapter 20, "What's in a Theme?" for more information about planning an outdoor reception.)

Traffic Jam

The traffic flow inside the facility is an important factor that shouldn't be overlooked. Your reception manager should be able to make suggestions, based on past experience, for the best traffic pattern for a wedding reception at that facility. Also check floor plans. I coordinated a lovely wedding a few years ago followed by an equally lovely reception—except for one small detail. The reception hall was on three different floors. There was an elevator, but most guests had to walk up and down three flights of stairs. Most of the food was set up on the first floor, and dancing and some finger foods were located on the third floor. The restrooms were located on the second floor. I remember trying to move a guest in a wheelchair through the crowd and wondering what I should do if anyone yelled "Fire!" That reception would have been so much nicer and easier for the guests had the bride made the reservation earlier and reserved a larger, one-floor facility.

What About Services and Restrictions?

Check with the manager about the restrictions the facility has for food and beverages. Can you bring in a caterer of your choice, or do you have to use the facility's *in-house caterer?* An in-house caterer is the caterer responsible for that facility's food service. An *outside caterer* is a person or organization not associated with the facility who comes to the facility to prepare the food.

Are there ample restrooms? Can they accommodate people with disabilities? (Most public facilities today must meet those requirements.) Are microphone hookups available? Will the DJ or band have any trouble setting up equipment?

What does the facility provide? Make sure you have that part in writing. Linens? Table skirting? Security guards? Get estimates on the price and what that includes.

Check about parking facilities. Are they adequate for the number of cars you expect? How far will guests have to walk? How far is the site from the ceremony location? Are there good, well-traveled roads between the two? Is parking available for people with disabilities?

Look at the "Choosing the Reception Site Worksheet" at the end of this chapter.

Who's in Charge Here?

Try to gauge whether you will be able to work with the reception manager. As I mentioned earlier, you don't want to hear, "That can't be done." Instead, "Let me see what we can do" is the response you want. You're going to be spending a lot of time (and money) with these people, and you want it to be a pleasant experience. After all, it is not the reception manager's wedding reception. You are the client, and her only job for that day is to make you look good. If you look good and are happy, the reception manager (and the facility) looks good.

Choosing a Caterer

After you select a reception site, the next step is to find a caterer. If the reception facility you reserved provides an in-house catering service, you have no choice. Most of the larger facilities, such as hotels, country clubs, colleges, or universities, provide in-house catering.

Bouquet Toss

The largest wedding dish ever prepared was a roasted camel. The camel was prepared in the following manner:

Eggs were stuffed into fish, fish were stuffed into chickens, chickens were stuffed into a roasted lamb, and the lamb was stuffed inside the whole camel.

The entire camel was then roasted and served to the wedding guests.

—*Guinness Book of World Records*

If you decide to hold your reception in a hall, art museum, home, church social hall, or outdoor setting, you must arrange for a caterer to provide the food. If the choice of caterer is up to you, then shop around and find someone who can give you the food choices you want at a price you can afford.

Friends, family, and recently married couples are your best bet when discussing possible caterers. Ask the reception facility manager, too. Sometimes facilities limit which caterers may come into their facility. They may give you their preferred caterer list and ask you to choose a caterer from that list. This usually means that those caterers are competent, provide quality work, and take care of the facility so that the reception manager doesn't have to worry about damage from the caterers.

Look at the "Choosing the Caterer Worksheet" at the end of this chapter. Chapter 11, "Eat, Drink, and Be Married," also contains detailed information about caterers.

May I Serve You?

Traditional etiquette says that the only thing you must offer your guests at the wedding reception is something to eat and something to drink, so cake and punch will do the trick. Indeed, the simplest type of wedding reception is a cake-and-punch reception, with some mints and nuts thrown in for good measure, if you so desire. Anything else is icing on the cake (pardon the pun).

You might want to move up one step and serve hors d'oeuvres and a limited bar. A *limited bar* means that you limit the selection of liquor: You may opt for only wine and soft drinks or beer. One step up from this would be an open bar and hors d'oeuvres.

Then there is the simple buffet for guests. A simple buffet includes one entrée, plus other side dishes. You can expand this into a more elaborate buffet by simply adding more entrées and other side dish choices.

The most elaborate reception meal you can offer would be a five- or six-course dinner served to guests, including wine with the meal. If you choose this option, consider hiring extra wait staff. If the facility's price normally includes one waiter for every two tables (20 guests), consider adding enough to have two waiters for every three tables (30 guests). This will speed the service and make the guests feel more special.

So, What Will It Cost?

After you decide on the kind of meal you want to serve, start getting price estimates. Most caterers figure their prices per person, except for hors d'oeuvres, which sometimes are figured per dozen. For example, you might order 15 dozen canapés at $8.20 per dozen. Other items may be priced per item, such as large fruit trays or blocks of cheese and crackers at $25 per tray.

Unless you have your heart set on particular food items, it often works well to give the caterer a price per head and let him be creative. He can choose the food, subject to your approval, based on seasonal availability. Also, be wary of caterers who refuse to deviate from their standard menu. Good caterers will be willing to take your favorite recipes and price them out for your reception. This is great if you have some foods you particularly like or that are family traditions (such as Aunt Eileen's traditional Irish soda bread). We'll talk more about actual menu selection in Chapter 11.

Ask about the caterer's policy on guaranteed numbers. This is an important concept for you to understand before you begin contacting caterers. If you plan to serve major food items, you must have an accurate guest count.

The caterer obviously isn't providing this food just for the pure pleasure of it; it comes with a price tag, and here's how it works. Most caterers give you a 5 or 10 percent window above or below your guaranteed number. If you guarantee them 100 guests and only 95 people show up, they bill you only for 95 guests. The same rule applies if you're substantially under your guaranteed number. If you guarantee them 100 guests and only 50 people show up, they still bill you for 95.

The caterer usually prepares food for only 5 or 10 percent above your guaranteed number. So, if you guarantee 100 guests and 120 show up, you will have enough food for only 110 (that's at 10 percent, which is on the high side). Thus, 10 guests are going to go without food. That probably doesn't leave a very good taste in your mouth. This is the biggest reason to make sure you have an accurate count for the caterer.

Bouquet Toss

Build in some extra time for checking out caterers and reception sites. This is one area of wedding planning that can carry a heavy price tag, and you want to find a facility and a caterer that offer you the best value for your wedding dollars.

Also, get the catering details in writing. This can save you a great deal of grief later as you try to remember exactly what was quoted, including the 5 or 10 percent window above and below the guaranteed number.

Liquor: To Drink or Not To Drink

The decision of whether to serve alcohol to your guests is solely a personal one. If you're going to offer alcohol with your reception, you need to engage either a caterer with a liquor license or a liquor-licensed dealer. This is a wise move, considering the liability issues presently in focus in the country.

Many states now make the host liable for accidents involving guests at a party. (Direct any concerns about local laws regarding alcohol to the liquor-licensed dealer.) Although all caterers are supposed to ensure that their bartenders comply with local laws, it may be wise to brief them (or have the wedding consultant do it) on specific guests they should watch for and to ensure that they know when and how to cut people off tactfully. (I'll talk specifically about designated drivers in Chapter 25, "Let the Party Begin!") If you're planning to serve champagne, also provide nonalcoholic sparkling grape wine so that those who do not wish to drink can have something bubbly for toasts.

Most religious facilities do not approve of liquor on the grounds. Again, that's why you need to read and understand the wedding policy booklets they provide. If you want champagne at your reception and the reception is scheduled for a church social hall that will not allow liquor, then having champagne is no longer a choice. Again, whether you offer liquor at your wedding reception is a personal choice; just because everyone else does it doesn't mean you have to.

If you're considering offering liquor at your reception, get the terminology down now so that you can ask intelligent questions.

➤ **Limited bar** means that you limit what is served to the guests. This is your choice. If you want to offer only wine and something nonalcoholic, that's fine. Often a limited bar will feature both wine and beer, plus soft drinks or maybe punch.

➤ **Open bar** means a bar containing hard liquor for mixed drinks, plus beer and wine and maybe even after-dinner drinks. Here again, you want to make sure you provide nonalcoholic beverages as well.

➤ **Cash bar** brings both smiles and frowns to people. If you offer a cash bar at your reception, your guests will pay for their drinks. You may offer wine and soft drinks, and then if guests want something else in the way of liquor, they can buy it from the bartender. Many people feel that a cash bar is insulting to their guests. You wouldn't make your guests pay for a drink in your home, so why make them pay for one at your reception? The other side of that philosophy is that if guests are paying for their own drinks, they may not be as free with the liquor and will watch their consumption. It's your call.

Pricing for liquor at receptions can vary. You want to know what system the caterer uses to arrive at the figure that appears on your bill. There are several methods; you just need to know what system he uses.

One method is for the caterer to charge a per-drink tab at the bar. Most bartenders aren't crazy about this system because it's time-consuming. When they have 200 guests to serve liquor to, it can become cumbersome to count drinks.

Another method is for the caterer to charge a price by the bottle. You choose the type or brand of liquor you want to serve. At the end of the reception, the caterer charges you for all the opened and empty bottles. The cheapest brands are house brands, the next step up are call brands, and the most expensive are the premium brands. The bottle price should include the fee for the bartender, mixes, and glassware.

The one other charging system I've run across is a per-person charge. The client who used this system was very satisfied with the price and didn't have to worry about counting bottles at the end of the reception. With this system, you are charged so much for each guest. It doesn't matter whether every guest drinks alcohol—you still pay a set price for each person. This system is supposed to strike a balance between those who drink and those who don't.

Keep in mind that if your caterer uses the open and empty bottle system, someone has to go to the bar at the end of the evening and count the used and open bottles. I've done this over the years for clients and had no problems until about a year ago. I told the bartender that I would count bottles at the end of the reception. When the reception ended, the bartender I had spoken with had the bottles all lined up in nice, neat rows. We counted together and came up with a total of 35 bottles that we had consumed. A second bartender then came along (I didn't find out until later that he was the owner) and started mixing up the lines of nice, neat bottles so that they were no longer even. Then he counted again.

I watched him very closely, because a big red flag went off in my head when he undid the even rows we had established. As he counted along, I watched him count one row twice. Okay, I was onto him, but I learned a long time ago that it's sometimes better to play dumb—at least for the moment. I coyly suggested that the other bartender and I had counted only 35 bottles, not 42 like he had, and that maybe we should count again. He started to count again, but I stopped him, and in my most motherly, demure voice said, "Oh, now look, we've got these bottles all out of line. Let's line them up nice and neat, and count them again. Your friend and I counted only 35." To say he was angry is an understatement. But guess what? I didn't care. He was trying to overcharge my client by seven bottles—and at $65 per bottle, it doesn't take a brain surgeon to figure out how much money he was going to make.

Bouquet Toss

The word **bridal** comes from the old English term *bride-ale*, which refers to the mead drink (a fermented beverage made of water, honey, malt, and yeast) consumed for 30 days following the marriage.

Moral of the story: Have the bottles counted by a neutral person, and watch carefully. At the next wedding reception I had with this liquor outfit, the owner saw me coming at the end of the evening and, without saying a word, had the bottles all lined up in nice, neat rows.

The Least You Need to Know

➤ Ask lots of questions about the physical layout for the reception. Make sure the facility can accommodate the number of guests you're inviting. Also check whether parking is adequate.

➤ Make sure the reception facility has a good traffic flow pattern. Too little room to comfortably allow for the number of guests you expect can be frustrating for everyone involved.

➤ Make a list of questions for the caterer before you meet with him. Get the details in writing of what the caterer will provide.

➤ Understand your legal responsibilities if you decide to serve alcohol at the reception.

Reception Site Worksheet

Reception site: _____

Contact: _____

Telephone: _____

Time for reception to begin: _____

Time for reception to end: _____

What the facility will provide (linens, skirting, mike hookups):

_____

_____

Fee for site: _____

Deposit made: _____

Floorplan layout: _____

_____

_____

Appointments with manager: _____

Choosing the Reception Site Worksheet

Facility: _____

Rental price:

_____

Includes:

  ❏ Linens   ❏ Tables   ❏ Security

  ❏ Skirting   ❏ Chairs   ❏ Plants, decorative items

Ample parking? _____

Distance from ceremony: _____

Catering requirements: _____

    In-house: _____

    Outside: _____

Number of restrooms? _____

Accessible to people with disabilities? _____

Date available: _____

Choosing the Caterer Worksheet

Name: _____

_____

_____

Referred by: _____

_____

_____

_____

Available on: _____

_____

_____

Pricing system: _____

Per person: _____

Per item: _____

Labor charges: _____

Linen charges: _____

Delivery charges: _____

Plate charges: _____

Menu format (buffet, hors d'oeuvres, seated dinner): _____

_____

Will incorporate family recipes? _____

Chapter 6

The Wedding Party—a Circle of Friends

In This Chapter

➤ Determining the size of your wedding party

➤ Deciding whom to include

➤ Finding other jobs for friends

One of the better parts of planning your wedding is telling your friends the good news and asking them to share this wonderful time with you. Most people consider it an honor to be asked to be part of a dear friend or family member's wedding. Because you're asking someone to stand with you on one of the most significant days of your life, be sure to put careful thought into choosing your wedding party. Also, think about asking other friends to help with the other wedding duties, such as being the guest book attendant. All these folks play a huge part in keeping your wedding running smoothly.

Wedding Party Size

A complaint I hear frequently is, "My groom wants to ask 14 guys to be groomsmen. I have only eight friends for bridesmaids. Where can I get some more maids?" Well, it's probably not a good idea to rent-a-bridesmaid, although sometimes it may seem like the only option you have left. The number of men and women in the bridal party does not have to match. Figure out exactly how many people the two of you want to

Teddy's Tips

Talk with parents or older relatives about their wedding party. How many of the friends they "just had to have" are still friends? Do they even know where some of them are today? How close are some of those "best friends"? Twenty years from now, will you look at the wedding pictures and wonder who those people are?

stand up with you, and then figure out which other jobs you can delegate to friends.

If the ceremony site has a large enough altar area to have 40 of your best friends lined up to be in the wedding party, then go for it. However, if the area will accommodate only a total of 12 people (that's the two of you, plus five bridesmaids and five groomsmen), you're going to have to prioritize who you want to do the honors. You need to coordinate the size of your ceremony area with the size of your wedding party. I've been church shopping several times to find a church large enough to accommodate a large wedding party. Armed with a tape measure and a couple assistants, we go into the sanctuary area and figure out how much room we have and whether a large wedding party will fit.

Size probably doesn't matter as much as your feelings for the family and friends you're about to ask to be part of one of the most wonderful days of your life. These should be people you feel especially close to and really want to participate in this occasion.

Finalizing the List

Your wedding party will consist of several groups of people. The first people you will ask will be the maid or matron of honor and the best man. You may refer to these people as the *honor attendants;* however, in current use, an honor attendant refers to a male maid of honor or a female best man.

The special honor of maid or matron of honor may go to a sister, a cousin, or a very close friend. You even can choose to have both a maid and a matron of honor. Just be sure to decide before the ceremony which duties each will perform. Maybe the maid of honor will hold the groom's ring, while the matron of honor will help arrange the bridal gown's train. Both can help with some of the preliminary duties, such as running errands, being a good listener, and organizing some parties. Of course, this all depends on whether the honor attendants live in your area.

Traditionally, the bridesmaids are young women who are close to the bride. These may include sisters, cousins, the groom's sisters, and good friends. Bridesmaids have no official function in the wedding party but are there to be supportive.

Likewise, the groom chooses a best man. He can decide to have two best men, although this is not as common as having both a maid and a matron of honor. The groom might even ask his father to be his best man. (What an honor for any father!)

The best man helps the groom prepare for the wedding, making sure he arrives at the ceremony site on time. He holds the bride's ring during the service and offers the first toast to the new couple during the reception.

Bouquet Toss

Choosing a best man keeps with the ancient custom of finding a good friend, most likely a tribal warrior, to help shield the bride from abductors known to prowl around the ceremony site.

The groom then chooses men to serve as his groomsmen. These can be brothers, the bride's brothers, cousins, or good friends. Groomsmen have no official function in the wedding party. They generally are not ushers, but simply are friends chosen to stand up with the groom and help witness the ceremony.

The remaining members of the main wedding party include the ushers, usually one usher for every 50 guests. Sometimes, the groomsmen double as ushers. There usually isn't a problem with this system, although it helps to have at least one usher in the back of the church to help with late arrivals or unexpected happenings.

If one of your attendants drops out of the wedding plans because of illness or other circumstances, you have a couple choices. You can ask someone else to step in if that person is agreeable and if (for the women) the dress fits the new attendant. Or, you can just go as is and not worry about having even pairs. As I mentioned before, you don't need to have matching numbers of attendants.

Other attendants making up the wedding party may include the flower girl and ring bearer, candle lighters, train bearers, Bible bearers, junior groomsmen, junior bridesmaids, and pages. You may give these assignments to children or young adults.

Using Children as Attendants

Children as members of the wedding can add joy to the day. They represent innocence and remind us of the circle of life we all share. They also can detract more than you think from the wedding ceremony. You need to remember that children in wedding parties are still kids—they're not little adults in children's suits. They think like children, they behave like children, and they will be unpredictable like children.

Kids Do the Darndest Things

Do not expect four-year-old Karen to walk down the aisle in front of 650 guests and not act timid. Unless she has maturity beyond her years, she will be shy. She may say, "No way, I'm not going down there—you can't make me!" (This happens frequently with flower girls.) Or, you could have the darling little ring bearer, dressed to the limit, who stops short of making it down the aisle, throws down the pillow, and stomps out because he's not used to so many people (and so many strangers), not to mention that funny-looking guy in the bathrobe—the clergyman—at the end of the aisle.

I coordinated one wedding in which the flower girl decided that the basket she was carrying was just too heavy for her to hold and asked the minister if he could hold it for her. He politely declined, saying he was busy at the moment. You must treat children as children. Have realistic expectations—do not expect children to be more than they are capable of being. Then you will not be disappointed when they don't perform as you had hoped.

Find the Right Jobs for Kids

When you consider including children in your wedding party, think about their age and maturity. A child of four—maybe even a very mature three-year-old—is probably old enough for the responsibility you're asking him or her to perform. Children much younger than three are a risk.

If you really want a particular young child, such as a niece or a nephew, to participate in the festivities, why not list her name in the program as "Honorary Flower Girl." An *honorary flower girl* is usually someone who is too young to do the job, yet the bride wants to "honor" her by giving her this title. That way, the child is being honored (which is what you're doing in the first place), and you don't risk a traumatic and nerve-racking experience. Don't put Junior in a situation he's not ready for and one in which he doesn't understand what you expect.

Here are some jobs you might consider assigning to special young people you want to honor:

➤ Ring bearer (age three to six)

➤ Flower girl (age three to six)

➤ Train bearer (age four to eight)

➤ Guest book attendant (age 12 and up)

➤ Program attendant (age 12 and up)

➤ Coat checker (age 10 and up)

➤ Gift attendant (age 13 and up)

➤ Candle lighter (age 10 and up)

➤ Altar boy or girl (Catholic service; age 10 to 15)

These tasks are all very important and can be used to show special attention to those whom you can't include in your immediate wedding party.

Assigning Other Fun Tasks

Okay, you have your wedding party all lined up, but you have some more friends you want to include in the festivities. Well, other jobs need attention, and guests usually are honored to be asked to perform them.

Some of the more obvious jobs are …

➤ **Guest book attendant.** This person, male or female, greets guests as they enter the ceremony site or reception site (depending on where you want the guest book placed) and asks guests to sign the guest book.

➤ **Birdseed, petal, or bubble attendants.** These are the folks who will distribute birdseed, petals, or bubbles to guests at the appropriate time (your exit) so that you can be showered with them.

➤ **Program attendant.** This person usually stands by the guest book and distributes the wedding programs; this person also acts as a greeter.

➤ **Readers (both scripture and poetry).** During the service, you may have several readings. This is a responsible job for the right person.

➤ **Gift bearer.** During a Catholic service, the gift bearer brings the bread and wine to the priest.

➤ **Personal attendant.** This is a close friend of the bride who is there to help, run errands, and be supportive.

➤ **Gift attendant.** At the reception, this person is in charge of taking gifts from the guests and placing them in the appropriate spot (either a gift table or a locked room).

➤ **Reception assistants.** These folks, usually ladies, are asked to help with the reception foods, mostly cutting and serving the wedding cake.

These jobs can be assigned to folks whom you want to include as honorees. Make all the people in your wedding party feel special. Whether someone is taking care of gifts at the reception or acting as maid of honor, they all need to know that you are excited that they have agreed to serve and that you really want and need their help.

Teddy's Tips

Small bottles of bubbles are now used as a release in place of birdseed or flower petals.

Consider asking friends to mingle at the reception. Tell those who are socially outgoing that you're counting on them to roam the reception, seeking out those who seem to be alone and then engage them in conversation, ask them to dance, or introduce them to others. It makes these friends feel special and helps all the guests feel more like family.

If you're not hiring a wedding coordinator, consider asking a very special friend with organizational skills to help oversee the reception, keeping an eye out for potential problems. It's a big responsibility, but one you (and your mother) won't have time for on the wedding day.

Getting a Little Help from Your Friends

Over the years, I've heard statements like these from time to time: "Aunt Shirley is going to cater my wedding." "My friend Ellen is doing the flowers." "Jennifer, my sorority sister, is going to coordinate my wedding." "Uncle Harvey likes to tinker with a camera and will be taking the pictures."

All these examples have two common elements: The couple thinks they're saving money, and they expect a professional job. They most likely will be disappointed on both counts.

Wedding Woes

Don't assume that, just because someone is your friend, she has the expertise to handle a particular task. Even with her best efforts, these jobs may be too much for her to handle. Unless your friend or family member is a florist, photographer, or caterer by trade, it's probably a good idea to leave these tasks to the professionals.

There's nothing wrong with asking your friend Ellen to take care of your floral needs. She's a good friend, and you know she'll do her best. The problem comes when she doesn't—or can't—deliver what you expect. When those flowers arrive, you find that Ellen wasn't really right for this task. The colors are all wrong, the arrangement doesn't look anything like the picture you showed her, and she forgot the main centerpiece for the head table at the reception.

One rather bleak example of using friends for tasks that they might not be prepared for involved a bride who was on a very tight budget. A good friend volunteered to prepare some food for the reception as her wedding gift to the couple. The bride couldn't afford a caterer and was grateful to her friend for offering. The friend volunteered to bring in enough meatballs, fruit trays, and cheese and crackers for 175 guests. Two days before the wedding, the bride called this friend to inquire whether the friend needed help with any of the arrangements. The good friend shrugged off the question with, "I changed my mind. I found you another gift instead."

Needless to say, the bride was devastated. Here she was without much of the food for her reception—and to make matters worse, the good friend didn't even seem to feel any regret or concern about not following through with her promise. That close to the wedding, it was too late to hire a caterer to come in and save the day. The stressed bride got lucky: The groom's aunt heard about the plight and volunteered to provide the necessary food. This situation could have been a disaster!

The moral of this story, and the point I want to make, is that you should be very careful when you ask friends or accept offers from friends to take on major responsibilities for your wedding. If that task is normally handled by a professional, then it's almost always better to let the professional handle it. If Aunt Charlotte is a florist and wants to give you a good deal on the flowers, go for it. Saving some pennies here and there is great. But if Aunt Charlotte just likes to play with flowers, you might want to use caution when you're discussing your wedding needs around her.

The Least You Need to Know

➤ Make sure the church or other ceremony site can comfortably fit the wedding party you're planning.

➤ Wedding party members should be those individuals you feel close to and want to include as a special part of your day.

➤ Use good judgment and common sense when you choose to include children in your wedding party. Remember, children will almost always act like children. That can make for some unpredictable moments.

➤ Be very careful when asking family and friends to do some tasks for your wedding that would be better left to the pros.

Chapter 7

Cast Party— Arranging the Rehearsal Dinner

In This Chapter

➤ Learning what's behind the tradition

➤ Determining whom to invite

➤ Incorporating your own personal style

The rehearsal dinner is another wedding tradition that has evolved over time. Its main purpose is to invite guests—usually family and the wedding party—to meet or gather after the wedding rehearsal and have fun. It serves several other purposes as well, including sometimes introducing family members for the first time, letting everyone involved with the wedding ceremony have a chance to meet each other, and generally celebrating the start of the wedding festivities. Read on and plan carefully, using the "Rehearsal Dinner Worksheet" at the end of this chapter.

Examining the Tradition

After you've reserved the church, reception site, and some of the fundamental elements of the wedding day (such as photographer, florist, and musicians), you should begin thinking about a place to hold the rehearsal dinner. Usually, the rehearsal dinner immediately follows the wedding rehearsal, although it can be held just before the rehearsal or even on an entirely different day.

Despite what some folks may think, the idea behind the rehearsal dinner is not just to make sure that the groom or his family has to pay for some part of the wedding. The rehearsal dinner is a time to get friends and family members together to relax, to get to know one another, and to celebrate this wonderful occasion. In some cases, a family member or close friend might even offer to host the rehearsal dinner.

Regardless of who is going to act as host and invite the guests to the rehearsal dinner, some coordination among all the players is important. The hosts—whether the groom, his family, or other relatives—need to work with the couple—both the bride and the groom—to determine their likes and dislikes. Even though the hosts can do what they want, they really need to make sure that the guests of honor are pleased with the plans.

Check with all the players involved with the rehearsal dinner to ensure that no one is accidentally left off the guest list. Usually, the bride's family submits a guest list to the groom's family.

Getting to Know You

Because nowadays it's not common to marry the boy or girl next door, the rehearsal dinner has become a very important part of the wedding activities. Many times, this is the first opportunity for the bride and groom's families to meet each other. It isn't unusual for the two sets of parents to live on opposite sides of the country, and getting them together before the actual wedding isn't always feasible. The rehearsal dinner is a time when you can bring everyone together to meet and get to know each other in a relaxed setting, before the formality and pressures of the wedding day.

As a couple getting ready to blend family and friends, you can use the rehearsal dinner to begin forging a united front. You want your parents, grandparents, aunts, uncles, and friends—people who are special to each of you—to get off to a congenial start. Take this time to make people feel welcome and at ease with each other. Try your best to make these special people *feel* special.

Even though the groom or his family traditionally hosts the rehearsal dinner, some thoughtful planning—and perhaps compromise—is in order. Because it's so important for all guests to feel comfortable, the setting for this dinner is an important factor—especially when your families come from different backgrounds.

In my situation, for example, my father was a businessman, part of the suit-and-tie crowd. My husband-to-be's parents were involved in agriculture; blue jeans and work shirts were their appropriate attire. When Floyd (my husband) asked for advice on the type of facility we should look into for the rehearsal dinner, we chose a restaurant in which both families could feel comfortable. If one family is accustomed to the country club and the other family is more comfortable with beer and pizza at the local pub, make a compromise for the rehearsal dinner. You want both families to feel at ease.

Whom to Invite

Your guest list for the rehearsal dinner should include all the key players who normally would attend the wedding rehearsal. That may include the wedding party and their spouses or dates, the parents, the grandparents, the officiant and spouse, and sometimes some of the other key players of the wedding team, such as the organist and soloist, if you know them well. Otherwise, while certainly a nice gesture, inviting the entire choir or string ensemble isn't necessary. You should include those out-of-town family members, especially close relatives, or close friends who arrive the night before the wedding, or close friends who live nearby and whose presence would make you feel more comfortable.

One thing you should avoid if at all possible is leaving out the spouses or dates of your wedding party. It's just plain tacky. Most likely they have come to your wedding with their spouse or date, and if they are not invited to the rehearsal dinner, they are left to sit at the hotel waiting for their bridesmaid or groomsman to return.

If one side has more guests than the other, who makes the call? Technically speaking, the person(s) who are hosting the rehearsal dinner make that determination but should *always* consult with you. If, say, the bride's side has 75 names on the guest list and the groom's side only has 25 and doesn't want to pay for more than 50, then if possible, make an offer to make up the difference. I remember one wedding where this very issue arose and the groom's mother wouldn't budge on the numbers game. She was leaving off dates and spouses and demanding that the bar be stopped when it reached a certain dollar amount. The couple finally said "enough" and told the caterer to put everything on their credit card. You can really get into some tight, uncomfortable situations, and you just have to weigh the pros and cons and try to come to some consensus. This is where a good bridal consultant can lend an ear and ideas on how to solve the problem.

Many couples choose to send invitations for their rehearsal dinner. As long as the invitation is not more formal than the wedding invitation, you can do what you please. Maybe a phone call inviting guests is enough for you, or maybe you've seen some wonderful informal invitations that go with the wedding theme. Some companies also offer some great rehearsal dinner invitations. Being a mother of two sons (I'll never be a mother of the bride—interesting …), I have envisioned different kinds of invitations to our sons' rehearsal dinners. We'll just have to wait and see what the two future Mrs. Lendermans think.

Young children who are part of the wedding party probably should not be included in the dinner unless they are old enough to enjoy it. However, even if they don't attend, do include their parents on your guest list. Basically, your guest list depends on what your budget will allow and the size of the facility you choose for this function. There are large guest lists for rehearsal dinners, and there are small, intimate guest lists. The choice of how large or small the guest list can be is ultimately the hosts'.

Giving It Style

The rehearsal dinner does not have to be a formal, sit-down affair. Some of the more successful rehearsal dinners that I've heard about have been very relaxed and informal. Brides and grooms sometimes choose to have picnics, pizza parties, cookouts, or even carry-in suppers instead of a formal dinner. Remember, the primary purpose of the rehearsal dinner is to get newly merging family members together in a relaxed, informal setting.

Wedding Woes

Unless there is a tight budget for the rehearsal dinner, out-of-town family—especially close family members such as aunts and uncles—should be invited to the rehearsal dinner.

Have It Your Way

Some couples go with a theme for the rehearsal dinner. One couple opted for an old-fashioned, Midwestern picnic supper on their lake property and finished the evening with a dramatic display of fireworks. To dress up this rehearsal dinner, they used red-and-white gingham-checked tablecloths and napkins, real china, and real silverware. Although they served hamburgers and hot dogs, the fine dinnerware made the event seem more special than if they had used paper plates.

Other ideas include a beach party rehearsal dinner. Those near the water may find a picnic on the beach with volleyball and hot dogs a fun way to get folks together. Or, how about a river cruise for the rehearsal dinner? If you're near a river and have access to a riverboat, it could be fun to take it sailing off into the moonlight.

Celebrate both families' heritages by serving foods unique to both families. Perhaps print up little booklets featuring the recipes, along with an explanation of why the foods are so special. Whether you choose to have the dinner inside or out, it can be a beautiful affair. With candlelight and soft music, you can turn the backyard or a formal garden into a magical place (can't you just see the fireflies buzzing by?). Of course, if you want an elegant formal dinner for your rehearsal dinner, then do it. Add place cards for each guest, some candles and floral centerpieces, and you can have a lovely affair. Remember the rehearsal dinner should not out shine or be more elaborate than the wedding reception.

Whatever you decide to do, just make it enjoyable for your guests. Make your guests feel relaxed, welcomed, and special. They are all nervous about meeting the other side, so try to put them at ease. You might want to assign a host or hostess to each table at the rehearsal dinner to help keep the conversation moving and to make sure guests are cared for. Another way to help avoid some extra stress for your guests is to assign them a seat for the meal. That way, you can put who you want next to crazy Cousin Cindy (every family has one, you know) and not worry about your future mother-in-law sitting next to her.

Another benefit of seat assignments is that they make people get to know each other. Often, guests like to be directed to a table assignment. The well-experienced and kind host will never place total strangers at the same table without at least two people who know each other.

What's on the Agenda?

Take the opportunity either at the beginning or during the meal to introduce your families to the others. The bride can take her side and the groom his side. Add a little personal comment about some of the guests to the introductions, to make them more personable. ("This is my Aunt Helen, who helped Mom make all the centerpieces for the tables tonight.")

You may want to add some fun activities to the evening as well. I know of several in-stances in which brides and grooms have shown home videos, set to their favorite music, during the rehearsal dinner. These videos showed the couple growing up, from babies up to the present. Although these sometimes can be tear-jerkers, they also can be tension-relievers. I have found that if the mothers cry at the rehearsal or the re-hearsal dinner, chances are good that they will be tearless during the ceremony.

Another rather fun activity you can add to the evening is for the couple to roast each other. Make sure that you have someone you both trust to act as MC for this portion of the evening. Handled in the right spirit and all in good fun, a roast can help make your rehearsal dinner both relaxing and unique.

One couple took one of the informal engagement pictures and had it matted. This was displayed on a table at the rehearsal dinner. As guests were having cocktails, they were asked to write their names or a message on the matting. The couple later had it framed, and even today, it hangs on their living room wall, a reminder of a great time.

A Time to Say Thank You

The rehearsal dinner is a good opportunity for both of you to give your attendants their gifts and to say your thank-yous to your family members for all their support.

The groom's father (if he's the host) should offer the first toast of the evening, and he should offer that toast to the bride. His next toast should be to the bride and the groom, as a couple. He most likely also will welcome guests and thank them for coming. The floor is open for additional toasts after those first two. This would be an appropriate

Wedding Woes

The rehearsal dinner should never be more formal or more elaborate than the wedding reception.

time for the father of the bride to welcome the groom to the family. At this time, the bride and groom also could offer a toast to their parents, thanking them for all their love and support.

The Least You Need to Know

➤ The rehearsal dinner should be a time when family and friends—the special people in your lives—come together in a comfortable setting to meet each other and to help you launch your new life together.

➤ Include all members of the wedding party and their spouses or dates. It's not mandatory to invite very young children from the wedding party, but do include their parents.

➤ Rehearsal dinners do not have to be formal. Make it whatever you want— sit-down dinner, picnic, carry-in supper—just make it a setting in which both families will feel comfortable.

➤ Use the rehearsal dinner as a chance to say thank you and to hand your gifts to the wedding party.

Rehearsal Dinner Worksheet

Place: _____

Address: _____

Telephone: _____

Contact: _____

Time to begin: _____

Time to end: _____

Menu ideas: _____

_____

_____

Meal price: _____

Bar charge: _____

Agenda ideas ("Roast the couple," slide show, etc.): _____

_____

Equipment needed: _____

_____

Invitations ordered: _____

Responses received:

Guest's Name	Address	# Attending
_____	_____	_____
_____	_____	_____
_____	_____	_____
_____	_____	_____
_____	_____	_____
_____	_____	_____
_____	_____	_____
_____	_____	_____
_____	_____	_____

Romance and Roses— Planning Your Honeymoon

Although it may be easy to overlook in the hustle and bustle of planning for the wedding itself, making your honeymoon reservations is one more thing you need to consider early in the planning stages. Depending on where you plan to take your honeymoon, you need to arrange reservations and details as early as possible. In this chapter, I'll talk about the type of honeymoon you want, explore some popular spots, and help you figure out your perfect honeymoon site.

Finally, Some Time Alone ...

Ah, the honeymoon. Finally, you'll be able to get away and be alone. The wedding and reception will be behind you, and your wedding day will be only fond memories and warm fuzzies. With all the pre-wedding parties, checklists, and appointments, the two of you won't have much time together. You're definitely going to be ready for some quality time alone.

Communication Is the Key

So, now you're planning for this wonderful time away, alone together for the first time as husband and wife. Where do you start? First, talk to each other and decide what your options are, how much time and money you have, and what your ideal honeymoon is. It's very important to discuss openly and honestly with each other what you want to do on the honeymoon.

When I was married, my soon-to-be husband wanted our honeymoon to be a trip to Mammoth Cave in Kentucky. Now, I don't get real excited about cold, damp, dark places where bats fly around freely and things slither on their bellies. I just didn't find this cave idea very romantic. So, we did some soul searching and some more talking and found out that we both really enjoy winter sports. We were married in January, so instead of heading south to a warmer climate, we ventured north to a wonderful mountain lodge complete with fireplaces, snowmobiles, cross-country skiing, and a huge toboggan run. We had a great time because we talked first and looked at our options, including what we could afford and what was within our reach. (By the way, just so you don't think I was totally insensitive to my husband's feelings, on our first anniversary we headed south to Mammoth Cave. It was actually a very nice place.)

Teddy's Tips

You will be tired. You will be physically exhausted from the wedding activities. Don't let anyone else convince you otherwise. Make sure your honeymoon plans include plenty of time to rest and regenerate after all the hectic months you've both just survived.

Whatever you choose for your honeymoon, whether it's a two-week cruise down the California coast, a luxury resort in the Hawaiian Islands, or a weekend in the big city, make it special. Make it your time to be alone together, to reflect on the wedding, to get to know each other, and to start out this marriage on the right foot. It doesn't have to cost you a bundle, either. Talk early on about the amount you realistically have to spend on this honeymoon. Stay within you budget. There is no reason to overspend on the honeymoon. Remember, you are in control of all pricing, including your honeymoon expenses.

Honey, Why Are You Crying?

A couple things to watch out for as you head out on your honeymoon: You may feel much more tense than usual, and you may even cry more easily. Relax and accept that these feelings are all part of normal wedding stress.

After our wedding and reception, as we were heading to our wedding night destination, I started to cry. I couldn't explain to my new husband why I was crying, and I couldn't stop. The more he asked what was wrong, the more I cried. In looking back on our wedding, I now know that it was nothing more than all the wedding stress coming out. The tension of keeping it together for those long months of planning finally had taken its toll.

I talk more about wedding stress in Chapter 19, "I Think I'm Losing My Mind." For now, the bottom line on your honeymoon is to make it special for both of you. Plan early, and find a good travel agent who knows what your budget is and will help you stick to it. Be sure to ask about special packages, especially those made just for honeymooners. Likewise, if you don't want to be identified as honeymooners, don't pick a honeymoon package or go to one of the traditional honeymoon locations. Make sure you get all details ironed out before you leave.

Bouquet Toss

The word **honeymoon** comes from the days of marriage-by-capture. A man would see a woman he liked, capture her (many times against her will), and hide out for a moon (30 days—one full moon to another full moon), or a month. During that time they would drink a concoction sweetened with honey—thus, honeymoon.

Get Thee to Paradise

As with any trip or vacation, deciding where to go on your honeymoon is a very personal decision for the two of you to make. You've probably heard about some of the traditional honeymoon spots, however, and you may want to give them some consideration. Following are a few of the current hot spots:

➤ **Hawaiian Islands.** All the islands offer the right weather with the right atmosphere for some very romantic times. These islands are about as close to Eden as you can get. The islanders have that "hang-loose," "don't worry," "it's going to be okay" attitude that makes you feel so welcomed and relaxed. Friends of ours traveled there earlier this year and were headed for the Big Island. They took the wrong island-hop plane, however, and landed on the opposite side of the island, more than three hours away. They called the hotel where their reservations were and told the manager, "We've got a problem. We landed at the wrong airport." The manager replied, "There are no problems on Hawaii, only solutions." Makes you feel good, doesn't it?

Having just returned from a "second honeymoon" to Hawaii, I can attest to the wonderful, laid-back attitude and beautiful scenery. When we finally arrived at our resort, we were behind our schedule. After we had checked into the hotel, the bellman had our luggage and I said to Floyd, "Come on, we have to hurry." The bellman stopped me and said, "Mrs. Lenderman, you are in Hawaii now. We have a much different philosophy from you on the mainland. It takes us an hour and a half to watch *60 Minutes.*" And he was right. We slowed down and savored every moment of our trip.

Watch for specials during the fall and in early January. This is an affordable vacation spot for lots of couples. If you watch for a price war on airfares, you can get some pretty good rates.

➤ **The Poconos.** This honeymoon capital of the world includes four counties located in northeastern Pennsylvania and consists of 2,400 square miles of majestic mountains, wonderful views, rivers and streams, and beautiful forests. There are many resorts to choose from in this region, and any of the four seasons are perfect for a stay in these resorts, which are made to fit all types of activities: winter sports, water-skiing in the summer, and walking along mountain paths in the fall foliage. They offer both earthy pleasures and fantastic accommodations. If you dream of a heart-shaped bathtub in your private cabin, then one of the resorts in the Poconos might be just right for you. If you've always wanted to spend the night in a 1900s farmhouse, a charming country inn, or a French chateau, then a resort in the Poconos may be just the ticket.

There's also lots of shopping here. More than 100 factory outlet stores are within driving distance of the center of the mountains. Don't forget your credit cards!

The Poconos area offers a Honeymoon Planning Kit. Simply call 1-800-POCONOS to receive the information.

➤ **Caribbean Islands.** Located on the eastern side of the United States and running from south of Miami to South America, the Caribbean holds many islands to choose from. Watch for specials during the low season (April to October); it rains more at this time of year, so prices run about 30 percent lower than the high season, which is November to April. Cruise several islands, or fly off to a remote island. They call this paradise, and there's a reason for that. With their gorgeous beaches, clear waters, and fun nightlife, many of the islands bid for the honeymooner business.

Jamaica is a popular honeymoon choice with a variety of accommodations and activities. There are six main resort areas in Jamaica, and they each have a different style. Montego Bay is Jamaica's primary port. Other cities famous for honeymooners are Ocho Rios, Negril, Port Antonio, and Kingston. Tucked away in the center of the island is Mandeville. While much will depend on what you want to do with your honeymoon time, each of these areas offers different points of interest to honeymooners. All inclusive resorts, such as Sandals, Couples, and Club Med, are popular in Jamaica and throughout the Caribbean. One price covers everything, including food, tips, and alcohol.

Other islands in the Caribbean area that can delight honeymooners are the Virgin Islands, Puerto Rico, Bermuda, and the Bahamas. All have wonderful beaches, terrific nightlife, and tremendous accommodations.

Teddy's Tips

Just as the Association of Bridal Consultants can provide names of consultants in your area, they also can provide names of destination and honeymoon travel specialists who are also members. Call 860-355-0464 for information.

➤ **Mexican Riviera.** South of the western United States, the Mexican Riviera boasts 2,000 miles of white-sand beaches. Some favorite honeymoon spots here include Acapulco, Cancun, and Puerto Vallarta. Again, they offer great nightlife and fantastic resorts.

➤ **Hilton Head, South Carolina.** This romantic city by the sea is fast becoming a popular honeymoon site. With a variety of condos and hotel prices to choose from, almost any couple can spend some time here walking along the beach, sipping a cool drink on the hotel balcony, or hitting one of the many golf clubs.

➤ **Las Vegas, Nevada.** Las Vegas not only represents a wedding ceremony site for many couples, but it also offers some excitement for honeymooners. You can find some of the most famous hotels in the world on "The Strip." The city's off-season is November to January. Some sites around the area include Death Valley, Grand Canyon West, Hoover Dam, and Lake Mead. For information, call the Chamber of Commerce at 702-735-1616 or the Nevada Commission on Tourism at 1-800-638-2328.

➤ **San Diego, California.** This city, which lies just north of the Mexican border, was once a remote Spanish mission. Famous must-see sites include Balboa Park and the San Diego Zoo. San Diego is full of history and has a near perfect year-round climate. Many people want to retire here, but don't let that stop you from considering it for a honeymoon spot—it has action, too.

➤ **San Antonio, Texas.** Located in south central Texas, this city's name means "Saint Anthony's City" in Spanish. One famous point in San Antonio is the Alamo, where Davy Crockett and Jim Bowie fought the huge Mexican Army.

The Alamo lies in the center of town along The River Walk. The downtown area is delightfully filled with cafés, boutiques, and hotels with tropical gardens. Call the San Antonio Visitor's Bureau at 1-800-447-3372.

➤ **Breckenridge, Colorado.** If it's snowy weather and skiing you dream of for your honeymoon, then you should venture to Breckenridge. The city actually got its start in 1859 with a gold rush discovery. Since then, the town has enjoyed activities for all seasons. There are many historical buildings in Breckenridge, and its Victorian charm lures honeymooners from all over. For more information, call 1-800-800-2732.

➤ **Cruise ships.** Many couples feel that an ocean cruise is the ultimate honeymoon idea. One price gets you almost everything (usually except for alcohol). You can be entertained, if you want, or left alone for a romantic walk about the deck in the moonlight. Hundreds of activities can fill up your day, including the sights and sounds of the neighboring islands (when in dock), along with swimming, sunning, taking exercise classes, doing aerobics, gambling, dancing in discos, and taking in cabaret shows. Other activities include board games, basketball, skeet shooting, Ping-Pong, saunas, country-and-western nights, a piano bar, a library, beauty shops, arts-and-crafts classes, massages, laundry services, midnight buffets, room service, duty-free shopping, movies, and endless eating.

Here are some points to consider if you're thinking about a honeymoon cruise:

➤ **Age group.** The age of passengers varies, not only on ship but also by area of the world. For example, travelers on cruises in the Caribbean usually are younger than those traveling in the Alaskan waters or the Baltic seas.

➤ **Ship size.** The size of the vessel will help determine what kind of cruise you want. Those carrying more than 1,200 passengers will offer more activities than the smaller ships.

➤ **Price.** Price is very important. Check with travel agents who specialize in cruise ships. They should be able to offer you all the information and help you to determine which line and what size ship is right you and your budget.

➤ **Departure days.** Departure days don't vary much; most cruise lines depart on Saturday. A few sail on Sunday, however, to accommodate the honeymooners who have married on Saturday.

➤ **Cabin accommodations.** Be sure to check with your travel agent about the cabin accommodations. If you want a king- or queen-size bed in your cabin, understand that not all cruise ships offer that option.

➤ **Shore excursions.** Check about shore excursions before you sail. In many places, these can be an unnecessary purchase. (Strolling through the local village market can be fun on your own; you might not want to go on-shore in a group.) In some cases, though, the excursion may catch your eye (hiking through a rain forest, riding horses on the beach, or snorkeling in clear blue waters). Ask your cruise travel agent for a list of ports where it would be better to go solo for sights and those ports where you will need a group tour.

➤ **Disney World.** If you want to feel like a child again, head south to Orlando for a time of fun and excitement amid the king of entertainment, Mickey Mouse. The various hotels in the area are geared to offer all the extras for the honeymooners, and you shouldn't be bored for lack of something to do.

Teddy's Tips

When packing for a cruise, consider shorts or slacks with elastic waistbands—with all the food available around the clock, you may need some room to grow!

Hints for Honeymooners

Here are some tips to help you take some of the worry out of your honeymoon travels:

➤ Take most of your money in traveler's checks. Be sure to get some in smaller denominations ($20) because some areas will not honor larger amounts ($50 and above).

➤ If traveling overseas, convert some cash to the foreign currency to cover initial expenses (transportation, tips, and more) before you leave. You really don't want to go out on your wedding night to convert currency!

➤ Overseas, it's best to use a credit card for purchases. The conversion rate usually is better than what you'll get at a bank, which is much better than what you'll get in stores and hotels.

➤ Keep a list of your traveler's checks' numbers, credit card numbers, and checking account numbers separate from where you keep the checks and cards themselves. Also take the phone numbers for these companies with

Teddy's Tips

Make sure you take $1 bills with you if you go to other countries. Many times you will find yourself wanting to purchase items that street vendors are selling and have to barter with them. American dollars are the best way to pay.

you. In case any of these items are lost or stolen, you can get help much faster if you have phone numbers and account information.

➤ Label luggage both inside and outside with your name, address, and phone number. Keep a list of luggage contents (for claims, if your luggage is lost).

➤ If you're traveling by air, take any medications and important papers (such as passports) in a carry-on bag.

➤ Rental car companies require a major credit card and have age restrictions. Check ahead of time.

➤ Make sure you have homeowner's or renter's insurance on your wedding gifts before you leave home.

➤ When making airline reservations, do not make the bride's ticket in her married name. Use the name she will have ID for, because you will have to provide it to security at check-in.

Most of all, remember that your honeymoon—whether it's two weeks on a remote island or two days in the local hotel—should be a special time for the two of you. Plan ahead, and make every minute count. Relax, get some much-needed sleep, and get your marriage off to a great start. (Use the "Honeymoon Worksheet" at the end of this chapter to make this special trip everything you've always dreamed it would be.)

Wedding Woes

If you travel to a sunny climate or to a climate with sun and lots of snow, be sure to take and use your sunscreen. Nothing can ruin a romantic getaway faster than a painful sunburn.

The Least You Need to Know

➤ Plan early. It takes a good travel agent and advance planning to get the best prices and accommodations.

➤ Be realistic about what you both want and what you can actually afford. Don't overstep your budget.

➤ Put a lot of thought into how you want to spend your first days as husband and wife. Choose a location you are both comfortable with, and then pick activities that you both enjoy.

Honeymoon Worksheet

Activities to include: _____

_____

_____

_____

_____

_____

_____

_____

Travel agent: _____

Telephone: _____

Budgeted amount: _____

Destination: _____

Hotel: _____

Mode of travel: _____

Meals included? _____

Extra expenses: _____

_____

Documents required (passports, IDs): _____

Luggage needed: _____

_____

_____

What to pack: _____

_____

_____

_____

_____

Planning Check-Off List

Six to Twelve Months Before the Wedding

_____ Announce your engagement.

_____ Plan the engagement party or make the announcement to the rest of your family and friends.

_____ Attend bridal shows.

_____ Talk with a bridal consultant/wedding coordinator. Make an appointment for a consultation.

_____ Together with both sets of parents, discuss wedding plans, including formality.

_____ Determine a budget.

_____ If you are sharing expenses, decide who will pay for what.

_____ Select a date and time for the wedding.

_____ Call the church or synagogue for an appointment with the officiant.

_____ If it will be a civil ceremony, call the officiant.

_____ Meet with the officiant.

_____ Ask friends and family to serve as wedding attendants.

_____ Start comparison shopping for services, such as florist, caterer, photographer, and videographer.

_____ Select wedding rings and make arrangements for engraving.

_____ Begin writing your guest lists.

_____ Gather ideas for reception: menu, beverages, entertainment, favors, and so on.

_____ Call the reception site and reserve it.

_____ Reserve your service providers: caterer, photographer, videographer, florist, musicians, limo, and so on.

_____ Shop for your wedding gown and headpiece. Also look at attendants' dresses.

_____ Begin to plan the wedding ceremony and reception music.

_____ Register with department stores for bridal gift registry.

Five Months Before the Wedding

_____ Select and order your gown, headpiece, and attendants' dresses.

_____ Discuss honeymoon plans with your fiancé, and send for travel information.

_____ Check samples of wedding invitations, announcements, and enclosure cards.

_____ Begin shopping for your wedding cake.

_____ Reserve blocks of rooms at hotels for out-of-town guests (include this information with invitations).

Four Months Before the Wedding

_____ Select and order your wedding stationery: invitations, announcements, enclosures, informals, scrolls, napkins, and thank-you notes.

_____ Get necessary travel documents (passport, birth certificate).

_____ Draw maps with directions to the ceremony and reception site for out-of-town guests.

_____ Make an appointment with the caterer or banquet manager to discuss your reception menu.

_____ Make an appointment with your bridal consultant to "touch base" and get your questions answered.

Three Months Before the Wedding

_____ Decide on honeymoon destination, and call for reservations.

_____ Begin shopping for your going-away outfit and honeymoon clothes.

_____ Finalize your guest list, check for duplicates, and correct spelling and addresses.

_____ Review musical selections with your musicians.

_____ Arrange for an engagement picture for the newspaper.

_____ Make an appointment with the florist to discuss floral budget and floral decorations.

_____ Check with local authorities about requirements for marriage license and blood test.

_____ Make an appointment with your doctor for a physical.

_____ Begin addressing the inner and outer invitation envelopes.

_____ Complete honeymoon plans: Buy air or cruise tickets.

Two Months Before the Wedding

_____ Order the wedding cake and groom's cake.

_____ Have a physical examination, blood tests, and any required inoculations for foreign travel.

_____ Accompany groom to the formal wear shop and choose formal attire for the male attendants.

Seven Weeks Before the Wedding

_____ Meet with the caterer or banquet manager and firm up reception details. Ask for a banquet room floor plan.

_____ Consult a party rental store if equipment is needed at the reception.

_____ Schedule an appointment with the bridal consultant.

_____ Talk with musicians and review your selections.

_____ Make an appointment with your photographer for your formal bridal portrait.

Six Weeks Before the Wedding

_____ Call the church or synagogue and confirm rehearsal date and time.

_____ Discuss music with the church organist and soloist.

_____ Plan the rehearsal dinner with the caterer.

_____ Visit the church and reception site and do a floor plan (if not done earlier).

_____ Have the males in the wedding party, including the fathers, rent their formal wear at the same store.

_____ If there are out-of-town male attendants, have the local store send them the tux information and a postcard to return with their measurements so they can order the tuxes.

_____ Order wedding programs.

_____ Order favors (if using).

Five Weeks Before the Wedding

_____ Mail all the invitations.

_____ Select and buy gifts for all attendants.

_____ Get swatches of attendants' dress fabric and have shoes dyed in one lot.

_____ If attendants live out-of-town, arrange for their dresses to be sent to them for fittings and alterations.

_____ Meet the florist and order your flowers. Take samples of fabric and pictures of your gown and attendants' gowns.

_____ Purchase or borrow bridal garter, guest book, pen, cake knife, and toasting glasses.

Four Weeks Before the Wedding

_____ Prepare the wedding announcement for the local newspaper.

_____ All invitations should be in the mail.

_____ Make an appointment with your hair stylist and a makeup artist to try out makeup and hair styles for your wedding day.

_____ Finalize arrangements for the rehearsal dinner.

_____ Finalize arrangements for the reception.

_____ Check with attendants regarding their accessories.

_____ Wrap attendants' gifts and have them ready to present.

_____ Make an appointment for the final fitting of your gown.

_____ Begin recording invitation acceptances and regrets.

_____ Begin addressing announcement envelopes.

_____ Select wedding gifts for each other.

_____ Arrange for transportation of the wedding party to the wedding and reception.

_____ Discuss the ceremony with the officiant.

_____ Make a seating plan for the rehearsal dinner and reception.

_____ Write place cards for the reception.

_____ Decide whether you will use a receiving line.

_____ If you are moving to another town after the wedding, call the movers and make arrangements.

Three Weeks Before the Wedding

_____ Have your final fitting.

_____ Notify all participants of rehearsal date, time, and place.

_____ Have your formal portrait taken.

_____ Check on honeymoon tickets and reservations.

_____ Set up a table to display your wedding gifts.

_____ Record gifts and continue to send thank-you notes.

_____ Get marriage license.

_____ Confirm transportation to ceremony and reception.

_____ Attend showers given in your honor.

_____ Arrange for bridesmaids' luncheon.

_____ Ask a friend to handle the wedding gifts at the reception.

_____ Make arrangements for gifts to be taken from the reception to your home or to storage.

_____ Hire a "house sitter" for the rehearsal and wedding day for your home, your parents' home, and your fiancé's home.

_____ Ask someone to be the guest book attendant.

_____ Check with cleaners about preserving your gown.

_____ Assign someone to take your gown to that cleaners.

_____ Pick up tickets and confirm reservations for honeymoon.

Two Weeks Before the Wedding

_____ Finalize hotel arrangements for out-of-town guests.

_____ Plan a "welcome" package for out-of-town guests to be in their hotel rooms when they arrive.

_____ Send your photograph and wedding announcement to the newspaper.

_____ Check on accessories for the groom and male attendants.

_____ Make an appointment with your hair stylist, makeup artist, and manicurist.

_____ Give addressed and stamped announcements to someone who will mail them the day after the wedding.

_____ Follow up on guests who have not returned their response card. You must have an accurate count for the caterer.

_____ Meet with your bridal consultant to go over all the details.

One Week Before the Wedding

_____ Eat right and get plenty of rest this week!

_____ Give the caterer a guaranteed count for the reception.

_____ Double-check all service providers: florist, photographer, caterer, church, and so on.

_____ Pay balances due on services required before the wedding.

_____ Have money or checks in envelopes for your consultant to hand to organist, soloist, musicians, minister, and anyone who needs to be paid the day of the wedding.

_____ Host the bridesmaids' luncheon.

_____ Remind everyone of the date and time of the rehearsal.

_____ Pack for the honeymoon.

_____ Give gifts to attendants (if not planned for rehearsal dinner).

_____ Spend some quiet time with your family.

_____ Have "something old, new, borrowed, and blue" ready.

_____ Explain any special seating to your bridal consultant.

_____ Attend the bachelorette party (*not* the night before the wedding).

Two Days Before the Wedding

_____ Check the weather conditions for the wedding day and make adjustments if needed.

_____ Lay out everything you will need to dress for the wedding in one place at home.

_____ Your bridal consultant should provide a care package: safety pins, thread, bobbi pins, hair spray, soft drinks, juice, crackers, and more for your use.

_____ Make sure the cars involved have gas.

One Day Before the Wedding

_____ Attend the rehearsal.

_____ Make sure you and your groom are comfortable with the rehearsal and have no questions.

_____ If you are leaving for your honeymoon directly from the reception, place your luggage in the car you will be driving and lock it.

_____ RELAX—take a hot bath. Have a glass of warm milk or hot tea and get a good night's rest.

The Day!!

_____ Have your bridal consultant get your gown, veil, and/or bridesmaids' gowns from the bridal shop and take them directly to the ceremony site (if the shop doesn't deliver).

_____ Eat a good breakfast—something that will last. You want to include protein items and some bread items (for energy). You might be too nervous to eat closer to the wedding time.

_____ Give yourself plenty of time to get ready. Don't rush! Enjoy this time. You may even indulge and have a makeup artist and hair stylist come to the ceremony site to apply makeup and do your hair.

_____ Your consultant should make sure that anything belonging to you that needs to go from the church to the reception will be taken there.

_____ *Enjoy this day!* You've planned well and now you can relax!

Best wishes for a lifetime of happiness!!!

Part 3

I Now Pronounce You ...
Ceremony Details

In Parts 1 and 2, I talked about some of the major items to be discussed and reviewed before you start spending dollars.

However, the biggest part of the whole day is the ceremony—and it should be of prime importance. After all, this is the legal part (and religious, too) of one of the most important days of your life.

In Part 3, I'll give you a general overview of some of the main religious services and go into detail about how to personalize your wedding service.

Chapter 9

Get Serious— Traditional Religious Services

In This Chapter

➤ Understanding different religious services

➤ Learning some of the traditions and terminology

➤ Accepting advice from the clergy

About 75 percent of all marriages take place in some form of religious establishment. That may be a church for Protestant, Catholic, and Orthodox services, or a synagogue or temple for Jewish couples. While I don't have a degree in theology and don't claim to be an expert, I do have a fundamental understanding of some of the primary parts of the various services. While the information contained in this chapter is intended to give you an understanding of the different religious ceremonies, it is only an overview.

The rules on getting married and what you can and cannot do are changing all the time. Much of what you do in your ceremony will depend on your clergy. He is your expert. Even in the same religion you will have some clergy who will not bend any rules while others will tend to be laid-back and more inclined to go with your wishes (as long as they don't offend anyone or go against the religious beliefs). So, keep that in mind as you read. This is general information not intended to be the "final" word on any aspect of the ceremony. That's between you and your clergy. In my research, I also came across some articles written and researched by the Association of Bridal Consultants (ABC). The ABC has graciously given me consent to use some of its material.

Eastern Orthodox

The churches of Orthodox rites, including Greek and Russian churches, hold services similar to a Catholic service. The priest and community control many aspects of the wedding ceremony, including what language is to be used. The traditional wedding service is firmly rooted in Byzantine ritual and is quite lengthy.

The Orthodox ceremony is full of symbolism. It's divided into two parts: the Betrothal and the service of Crowning.

The Betrothal

The Betrothal begins with the blessing of the rings by the priest, who takes them in his hand, makes the sign of the cross, and says, "The servant of God (groom) is betrothed to the handmaiden of God (bride), in the name of the Father, and of the Son, and of the Holy Ghost."

The best man exchanges the rings, taking the bride's ring and placing it on the groom's finger, and then taking the groom's ring and placing it on the bride's finger. The rings are the ancient symbol of betrothal. The exchange signifies that, in married life, the weakness of one partner will be compensated for by the strength of the other partner. The Orthodox belief is that, by themselves, the individuals of the newly betrothed couple are incomplete; together, they are made perfect.

During the rest of the service, the couple holds candles to symbolize the Lord's light. The bride's bouquet is either held by an attendant or placed on a table.

The Crowning

The Crowning is the climax of the wedding service. Wreaths or crowns are placed on the couple's heads. The bride's headpiece must be removed and held by an attendant if it interferes with the crown.

Usually, two crown bearers are included in the wedding processional and walk side by side because the crowns are joined with a ribbon, again to signify unity. The crowns are a sign of the glory and honor with which God crowns the couple during the sacrament. When the crowning takes place, the priest takes the crowns and, holding them above the couple, says, "The servant of God (groom) is crowned unto the handmaiden of God (bride), in the name of the Father, Son, and Holy Ghost. Amen."

The rite of Crowning is followed by the reading of the Epistle and the Gospel. Wine is given to the couple in a common cup, denoting the mutual sharing of joy and sorrow. Drinking from the common cup reminds the couple that, from then on, they will share in everything in life.

The priest then leads the couple and the honor attendants around the table on which the Gospel has been placed, symbolizing the Word of God and the redemption by Christ. They circle the table three times to signify the Trinity.

The final part of the service takes place while the priest is leading the couple around the table. The first of three hymns begins. The first hymn celebrates the incarnation of Christ and praises the Mother of God. The second hymn asks the victoriously crowned martyrs to pray for the couple's salvation, and that the couple may live a life worthy to be crowned in heaven. The third hymn glorifies Christ.

Orthodox Church members must receive Communion on the Sunday before the marriage ceremony. The Church allows interfaith marriages, but one partner and one witness must be Eastern Orthodox.

It's helpful to have detailed wedding programs printed so that your non-Orthodox guests can understand the symbolism of the service. The service is a very moving and lovely ceremony; guests will appreciate it all the more if they know and understand what is happening and why.

Protestant

When you talk about Protestant services, you're talking about many different denominations: Baptist, Methodist, Presbyterian, Church of Christ, Episcopal, and Lutheran, to name just a few. Add to that the many independent and nontraditional branches, and it becomes quite difficult to provide a "typical" Protestant service.

Because I'm Presbyterian by choice and come from a long line of Presbyterians, I will refer to the *Book of Common Worship* as my guide for a standard Presbyterian marriage service. Other Protestant denominations have their own guidelines and may have different requirements for their services. Be sure to check with your minister or officiant; some ministers are very rigid and will not give or take on any point of the service, while others are willing to work with you to make the service unique to both of you.

The standard Protestant service begins with the Words of Welcome in which the minister greets the congregation, announcing that they have come to see the bride and groom united in marriage. This is followed by the Call to Worship. The traditional words here are, "We are gathered here today to witness the marriage of John and Sally in Holy Matrimony ...."

Following this opening, you may select a reading or two. These readings can be (depending on your minister) Biblical verses, a favorite poem, or some other piece of literature that is appropriate for a religious service. One Bible verse that couples often choose is I Corinthians, verse 13 ("and the greatest of these is love").

At this point, the minister may offer a short sermon to the couple. He may talk about marriage as a commitment or refer to some part of the couple's life in which there has been struggle and they have overcome that struggle. A good minister can make a lovely sermon a very meaningful part of the service.

Next in the service, the minister will ask the couple to declare their intentions. He will ask a series of questions to which the bride and groom either answer "I do" or "I will."

Following this, the minister will ask, "Who gives this woman to be married to this man?" Whereupon, the bride's father, choking back tears, says, "Her mother and I." More frequently these days, the minister says, "Who brings this woman to be married to this man?" rather than, "Who gives this woman?" because it doesn't sound quite so possessive. I've seen a lovely variation on this question in several recent services. Rather than "who gives" or "who brings," the minister asks both families if they will support the union and give it their blessing. The minister may say, "Do you, the parents, accept both (bride) and (groom) as your own? Do you give your loving support to their marriage, and do you acknowledge that from this time forward, their loyalty shall be to one another?" The families then (hopefully!) both answer, "We do."

The next part is the biggie: the marriage vows. Within each denomination, you should have a couple choices. Sometimes, ministers will let you write your own vows (we'll talk about that in Chapter 10, "I Do, I Really Do"). If you're creative and want to make the service more meaningful, try your hand at that.

After the vows segment, the rings are blessed and exchanged. Usually, the minister will say a few words about the ring being an unbroken circle symbolizing unending and everlasting love.

If you're incorporating a unity candle into your ceremony, this is the point at which you light it. A unity candle is a candle that remains unlit on the altar table. Then, after the vows and the ring segment of the ceremony, the bride and groom light it to signify the unity of their marriage. Sometimes, the parents also light family candles before the service to represent both the bride's family and the groom's family. Some churches do not permit a unity candle because it holds no theological significance, so be sure to check with your officiant.

A unity candle with family candles to the side and simply decorated with bouquets, which can be used later at the reception.

(Colter Photography)

At this point in the service, the minister offers a Prayer of Thanksgiving and usually concludes with the Lord's Prayer. Your congregation can join in saying the Lord's Prayer, or sometimes the Lord's Prayer is sung.

The minister may ask the bride and groom to kneel for the benediction. Some ministers place their hands on the couple's heads for the blessing; others wrap their stoles around the bride and groom's hands as a sign of support.

Following the benediction, the minister, if allowed, announces the couple as Mr. and Mrs. John Smith, and the recessional begins.

Roman Catholic

In many respects, the Roman Catholic wedding rite resembles that of the Protestant denomination, with the blessings, prayers, and exchange of vows and rings.

The Roman Catholic ceremony, however, is also the Sacrament of Matrimony, one of the seven sacraments Catholics believe are channels of God's grace. The ceremony consists of at least three readings, the nuptial blessing and concluding prayers, and the Sacrament itself.

Bouquet Toss

The reason the bride stands to the left of her groom dates back to the Anglo-Saxon times, when the groom, fearing attack from fire-breathing dragons and other menaces, had to keep his right hand free to grab his sword.

The Sacrament often is included in a Mass, referred to as a Nuptial Mass. Nuptial Masses usually are celebrated in the morning, but the Sacrament of Matrimony may be celebrated at any time. When an afternoon or evening wedding is scheduled without a Mass, it's customary for the couple and other Catholic bridal party members to participate in a morning Mass and to receive Communion at that time. It's also customary to receive the Sacrament of Reconciliation.

Marriages are announced by banns, read during Mass or published in a church bulletin. This replaces a traditional Protestant question that's asked at the ceremony: whether anyone knows why the marriage should not take place.

The Catholic Church encourages the couple to help develop and personalize the ceremony, within constraints. Particularly appropriate readings from the Scriptures, prayers, and hymns have been identified and may be used. Other modifications are possible.

After the exchange of vows comes the exchange of rings. The best man gives the bride's ring to the priest, who blesses it and gives it to the groom, who then places it on the bride's finger.

In a double ring ceremony, after the bride receives her ring, the maid of honor gives the groom's ring to the priest; the blessing and presentation are repeated.

The Roman Catholic Church has relaxed many of its former stringent rules regarding marriage to non-Catholics. Restrictions do apply, however, some based on church rules and others regulated by the local diocese or parish. It's possible to have two religious ceremonies follow one another or to have an ecumenical service, with another faith's officiant participating.

The Roman Catholic Church prefers both the best man and the maid of honor to be Catholic, but requires only one to be. The other attendants don't have to be Catholic, but they will be instructed in the required courtesies and reverences.

The Catholic partner is required to promise to continue observing the Catholic faith and to raise children as Catholics, but the non-Catholic partner no longer is required to make that promise.

Some Common Threads Among Christian Weddings

Some common elements among all Christian wedding services include the processional, the recessional, and the placement of the wedding party at the altar. Although individual denominations or churches may have developed somewhat unique versions of these parts of the ceremony, they usually are simply a variation of a standard theme.

The Christian Processional

In the standard Christian processional, the groomsmen and the groom enter first, followed by the bridesmaids. The maid of honor is the last adult attendant to enter and is followed by any children in the party, such as a ring bearer or flower girl. The bride is the last member of the wedding party to enter the church and usually is escorted by her father or other close male relative or friend.

This example shows the groom and groomsmen (or ushers) in pairs leading the processional. They can walk single-file or can make their entrance at the front of the altar area with the priest. Next come the bridesmaids, who can walk in pairs or single–file (depending on the officiant), followed by the maid or matron of honor, the flower girl and ring bearer, and finally the bride and her father or other escort.

Notice how the aisle candles were used to block off a part of the church this couple didn't need for guests.

(Colter Photography)

The Christian processional.

Legend
1 = Bride
2 = Groom
3 = Maid of Honor
4 = Best Man
5 = Bridesmaid
6 = Groomsmen/ushers
7 = Flower Girl
8 = Ring Bearer
9 = Father of Bride
10 = Mother of Bride
11 = Father of Groom
12 = Mother of Groom
13 = Officiant
14 = Cantor
15 = Bride's Grandfathers
16 = Bride's Grandmothers
17 = Groom's Grandfathers
18 = Groom's Grandmothers

Bouquet Toss

In the Roman Catholic ceremony, the bride's father escorts her up the aisle. When the father gives his daughter's hand to the groom, he joins his wife in the first pew. If a bride's father cannot perform this duty, a brother, uncle, godfather, or close family friend can take his place. In rare cases, a bride could ask the groom's father to take the role. The escort, by tradition, is a man. If the bride has no one for the role, she traditionally walks up the aisle alone.

Positions at the Altar

When the bride and her escort arrive at the front of the church, she lets go of his arm and moves her flowers to her left hand; she gives her right hand to the groom. He puts it through his left arm, with her hand near his elbow. It's also acceptable for the couple to simply stand side by side holding hands.

As for the remainder of the wedding party, you can move them around to accommodate your personal wishes (with the blessing of the priest or minister, of course). Wedding party placement varies depending on your church and its physical setting. The following illustration shows one example of the basic positioning of the wedding party as it arrives at the altar.

Notice the placement of the wedding guests as they are gathered in a circle around the couple. Also notice another way to use a unity candle in a nontraditional setting.

(Classic Contemporary Photography by Geno)

There are no rules for arranging the wedding party; the decision usually is made by the bride, who relies heavily on the priest's advice and recommendations from her bridal consultant, if she has one. It should be obvious here that a rehearsal is essential.

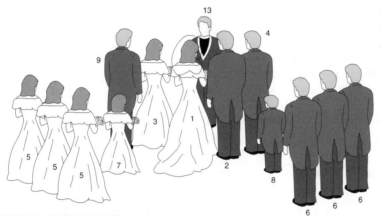

Traditional positions at the altar for a Christian ceremony.

Legend
1 = Bride
2 = Groom
3 = Maid of Honor
4 = Best Man
5 = Bridesmaid
6 = Groomsmen/ushers
7 = Flower Girl
8 = Ring Bearer
9 = Father of Bride
10 = Mother of Bride
11 = Father of Groom
12 = Mother of Groom
13 = Officiant
14 = Cantor
15 = Bride's Grandfathers
16 = Bride's Grandmothers
17 = Groom's Grandfathers
18 = Groom's Grandmothers

Jewish

To understand the Jewish wedding, it helps to have a general understanding of the differences among Jews and Jewish observances. Jewish people divide themselves into Ashkenazi Jews (descended from Eastern European Jews) and Sephardic Jews (descended from Middle Eastern or Spanish Jews). The two sects have very different customs, evident in the celebration of holidays and life cycle events, such as weddings.

Judaism is divided into three basic groups. Jewish weddings differ depending on whether the rabbi and/or congregation is Orthodox, Conservative, or Reformed and depending on whether the customs are Ashkenazi or Sephardic. Even with the varying customs among these groups, all Jewish weddings still have much in common.

The wedding ceremony may be conducted in a temple or other location of the couple's choosing; many Jewish weddings are held at the same site as the reception.

Weddings may not be conducted on the Sabbath (sundown Friday to sundown Saturday), on other religious holidays, or during historical mourning periods. The bride and groom should meet with the rabbi shortly after they become engaged to select a date. Because the Hebrew calendar is lunar, holidays are celebrated on different dates each year, so this visit to the rabbi is very important.

According to the most ancient Jewish law, the state of marriage could be attained by the performance of any of the following acts (with witnesses):

➤ Cohabitation

➤ The delivery of a document (*ketuba*) by the man

➤ Presentation by the man of an article of value to the woman

Most ceremonies today include the last two of these three, plus the exchange of a specific vow.

The marriage document, called a *ketuba*, is a contract written in Aramaic that outlines the groom's responsibility for and to the bride. It is signed by the bride, groom, rabbi, and two witnesses. Couples sometimes commission artists and scribes to create beautiful *ketubas* and then have the work of art framed and hung in their homes.

In ancient times, "something of value" often was a coin, but today it's usually a ring. The ring must be of solid gold, with no stones or gems, and it must be the groom's property at the ceremony. Today, when many couples select diamond wedding sets, it's often necessary for the couple to borrow a family ring for the ceremony. To do this and meet the ownership condition, the groom must buy the ring from the family member and sell it back after the wedding.

After the *ketuba* is signed and the item of value has been presented, the rabbi and the two fathers lead a procession of the groom and male guests into the bride's chamber for the *badekan* (veiling) ceremony. This custom comes from the Biblical story of Jacob, who worked for seven years to marry Rachel, only to discover that her father had substituted the older, blind Leah under heavy veiling. A groom still comes to look at his bride before the ceremony and actually places the veil over her.

Once the bride is veiled, the ceremony is ready to begin. How the rabbi and cantor enter is determined by local custom. If the grandparents choose to be part of the processional, they lead off, with the bride's grandparents walking first. The groomsmen follow, one at a time. Following the groomsmen is the best man. Then the groom enters, escorted by both his parents. The bridesmaids enter single-file; then comes the maid of honor, the flower girl, and the ring bearer (if you're using children). They are followed by the bride, who is escorted by both her parents. The following illustration shows a traditional Jewish processional.

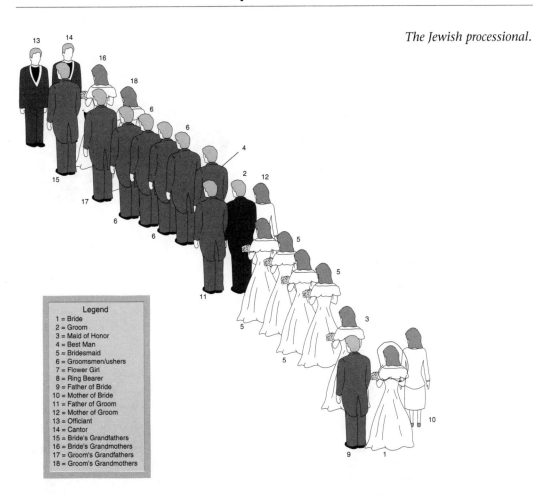

The Jewish processional.

Legend
1 = Bride
2 = Groom
3 = Maid of Honor
4 = Best Man
5 = Bridesmaid
6 = Groomsmen/ushers
7 = Flower Girl
8 = Ring Bearer
9 = Father of Bride
10 = Mother of Bride
11 = Father of Groom
12 = Mother of Groom
13 = Officiant
14 = Cantor
15 = Bride's Grandfathers
16 = Bride's Grandmothers
17 = Groom's Grandfathers
18 = Groom's Grandmothers

The wedding party usually stands to the left of the *chuppah* (canopy). The *chuppah* generally is supported by four poles in stanchions, but it also can be held by four men during the ceremony, as is frequently done in the Sephardic tradition. Sometimes, a large *tallis* (prayer shawl) is put on the poles and held above the couple to create the *chuppah*. The *chuppah* symbolizes the home the couple will establish.

When the bride and her parents reach the *chuppah,* the parents may lift the bride's veil and give her a kiss. They then replace the veil and walk up under the *chuppah* on the right side. When her parents are in their place, the bride takes three steps on her own, symbolizing her decision to enter the marriage, and the groom comes to escort her under the *chuppah.* The groom turns as he joins her, so she is on his right.

The following illustration shows the placement of the wedding party after the processional for the Jewish service.

Jewish wedding party positions at the end of the processional.

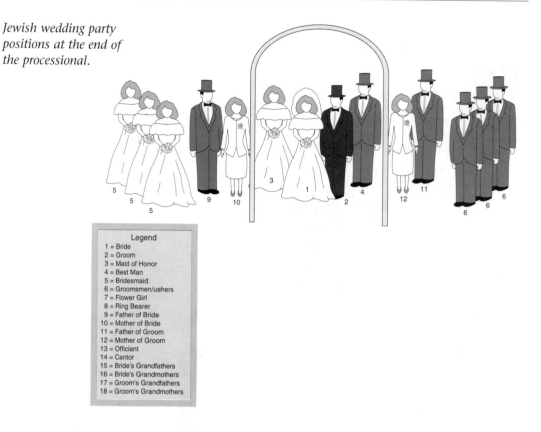

Legend
1 = Bride
2 = Groom
3 = Maid of Honor
4 = Best Man
5 = Bridesmaid
6 = Groomsmen/ushers
7 = Flower Girl
8 = Ring Bearer
9 = Father of Bride
10 = Mother of Bride
11 = Father of Groom
12 = Mother of Groom
13 = Officiant
14 = Cantor
15 = Bride's Grandfathers
16 = Bride's Grandmothers
17 = Groom's Grandfathers
18 = Groom's Grandmothers

During the ceremony, the rabbi reads the *ketuba* in both Hebrew and English, and the couple drinks wine. Sephardic rabbis usually wrap the couple in a *tallis,* symbolizing their becoming one. The bride (and sometimes the groom) receives a ring. In most ceremonies, the groom repeats a Hebrew vow after the rabbi, with the giving of the ring. The groom declares, "Behold, thou art consecrated to me with this ring, according to the law of Moses and Israel."

At the conclusion of the ceremony, the rabbi will ask the best man to place a wine glass, wrapped in a white cloth or in a special bag the couple provides, under the groom's right foot. The groom will step on it to break it, symbolizing the destruction of the temple in Jerusalem, although there are nearly as many interpretations of the meaning of the breaking of the glass as there are rabbis. The bride and groom will kiss immediately after being declared man and wife and then run up the aisle into a *Yichud.*

The *Yichud* is a brief seclusion where the couple can spend a few moments together before joining their guests. If the couple has fasted until the ceremony, this is their opportunity to break that fast. Even couples who have not fasted appreciate a few moments alone in what is usually a hectic and emotionally packed day. Because of this brief seclusion, Jewish weddings usually don't have receiving lines.

Summing Up

This chapter has been an overview of wedding ceremonies of four major religious groups in the United States—it is not intended to be the final word on any of them. Your own minister, rabbi, or priest can be a great help in explaining why something is done the way it is or in giving you additional information about the various parts of a particular service. I urge you to seek his or her counsel.

Just some final thoughts: No matter what kind of religious tradition you follow, remember that this is your ceremony. Don't be afraid to ask questions. Make sure that you understand what you're saying and why you're saying it. You may be bound by certain rituals and rules, but you can still put a lot of thought and love into this important celebration.

The Least You Need to Know

➤ Even though parts of the wedding service may be quite similar, various religions and denominations can have very distinct rules and requirements.

➤ Meet with your minister, rabbi, or priest early in the planning stages so that you have time to meet any prewedding obligations (for example, Pre-Cana classes).

➤ Most often, the officiant has the last word when it comes to making decisions about the wedding service.

Chapter 10

I Do, I Really Do

> **In This Chapter**
>
> ➤ Writing your own vows
>
> ➤ Deciding what to include in your wedding service
>
> ➤ Taking that first step down the aisle
>
> ➤ Choosing whom to include in the receiving line

Many couples sit in my office and tell me they are going to write their own wedding vows. They know exactly what they want to say to each other, and the traditional versions just don't make sense to them. When push comes to shove, however, they find out rather quickly that they can't do it because their officiant won't allow it, they find it too difficult because they have no experience in writing, or they simply run out of time.

Before you even think about writing your own vows, check with whomever is going to perform your wedding ceremony. If that individual gives you the go-ahead, get some reference books (I suggest several in this chapter) and then sit down with each other and try to decide what exactly it is you want the whole world to know and understand about your love for each other.

Writing Your Own Vows

When you decide to write your own vows, you need to sit down someplace (jointly or individually) where you won't be disturbed and think about the things in this world that mean something to you. What do you want to include? Do you want to totally rewrite the vows segment or add only a few words?

Before you can begin this task, you must know where the two of you are coming from and where you want to go. Is tradition important to you? Do you want to be completely spontaneous and go with the moment? Is it more important to include readings and poetry that have meaning to the two of you? There are many choices out there—that's the easy part.

The hard part is putting all the pieces together. One good resource on this topic is a book titled *With These Words … I Thee Wed,* by Barbara Eklof (Adams Media Corporation, Inc., 1989). This is a great book to sit down with and has vows that cover a wide range of feelings and emotions. The book even provides a questionnaire in the back for each of you to fill out so that you can see where the two of you have similarities and common threads. Working through this questionnaire should give you some form of theme for your vows.

After you have the go-ahead from your officiant and have decided what's important, your next task should be to look at some sample vows for ideas.

Wedding Woes

Never simply assume that you can change any part of your wedding service, including the vows segment. Always clear service changes with the officiant.

I, Mary, Take You, John

If you're a traditional couple and want to keep that flavor, you might want to change only a word here or there and keep most of the traditional words.

One of the more traditional vows segments goes like this:

I, (name), take thee, (name), as my wedded husband.

You can probably find several variations on this line. A vows segment from *The Protestant Wedding Sourcebook,* for example, reads as follows:

Before God and these witnesses, I, (groom), take thee, (bride), to be my wife, and I promise to be true to you, and to be faithful to you as long as we both shall live.

Another selection from the same book reads:

I, (groom), take you, (bride), to be my wedded wife; and I do promise and covenant to be your loving and faithful husband; for better, for worse, for richer, for poorer; in sickness and in health; so long as we both shall live.

These examples, while still quite traditional, add a word here and there to give the vow more meaning. Sometimes, just changing a word to a more modern term can make the vow seem more personal—for example, insert "you" instead of "thee."

Get some ideas from these samples and change the words around to put your feelings and thoughts about each other into words with which you are comfortable.

Mary, Join Me as We Venture into the Cosmos

If you're not a traditional couple and want something very different and unique, you have some more work to do.

Your best bet could be to pull out parts of several vows segments, mix and match them to fit your needs, and then see what you come up with. This takes time and concentration, but the end result may be something the two of you can cherish the rest of your lives.

Bouquet Toss

The following books can help you get started if you want to write your own vows:

➤ *The Protestant Wedding Sourcebook*, by Sidney F. Batts, Westminster/John Knox Press, 1993.

➤ *Weddings: A Complete Guide to All Religions and Interfaith Marriage Services*, by Abraham J. Klausner, Alpha Publishing Company, 1986.

➤ *Wedding Readings*, by Eleanor C. Munro, Penguin Group, 1989.

➤ *Words for Your Wedding*, by David Glusker and Peter Misner, Harper & Row, 1983.

➤ *The Christian Wedding Planner*, by Ruth Muzzy and R. Kent Hughes, Tyndale Publishers, Inc., 1991.

One couple chose an outdoor setting for the ceremony and asked an officer of the court to preside. They wanted to limit the religious aspects of the service, but still have something meaningful to the two of them and to their families. They also wanted to keep some traditional elements. They studied several books, and after much cutting and pasting, they came up with these vows:

I, (name), acknowledge my love for you in front of our family and friends. I respect you as a person and, in doing so, invite you to share in my life as I hope to share in yours. I promise always to recognize you as an individual. I promise to be true to you in good times and in bad, in sickness and in health. I will try through kindness and understanding to work with you for the life we have envisioned. I will love you and honor you all the days of my life.

This couple did an excellent job at sharing their feelings with the guests. The vows meant more to them because they had such a large part in putting them together.

Customizing Your Service

Even if you can't change the wording of your vows, you can add other items to your service to make it more personal (if you have the blessing of the officiant). Some couples are just too overwhelmed to even consider rearranging the actual ceremony, but others do little things here and there to make the ceremony truly their own.

A Song for You

You can expand on several areas within the ceremony to give your wedding a unique flair. Music is one of the easiest ways to add some personality to the service. Again, check with the musicians at the church or site to make sure you're not breaking any rules, and then let your imagination soar.

One couple sang to each other during the service, which was beautiful because they were both professional musicians. (You might not want to try this one if your singing experience is limited to the shower.)

Wedding Woes

Be careful that you don't add anything to your ceremony that greatly increases the pressures of the day. You already might be on emotional overload, so don't make it harder on yourself. Don't consider singing at your own wedding, for example, unless you know you can deal with the added pressures of performing.

I've actually had several couples use singing as a way to make their wedding ceremony unique to them. One father sang to his daughter after they reached the altar. He chose "Climb Every Mountain" from *The Sound of Music,* and it was very moving—when he reached the part, "… 'til you find your dream," there wasn't a dry eye in the church. In a later chapter I'll tell you about a bride who burst into "When I Fall in Love" at her wedding. Her groom didn't know it was coming, and the look on his face was priceless. If you aren't into singing or having songs performed by someone else, think about using music in other ways to make your service truly yours. See if you can add chimes or a bell choir (a group of musicians who play bells); either would be very fitting for a wedding.

One groom had a very strong Scottish heritage. As a surprise, the bride's family hired a bagpiper to lead the recessional from the church. It was a wonderful moment (and was captured on film). You could see the tears well up in the father of the groom's eyes as the bagpiper began to play.

A Special Passage

Readings are another way to make the service more individual. In many cases, you may choose either a religious or a traditional piece, or both. Be sure to check with the officiant first.

One bride hired an actor to read Elizabeth Barrett Browning's famous sonnet, "How Do I Love Thee?" Before that reading, I had never been particularly fond of that piece. After hearing it read as it should be, however, I definitely changed my mind. Selections from "The Prophet," by Kahlil Gibran, are also popular contemporary readings, or you might like a particular e. e. cummings piece and want to work it into your service. Or, if you have a talent for it, you might want to write something yourself for the service.

While a professional actor might be a nice touch, readings are a great way to include close friends who are not otherwise part of the wedding party. One bride asked a close friend whose mother had died tragically two months earlier to do one reading. Then, in the "Prayers of the Faithful" at the Nuptial Mass, the congregation prayed for the reader's mother. This was a nice, thoughtful touch showing that the bride—even on *her* day—was a caring, loving person.

That Special Touch

One bride I worked with had her wedding gown made. She then took some of the leftover material and made small handkerchiefs for both mothers. She had their initials embroidered on the hankies and wrapped a single rose in each one. On her way down the aisle, she stopped first to present one to her mother-in-law and then stopped to give one to her mother. It was very touching, and I'm sure those hankies will be treasured always.

Illuminating the Ceremony

One of the most memorable wedding ceremonies I've ever witnessed was a wedding I coordinated before I had even considered getting in the business. This couple worked very hard on the various parts of the service and thought through the rationale for why they wanted things the way they did. They did their homework, and each part of the ceremony had meaning.

The highlight of the ceremony was a candle-lighting service. Not only did the couple light a candle, but they also shared their light with the ushers, who lit candles and then walked down the aisles lighting the candles of every guest on the end of each pew. That guest then turned and lit his neighbor's candle, and so on. The light spread across that church with the feeling of a warm blanket covering you on a cold night.

The minister had just concluded a lovely sermon in which he talked about the inner light we all have and how we must pass that light on and make the world a better place. When all the candles were lit in the church, 500 guests sat in the glowing candlelight while the couple turned toward the congregation. With a look of love and hope in their eyes, they raised their candles up and the congregation followed suit. That entire church was lit by candlelight. There was the feeling of togetherness and hope for the future, not only for the couple, but for each member of the congregation as well. To this day, when people talk about that wedding, they always comment on the candle-lighting service.

Where to Draw the Line

Okay, you want a truly unique service. You want a service that causes your guests to say as they file out: "Oh, that was wonderful. The ceremony meant so much to them (the bride and the groom)." You want to make it *your* ceremony, not some carbon-copy script that half the brides and grooms in the United States use—but you don't want to go overboard.

It's as easy as K.I.S.S.—keep it simple, sweetie. Just because you love music does not necessarily mean you should engage the Philharmonic Orchestra, the Mormon Tabernacle Choir, a string quartet, two trumpeters, and an organist. No, let's do one or two of these and call it quits.

Adding one or two unique features to your service is probably enough. You don't want guests so overwhelmed by the individuality of the service that they lose track of what's really taking place.

So, K.I.S.S., and enjoy!

This Is It: The Ceremony!

All systems are go. You've been through the rehearsal. You got a good night's sleep. You even ate a little breakfast this morning. Now, you're in the back of the church holding on for dear life to your dad. Your guests are all seated. Your groom's mother and your mom have been seated. The candles are lit. The music is playing. Your heart is beating faster and faster; you may even have little beads of sweat breaking out on your upper lip. The processional music starts for the bridesmaids, and then you hear the trumpet fanfare and take that first step. You know what they always say—that first step is a big one.

Take a deep breath—seriously. Controlling your breathing has a calming effect on your body and your mind. Relax and walk *slowly*. After all, this is one walk you want to make the most of. You want to get mileage out of this trip down the aisle. You want to be poised, proud, happy, maybe even a little teary-eyed. This is your moment. If you haven't seen your groom before the service, this will be the first chance you have to gaze at each other (although, it will be a quick gaze).

As you walk down the aisle, make eye contact with your guests. Let them know, visually, that you're glad they're here. One of my favorite pictures from our wedding is the one of my dad and me walking down the aisle. In keeping with my character, I'm just chatting away to guests along the aisle. But that's me, and the photographer captured the moment perfectly.

Bouquet Toss

"The Wedding Song" (you know, the one that begins "As it was in the beginning ..."), written and sung by Neil Paul Stookey of Peter, Paul, and Mary fame, is a popular wedding number. But did you know that Stookey has never profited from royalties? Actually, neither has anyone else. Stookey set up a foundation that receives all proceeds from royalties, and millions of dollars have gone to this special charity. That's a true humanitarian.

When you reach the altar, depending on what type of service you have, you may either leave the arm of your father or stay with him until the officiant asks the famous "Who gives this woman ..." question. When you reach the altar area in a Catholic service, your groom comes over to you, you give your dad a kiss, and then you turn to walk up to the altar with your groom.

Now you're in the hands of the officiant. And, trust me, he has probably done this about 1,000 times and likely hasn't lost a couple yet. Just take your time, wait for the officiant's lead, and try to remember every moment of this most wonderful experience. Personally, I remember nothing except walking down the aisle, talking to guests as I passed, saying "I do" several times, and then kissing so loudly at the end of the service that I thought I would die of embarrassment. It did give a humorous pause to an otherwise very serious ceremony.

During one service, in which my favorite Catholic priest was presiding, the priest asked the best man for the ring. From my vantage point in the back of the church, I could see the best man digging in his pocket for this ring. Next I heard a "plink" and the sound of something rolling across the wooden floor near the altar. As I looked toward the altar, I could see the priest chasing this now wildly rolling

Wedding Woes

As you're standing during the ceremony, do not lock your knees—keep them flexed. Locked knees lead to only one thing, and that's fainting. You don't want *that* during your wedding service!

ring all over the altar area. Finally, he stomped on it to stop its forward motion, picked it up, and walked back to the wedding party. He stood there for a moment, looked the groom right in the eye, and said, "And *this* is your best man?" The wedding party burst into laughter. The congregation also laughed—and it was wonderful because it was natural. It wasn't made up or planned; it just happened. Instead of getting all upset and distressed, go with the flow of things. Let the officiant guide you through, and make sure your best man doesn't have slippery fingers.

The ceremony is complete now, and you're about to leave the altar area. You have just pledged your life to this wonderful man, now your husband. Having planned ahead of time what would happen next, the officiant pronounces you husband and wife (not man and wife anymore), and you hear the chimes, or the peal of bells and music, and you're off down the aisle.

Oh, My Aching Hand!

If you decide to use a traditional receiving line, you have to determine in advance where it will be and who will participate. It once was considered proper etiquette for all the bridesmaids to stand in the receiving line. While not wanting to incite those who still believe in the etiquette police, there really is no reason to include all the bridesmaids. That's part of the old etiquette standard that needs some help being revised. Guests are more interested in seeing the bride, the groom, and your respective parents than in shaking hands with 10 of your closest friends that they may never lay eyes on again.

The men in the wedding party seldom stand in the receiving line—except, of course, for the fathers, who may or may not take part. They may choose to mingle with the guests instead.

After you have decided where to place the line and who will stand in it, build in some extra time for that whole process to happen. If you're on a tight schedule, for whatever reason, you want to make sure that you have the time to accomplish a formal receiving line. If you expect 200 guests for your wedding and are doing a traditional receiving line, expect that process to take about 40 minutes. Sometimes, it may take less time or more time, depending on the guests and (don't ask me why) the weather outside. If it's hot or rainy, the line will move slower; if it's sunny and cool or even cold, it will be quicker.

Teddy's Tips

Long before you start back down the aisle, you need to decide whether you're going to have a receiving line. A receiving line is a traditional way for guests to greet you, your parents, and possibly some of the wedding party after the wedding. You form a line outside the ceremony area—someplace with easy access and a good traffic flow (people, not cars). Guests move through the line, introducing themselves, shaking hands, and giving out hugs and kisses.

Bouquet Toss

The receiving line comes to us from the ancient Greeks, who believed that the bride on her wedding day was blessed. The blessing rubbed off on those who touched her.

The following illustration shows one way to have the parents and the bride and the groom line up for the receiving line. It's optional for the fathers to stand in the line. Guests enter the receiving line from the left and move to the right.

mother of the bride   mother of the groom   bride   groom

Positions of participants in a traditional receiving line.

If someone in your family is divorced and you don't want to put parents in a receiving line, consider just you and your groom releasing the rows and greeting your guests there. In this case, instead of the ushers returning after the recessional and escorting the mothers out and then letting the rows leave systematically, the wedding party exits and then the couple comes back in and releases the rows. You would start with the bride's side. Your parents stand, come greet you in the center of the aisle, and then exit. You then move to the groom's parents and do the same thing. You then zigzag your way to the back of the church. I have found that this system works beautifully in divorced families or in weddings with a large attendance. The couple still has the opportunity to greet guests, but it moves much more quickly than a traditional receiving line. The following example illustrates this method of releasing guests.

After you have released the rows or finished with the receiving line, one of two things happens: Either you are either needed for more photography if it wasn't all taken beforehand, or you can exit the ceremony and head for the reception—it's party time!

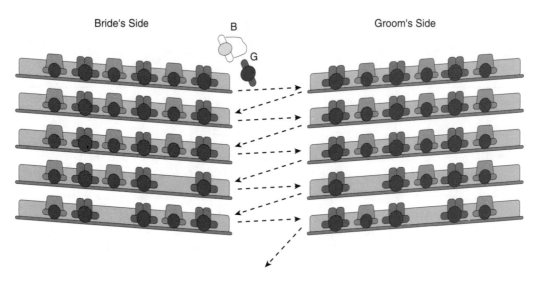

Bride's Side   Groom's Side

Greeting guests while releasing rows at the end of the ceremony.

Taking the time to carefully plot the order of events that will occur at the ceremony site will help your day run as smoothly as possible. (And you can reduce your stress level!) This is where expert advice from professional folks who have been through this before will help. Even if you buy only a couple hours of time to meet with a wedding coordinator, I think you will find it very beneficial to your planning.

The Least You Need to Know

➤ Get advice from your officiant before you start working on writing your own vows. Make sure it's okay for you to vary the traditional words.

➤ You don't have to go all out to make your wedding ceremony unique. You can add little touches here and there to make it reflect both your personalities. Some great books are available that can give you some ideas.

➤ Don't go overboard. Remember to K.I.S.S. (keep it simple, sweetie).

➤ Decide early whether you want to include a receiving line in your plans. Consider your time factor, the number of guests, and the physical area you have to work with. An alternative to a receiving line is for the couple to greet guests as they release the rows one by one after the recessional.

Part 4

Putting It All Together

Parts 1 through 3 discussed searching for the various wedding vendors and service providers you have to work with during the planning stages of your wedding. I suggested some questions you can ask vendors as you try to figure out which vendors can provide the services you want at a price you can afford. I also talked about the order in which you must reserve facilities and book vendors.

In Part 4, I'll review some of this material and provide additional information to help you on your wedding planning journey. I'll guide you along the path of catering and offer you some sample menus. I'll talk about how to choose the right florist and musicians. I'll talk about dressing your wedding party and finding the right photographer and videographer to help capture your special day. I'll also offer advice on the wedding invitations, including wording samples. You'll read ways to make your wedding more unique through the use of programs and newsletters, and, finally, you'll discover how much fun incorporating favors can be. And don't forget to check out the worksheets that will help with the details of these tasks.

Chapter 11

Eat, Drink, and Be Married

In This Chapter

➤ Working with the caterer to serve the foods you like and still stick to your budget

➤ Looking at sample menus to get your creative juices flowing

➤ Choosing the wedding cake and groom's cake you've always wanted

➤ Finding out what you need to know about serving liquor

We're moving right along and starting to get into the nitty-gritty. Regardless of how simple or fancy you want the reception to be, menu planning takes time. I keep stressing *time* because the wise wedding consumer allows enough time to shop for comparisons.

Working with the Caterer

Whether the facility provides an in-house caterer for you to work with or you bring in someone of your choice, what's your next step? As you might recall, I talked in Chapter 5, "Seeking Your Soirée," about the differences between an in-house caterer and others. *In-house* refers to a caterer that provides the food for functions within a particular facility. An *outside caterer,* as the name implies, is an independent caterer you hire on your own, from outside the facility.

When working with either the inside or outside caterer, go into the first consultation with some notion of what kind of reception you are looking for. You should have some idea whether you're thinking a formal seated affair or food stations. Have some plan in mind. Then let the caterer guide you with what works best in his facility. Don't let him tell you it can't be done—ask questions to see if it can be. If something you've had your heart set on is a "No" in his book, ask why. But please, ask "Why?" respectfully. You are going to be spending not only time but also money with this person and you want to be on the best terms possible.

There is really no difference in dealing with either the onsite caterer or the outside caterer. The only difference is that the onsite caterer knows the property like the back of his hand and the outside caterer has to move from reception site to reception site. Most facilities that do not provide catering will provide a list of approved caterers their facility will allow to work the event. There is a reason they are approved. They've done a good job before and the facility wants them back.

What's on the Menu?

After you've decided which caterer you'll be working with, choose your menu carefully. Make good use of your food choices. If you're on a limited budget for the reception (and who isn't?), then make sure you thoroughly consider the time of day you choose for your wedding and reception. (Refer to Chapter 3, "Simple or Extravagant—Setting Your Budget," for more information about when to hold your wedding and reception.) The time of day your reception occurs has much to do with what your menu will be and can help determine how much money it's going to cost you.

The following paragraphs explain in greater detail the various kinds of receptions that I touched on in Chapter 5. They also provide some sample menus to help get your creative juices flowing.

Bouquet Toss

The custom of serving food at a wedding reception actually dates back to the ancient Greeks; they had the bride and groom share a quince (fruit). The Greeks thought that by having the couple eat this fruit, which has a bitter and sweet taste, the bride and groom were accepting the good and bad times that come with marriage. Other cultures also have used the tradition of consuming food on the wedding day as a prerequisite to a good marriage. The ancient Brittons drank "marriage ale" for 30 days following the wedding. Those native to the South Sea Islands, such as Bali, feasted on fruits and flowers for 30 days. At the end of that time period, the couple was considered to be married.

Cake and Punch

Obviously, the simplest type of menu is a cake and punch reception. You can serve a lovely wedding cake with some delightful fruit or champagne punch, or maybe champagne by itself. With that menu, you can include assorted nuts and mints (either chocolate or candies in other colors). The only supplies needed would be plates, cups or glasses, napkins, forks, the table linens, a few nice serving bowls or plates for the mints and nuts, a cake knife for the cutting ceremony, and some friends to help serve. This is one type of reception that you can take care of yourself or with help from family and friends.

Hors d'Oeuvres

An hors d'oeuvres reception is another popular menu selection. Food items for this type of reception include various finger foods, which can be eaten without forks and knives. Normally, the caterer places fancy wooden picks in attractive little cups by each food item so that guests don't have to use their fingers if they don't want to. Some hors d'oeuvres may require a fork; if they do, a basket of forks is placed next to the food.

You can serve hors d'oeuvres to your guests for relatively the same price as a buffet. The biggest advantage to having an hors d'oeuvres reception is that it allows for a more relaxed atmosphere than a formal dinner or even a formal buffet. Guests can help themselves to the spread throughout the evening.

You'll want to include a variety of foods, both hot and cold, with an array of textures, colors, and presentation. (Presentation means how well they look on the serving plate and also how well that particular item holds up after several hours on a serving plate.) The chef or caterer should be able to answer your questions and guide you in selecting a well-rounded menu. If you want to include any ethnic foods, be sure to ask if they can be incorporated. Some caterers do allow you to bring in some food to the reception but may not allow it to be served on their table. (Something about health laws.) Just do yourself a big favor and check with the caterer regarding these details ahead of time.

Wedding Woes

Be sure to check with the caterer about floor layout if you want to use the food station concept. Traffic flow here is crucial. If your facility does not lend itself to this type of layout, you probably should stick to a more basic setup. You may opt for dividing up the food into two areas and offering the same items in both places. This helps move guests through the lines without so much delay.

Food Stations

The food station concept is quite popular for receptions around the country. This setup enables you to offer different types and styles of food at various "stations" throughout the room. In different areas, you may have a seafood table, a fruit and cheese table, a pasta table serving several types of pasta and sauces, a carving table with roast beef for small sandwiches, some tables set with other types of hors d'oeuvres, and then a table set for sweets, which can include your wedding cake.

Buffet

A buffet reception features a table (or more) filled with more substantial dishes, where the guests help themselves to the food. The difference between a buffet and an hors d'oeuvres menu is that the buffet is generally more of a complete meal. You can serve a variety of items on your buffet: some simple sandwiches and salads for an informal reception, or several entrée choices for a more formal reception. Guests serve themselves and may return as often as they want for refills. This is usually a less-expensive meal than the served dinner because of reduced labor costs—your labor costs will be much lower with a buffet for 200 than at a served dinner for 200 because fewer workers are required to serve the meal.

If you attempt a buffet reception on your own without the help of a caterer, you must provide plates, serving pieces, chafing dishes, napkins, linens, silverware, glasses, and back-up help to replenish the tables as they become empty. It's a big undertaking. Be very sure you have competent people who can handle pressure and understand the meaning of the word *work*. Serving a meal—even buffet style—is lots of work.

Formal Dinner Reception

A formal dinner reception consists of several courses, with each course served to the guests at their seats. This is the most formal type of wedding reception meal and also the most expensive, mostly because more labor is required in the form of servers.

A formal dinner usually is served in courses. The meal normally begins with an appetizer, followed by (depending on your region) either a fruit course or a salad course. The entrée, or main course, is served next. Sometimes at very formal dinners, your guests can choose among several entrées. They must specify their preference on the response card included with the invitation. Dessert is the last course and is served with assorted coffees and teas. You might want to offer wine with dinner and also serve champagne during the dessert.

You can limit the dessert portion of your reception to wedding cake, or you can decide to set up a sweet table. Several different types of sweets are available on a sweet table, and guests can help themselves to whichever dessert they prefer. The wedding cake would be the main attraction for the dessert table, but you also can include some petit fours, heart-shaped cookies, mini-cheesecakes with various fruit toppings, chocolates, dipped fruit, or whatever your sweet tooth dictates. Consult with your caterer to find out what your options are.

Thinking Through Your Food Options

Suppose that you're going to have an hors d'oeuvres reception with a limited bar. Your test now is to make good use of your money as far as food selection goes. Offering liquor always means you must serve some substantial food. You don't have to serve meat and potatoes—especially for an hors d'oeuvres reception—but you do need to provide something filling so that guests don't drink on empty stomachs.

You might opt for some pita triangle sandwiches (pita bread cut into triangles and filled with various fillings). You could add a fruit tray with a yogurt dip. To that, you could add some water chestnuts wrapped in bacon and cooked in a brown sweet-and-sour sauce (mmmm, one of my favorites), and so on. The catering manager should sit down with you and find out what your favorite foods are and how to incorporate them into the menu.

Bouquet Toss

One of the most well-known champagnes in the world is Dom Perignon, from France. Champagne was discovered by a monk in a northeastern region of France called Champagne. This monk found that by sealing wine in a bottle for several years, the wine would begin to ferment and sparkle. That monk's name was Dom Perignon. Today, Dom Perignon is a very famous champagne and a very expensive addition to your wedding reception.

One of my favorite catering managers always asks for family recipes to duplicate and serve at the reception. Clients are thrilled to have someone who cares that much and wants to make the reception special for them. One recent wedding reception combined a Spanish family with a German family. The catering manager took treasured family recipes from both sides and duplicated several dishes. Then, for an added touch, the couple used menu programs and added side notes about the family recipes and their origins.

When talking to the caterer about how much this wonderful menu will cost, ask whether the cost includes add-on items, such as tips and gratuities. If the linens aren't part of the reception hall billing, then they also might be included in the catering bill.

Also, ask to see pictures of the caterer's previous receptions. Often, the way the caterer displays the food can mean the difference between a good reception and a wonderful reception. Will the caterer garnish the serving tables with ivy or other greenery to make them more appealing? Does the caterer have access to votive candles or colored linens, if that is what you want?

Can you taste the food prepared by the caterer? Many times, you can make an appointment to come for a tasting or sampling of the foods prepared, or caterers might offer a tasting at certain times of the month. This is usually not a concern if the caterer is affiliated with a hotel or restaurant that serves meals consistently to the public. You can simply go out for dinner to sample the menu.

Playing the Numbers Game

Talk to the caterer some more about what the guaranteed numbers mean. (Refer to Chapter 5 for more information about guaranteed numbers.) Find out what percentage the caterer will go under and above the guest count that you provide. Make sure that you understand how this process works and what it means for your reception.

At a recent wedding reception I coordinated, the mother of the bride had given the caterer a guaranteed number of 125. She guesstimated the number of expected guests. When the guests at the church numbered only 70, I was concerned that her count was high and that we would have many extra places at the reception. I was right. She was very upset that guests hadn't shown up when she thought they would. And, she was stuck with a bill for 50 extra guests (at $25 per person) because she had not taken the time to get an accurate response count.

This story illustrates how important it is to have an accurate count for the caterer. *Do not guess.* So many times brides will say, "Oh, I know they're coming to the wedding," or, "I think we'll have about 150 people." Hey, save your guesses for the lottery or the racetrack. "I think" and "I guess" are two phrases you don't want to use when it comes to guaranteeing your guest total for the caterer. This number equates to money—at times, *lots* of money. (Turn to the "Catering Worksheet" at the end of this chapter when you're planning the food for your reception.)

Wedding Woes

Never guess at numbers for your reception count. Guessing can destroy your food budget and leave you feeling angry, disappointed, or even embarrassed. Even the best caterers cannot afford to supply your reception with unlimited amounts of food.

That Fantasy Creation: The Cake

Perhaps one of the creations given the most thought during the wedding planning stages is the wedding cake. Maybe you've dreamed about a five-tier creation with fountains and lights or a simple, stately, stacked cake with fresh flowers adding the only color. When you're shopping for your wedding cake, be sure to ask for suggestions and recommendations from family and friends who have recently married. The caterer you're working with also might offer a wedding cake service, or he may be glad to provide you with names of competent bakers if you just ask.

So Many Choices ...

Today, you can select a wedding cake in a variety of flavors and fillings—again, another way to make a particular wedding unique.

Gone are the days of only a white wedding cake. You might want a layer of carrot cake with cream cheese filling, a layer of chocolate cake with raspberry filling, or maybe even lemon cake with an orange-flavored filling. You can even mix different flavors on different layers so that all guests can have a choice. The sky is the limit when it comes to choosing flavors and fillings for your wedding cake.

Bouquet Toss

The first wedding cake goes back to ancient times, when the cake was actually a mixture of sesame seed meal and honey. Then, as Western Europe developed, the cake consisted of a small, unleavened biscuit. In the 1600s, a French chef tried an experiment with small cakes he stacked together and held in place with a white sugar icing. And, before the Civil War in this country, the wedding cake was actually a fruitcake.

Maybe you love the look of rolled fondant icing—it's pure elegance. Fondant consists of a layer of icing that is literally rolled over the cake layers. It's completely smooth all the way around. When you meet with the baker, ask to see pictures of his creations. Take pictures with you of cakes you think are particularly pretty or that have caught your eye. Ask if he can duplicate these. When my parents celebrated their thirty-fifth wedding anniversary, I took a picture of their wedding cake and gave it to the baker with a description of the flowers my mother had used. The baker almost perfectly created their wedding cake, complete with the cake top. They were thrilled.

A beautifully stacked wedding cake adorned with fresh flowers.

(Stephanie Hogue Photography)

Bargaining with the Baker

Just as important as any vendor on your wedding list is the baker. Here are some questions to ask as you make your decisions:

➤ **Fresh or frozen?** Ask whether the baker bakes fresh or works from frozen cakes. Some bakers bake early in the week and then freeze their cakes and decorate them on Friday, with finishing touches the day of the wedding. I personally prefer fresh because I think the cake tastes better, but that's something you will have to decide for yourself. Get all the information; it never hurts to ask questions.

➤ **Pricing?** Wedding cakes usually are priced per person (meaning how many people the cake will feed), and your locale determines what that per-person charge will be.

➤ **Delivery?** Ask whether the baker will deliver the cake or whether you must arrange to pick it up. Is there an extra charge for delivery to the reception site? Trust me, picking up a wedding cake and hauling it across town is not a pleasant task. Every bump you hit makes you wonder what the cake will look like when you arrive at your destination. I do this only for clients when we have no other choice. Most bakers will deliver; they may charge for that service, but it's probably worth it.

➤ **Deposit and return?** Ask the baker if there is a deposit on the cake stands and pillars. Also, check how the wedding cake pieces (plastic pillars, the layer pieces holding the cake together) are to be returned. Find out whether the caterer will take care of that for you or whether you are responsible. You don't want to have to play with icing and cake pieces as you're trying to leave for your honeymoon, so take care of this item before your wedding day arrives. Designate a family member or friend to help.

➤ **Cutting the cake?** Finally, ask if the caterer will cut and serve the cake for you. Again, there may be a charge for that, but cutting a wedding cake is an art. If the baker doesn't offer that service, the catering people most likely will.

Be sure to use the "Wedding Cake Worksheet" at the end of this chapter.

Yes, this is a wedding cake. Notice how most of the decorative touches are done with icing while the base of the cake is covered with flowers.

(Colter Photography)

The Groom's Cake

The groom's cake, which was once a part of every wedding reception but slowly lost its popularity, is making a big comeback. At the turn of the century, the groom's cake was similar to a fruitcake, heavy and rich with dried fruits and nuts. A small piece was served in small white boxes, and guests took a piece as they left the reception. Unmarried female guests placed the box under their pillow; supposedly, as legend goes, the man they dreamed of would become their husband.

Bouquet Toss

The wedding cake chosen by Linden Johnson's daughter, Luci Baines Johnson, and Patrick Nugent in 1966 weighed a whopping 300 pounds and was 14 tiers high. The icing posed a problem as the couple tried to cut the first piece: They couldn't cut through it. Finally, the president himself had to step in and make a stab at it.

Today, groom's cakes appear in all kinds of shapes, sizes, flavors, and themes. Grooms have used basketball and football themes for their cakes. One groom who loved to play bridge had his groom's cake designed like a huge hand of cards. Remember the red velvet armadillo in *Steel Magnolias?* That was an original (if not odd) groom's cake. One couple who was heading to Florida for their honeymoon chose a groom's cake made like the island they were going to visit. Complete with sugar "sand" and blue icing "water," a doll-sized hotel and people, and a toy red convertible, it was the focal point of the lobby area of their reception. They didn't want to take away from the elegant, stately wedding cake in the ballroom, but they did want their guests to view the creation and have fun enjoying it.

Chocolate seems to be a very popular flavor with grooms, but I've also seen cheese-cakes served with luscious fruit toppings as a groom's cake. Experiment and have fun with this. If your budget will allow it and you want some creative way to express yourselves, consider having a groom's cake.

Those Luscious Libations

One of the hardest questions for folks to answer when planning their wedding reception is, "Do we want to serve liquor?" Sometimes the answer to that is an overwhelming "Yes." Sometimes the answer is "No," but there are many fence-sitters on this issue.

Traditional etiquette says only that you must offer your guests something to eat and something to drink at the reception. If that something to drink is alcohol, that's your choice, and yours alone.

Look at All Your Options

If you decide to offer alcohol at the reception, you can choose from the following methods:

➤ **Open bar.** You can offer a full bar outfitted with the liquor you choose. The bar consists of mixed drinks, wine, beer, and soft drinks. You also can choose to serve some after-dinner liquors. With an open bar, you pay the bill.

➤ **Limited bar.** You limit what you serve your guests. You can choose to serve wine, beer, and soft drinks only, or you can serve a combination (wine and soft drinks or beer and soft drinks). You also can limit the time the bar remains open. For example, if your reception is scheduled to start with cocktails at 6:30 and dinner is served at 7:30, you may decide to have the bar open from 6:30 to 7:30, close it from 7:30 until 9:00, and then open it again at 9:00 until a half hour before the reception ends. You pay the bill with a limited bar as well.

➤ **Cash bar.** In this case, a bar service is available, but guests pay for their individual drinks. Many families have trouble with this concept, but, as I said, if you meet your obligation with "something" to drink, then don't worry about it. Another option is to offer wine and beer as a freebie and then have a cash bar on top of that. If they choose, the guests can have a mixed drink, but they pay for it themselves.

Remember, you do not have to offer liquor at all—that is a personal choice. Some couples offer only champagne for the toasting part of the festivities; you can have champagne served to guests or place open bottles on each table. (Turn to the "Liquor Worksheet" at the end of this chapter for help in this area.)

Don't Take Your Responsibilities Lightly

Make sure you have a reputable liquor dealer serving the alcohol. Liability laws differ from state to state. If you hire a liquor dealer to serve your guests, some of the liability that could otherwise fall to you then falls to the dealer.

Over the past seven or eight years, I have observed a much more conscious society as far as drinking habits go. When I first started out in this business, it was not unusual for some guests, provided with all that free-flowing liquor, to drink too much and dampen the party. I haven't had as many problems in the past few years as I had early in my career. People are just more understanding of the responsibilities that go along with serving alcohol, and guests are more conscious of their responsibilities, too. Certainly, the potential for abuse is still there, and you need to be aware of this and watch out for possible problems at your reception (or appoint a responsible friend or family member to watch the guests for you). Our society on the whole, however, does seem to have matured a little in this area. Always make sure that if you do offer liquor, you have someone assigned to watch for those individuals who might need help returning home. Be sure you have adequate designated drivers.

Call in the Chefs!

Here are some sample menus provided by several of the professional chefs I work with. These menus should get you thinking and give you some ideas about what you might want to serve.

Cake and Punch Reception

> Wedding cake
>
> Champagne punch
>
> Fruit punch
>
> Assorted chocolates
>
> Mixed nuts

Hors d'Oeuvres Reception

> Shrimp cocktail served in an ice sculpture
>
> Assorted cheeses and crackers
>
> New potato skins filled with a mixture of cream cheese, sour cream, herbs, and dill
>
> Roast turkey and beef tenderloin mini-sandwiches
>
> Banana Rumaki
>
> Fresh-fruit-and-cheese kabobs
>
> Bacon-stuffed cherry tomatoes

Buffet Reception I

> Fresh fruit salad
>
> Spinach salad

Carved tenderloin of beef with sour cream and horseradish sauce

Chicken Mandarin with puff pastry shell

Pear potatoes

Fresh cold vegetables vinaigrette

Glazed baby carrots

Assorted rolls and butter

Buffet Reception II

Farmer's market salad with choice of three dressings

Herb roasted beef carved to order

Baked trout with lemon butter and capers

Herb grilled chicken breast

Orange glazed julienne carrots

Buttered potatoes will dill

Assorted rolls and Irish soda bread

Chocolate raspberry bash

Fresh fruit platter with lime sherbet

Home-style carrot cake

Formal Dinner I

Field green salad with wild mushroom vinaigrette

Almond crusted filet mignon with a roasted Vidalia onion demi glaze

Grilled salmon fillet with a dill Chardonnay wine crème sauce

Petite roasted Yukon gold potatoes

Fresh medley of spring vegetables tossed with tarragon butter

White chocolate swan filled with raspberry mousse

Crisp shortbread cookie

Painted plate with crème Anglaise with dark chocolate

Formal Dinner II

Hors d'Oeuvres

>   Pea pods with smoked trout

>   Artichoke hearts with curried egg or chicken salad

>   Cucumber slices with herbed cream cheese and shrimp

Cocktails

First Course

>   Fresh pasta with sautéed vegetables, topped with fresh basil and a choice of salmon or black caviar

Second Course

>   Raspberry sorbet

Main Course

>   Filet of beef tenderloin

>   Mushroom turnovers with thin mushroom sauce

>   Fresh asparagus with slivered almonds

Fourth Course

>   Fresh green salad of bib lettuce and watercress, with sliced strawberries and purple onions with poppy seed dressing

>   Individual loaves of French bread, whole wheat, and rye

>   Butter rosettes

Dessert Course

>   Pears Cranbrook (pears poached in white wine and then peeled, cored, and stuffed with cream du macaroon; then served on a bed of whipped cream and chocolate fudge sauce)

>   Wedding cake

>   Champagne

>   Assorted coffees and teas

The Least You Need to Know

➤ Get referrals from family and friends of the vendors whose services they have used recently.

➤ Ask about add-ons with the reception site and caterer.

➤ Ask the catering manager and the baker if you can sample the cakes and reception food.

➤ Always give an accurate count to the caterer; never guess at numbers for your guaranteed count.

➤ Give careful consideration to whether you want the expense and responsibility that accompanies the serving of liquor at your reception.

Catering Worksheet

Caterer: _____

Telephone: _____

Menu format:

    ❏ Buffet   ❏ Hors d'oeuvres   ❏ Sit-down dinner

Menu ideas:_____

_____

_____

_____

Cost per person: _____

Deposit made: _____

Next appointment with chef: _____

Liquor Worksheet

Dealer: _____

Telephone: _____

Address: _____

Contact: _____

Requested:

     ❏ Open bar   ❏ Limited bar   ❏ Cash bar

Method of accountability: _____

_____

Liquor requested: _____

_____

Number of bartenders needed: _____

Time for setup: _____

_____

Questions: _____

_____

_____

_____

Wedding Cake Worksheet

Baker: _____

Telephone: _____

Price: _____

Delivery fee: _____

Deposit on cake pieces: _____

How to get items back to baker: _____

Number of servings: _____

Description of cake and fillings: _____

_____

_____

Groom's cake description: _____

_____

Flavor and fillings: _____

_____

Price: _____

Number of servings: _____

Questions for the baker: _____

_____ _____

_____

Snapdragons and Song

In this chapter I will focus on two important aspects of your wedding: the flowers and the music. Both items are filled with choices. I'm going to talk about what you need to include in your floral order, from bouquets to centerpieces; give you hints on how to get the best value for your wedding floral dollars; and give you some extra tips on how to spice up the reception site.

I'll also look at your options for the music for your wonderful celebration. Music can really set the mood, and you want to make sure it's not only the mood you want, but a mood well spent!

Deciding on a Florist

Under normal circumstances, you don't really have to decide on flowers until two or three months before the wedding. If you're being married in a prime wedding season (May, June, or August), or if you're being married around a holiday (Christmas, Valentine's Day, or Mother's Day weekend), however, it's wise to go ahead and reserve your florist for your wedding day. Some florists will service only one or two weddings a weekend during the peak seasons because weddings are such labor-intensive productions.

My personal pet peeve is a florist who says to the bride-to-be—who has no idea which flowers she wants or even knows the available options—"Oh, honey, we'll do anything you want." No, no, no—you're paying that florist for his ideas; you're paying for his expertise. This attitude is fine when and if you know what you want, but if you're like most brides, you do not know what you want or what your options are. Try to stay with seasonal flowers if at all possible. Tulips in December will be expensive and won't be the quality of tulips in April, when they're in season.

Bouquet Toss

The very first types of bridal bouquets included not only flowers, but also herbs and spices. Especially popular were strong-scented ones, such as garlic, to ward off evil spirits.

Various kinds of flowers have different meanings. Ivy represents fidelity, lily of the valley represents purity, red roses mean love, violets represent modesty, forget-me-nots mean true love, orange blossoms represent fertility and happiness, and myrtle is the symbol of virginity.

My favorite florist story goes back many years, before I was officially in this business. I was planning my out-of-town sister's wedding and was meeting with the florist to finalize the wedding flowers. I went to the appointment armed with a picture of my sister, a picture of her gown, and a swatch of the fabric from the bridesmaids' dresses. I sat facing the florist, who was seated at his desk. While I talked and described the wedding, the reception site, the number of bridesmaids, and the formality of the wedding, Mr. Becker was drawing on a pad. When I finished describing the details, he handed me the piece of paper he had been working on. There in black and white was a sketch of my sister, in her wedding gown, with the appropriate bouquet that would not only complement the gown, but would also complement her. He then drew pictures of the bridesmaids' dresses and their bouquets and what he saw to be the total picture. It was perfect, and it all blended and fit together wonderfully.

Now, obviously, most florists don't have the ability to sketch out the bride with her bouquet, but I think you get the point. Good florists will assist you in determining what you can and cannot do with your flowers for your wedding. They will offer suggestions and ideas, and they will help you work within your budget. Before you meet with them, ask if they are familiar with the ceremony and reception site. If they are not, ask if they can visit the sites before your appointment. At a minimum, provide the florist with photos of the sites. That will help you be more practical when you discuss the options you have for decorations.

By the Dozen

Make sure you ask the florist whether she uses a contract. Also, find out how pricing is done. Usually, you will pay per item. If you're having six bridesmaids and each of their bouquets will cost $20, then 6 × $20 = $120 in bridesmaids' bouquets. The only other charge that might come into play—and that depends on each individual florist—is a labor charge for extensive setup. Often, the labor charge is built into the flower pricing. As with any vendor, check references.

Nipping Your Floral Bill in the Bud

Your floral bill can consume a significant portion of your wedding budget. You can make the most of your wedding dollars, however, by using your imagination and finding a good florist to help you stretch your dollars. (Use the "Floral Worksheet" at the end of this chapter to help you with your planning.) References here are crucial. Ask those same friends and family members who have recently had weddings which vendors they used and how they liked a particular florist. Don't ask if the flowers were pretty; ask how the florist was to work with. Was he reliable? Did he show up on time? Did he label the flowers? There is nothing worse than having a box of 30 boutonnieres and no idea whom they go to.

A good florist should be willing to assist you with ideas and ways to make your floral dollars go further. Is the florist familiar with the ceremony site? Has the florist previously provided flowers for your reception facility? How can you make your reception hall pretty without spending a fortune on centerpieces? It can be done, but you'll need help.

If you want silk flowers, find out what quality of silks the florist uses. You want to make sure you use good-quality silk flowers; there is nothing worse than cheap-looking silk flowers. And speaking of silk flowers, be very sure that none of your guests are allergic to the odor of some silk flowers. They can sometimes, literally, stink.

Buds of Beauty

Flowers used during the ceremony are divided into two sections. One set is referred to as "body flowers" and are the bouquets, boutonnieres, and corsages. We're going to find some ways to make the body flowers something you want to carry or hold, not something you saw in a bride's magazine that doesn't even begin to go with your total look. The second set is the flowers used at the sites, both ceremony and reception.

Bouquets and "Boots"

The two main body flowers for weddings are the bouquets and the boutonnieres, or as they're more fondly referred to, "boots." The first bouquet you should consider is the bouquet style and colors you want your maids to carry. Tell the florist your overall theme. Be sure to show him samples of fabrics, a picture of the dresses, and describe to him what you envision. Color in bouquets is very big; we have moved away from pastels. Look at some of the floral pictures in this book and you will see how bold the color for flowers can get. Some sample styles of bouquets for your maids are nosegays, small crescent shape, arm bouquet (simply put, it lays in the crook of your arm), or a single, long-stemmed flower, maybe tied with an elegant ribbon. Let the florist help you with your decisions. Ask for his advice. That's what you're paying him for.

For your bouquet, there will be several things the florist will need to keep in mind as he designs your arrangement. First of all, he will note your physical size. I am 5'9" and wear a size 10 dress. I can carry a long, cascading bouquet. My assistant Jean is about 5' and can't weigh more than 90 pounds soaking wet. She would be much better suited to carry a small nosegay type bouquet or something equally proportioned to her size. You don't want a bridal bouquet that you find yourself dragging down the aisle. The next thing the florist will want to see is a picture of your gown. The bouquet is only meant to accent the gown, not take away from it. He can also tell from the lines of the gown how the lines in the bouquet should run. Remember, this is an art form, and it takes a good, experienced florist to pull the total look of a wedding together.

You need boutonnieres for the men in your wedding party, including the fathers, ushers, groomsmen, ring bearer (make his small!), and, of course, the groom. The groom's should be different from the others. Tradition suggests that his boutonniere be made of some of the flowers from the bride's bouquet.

The final body flowers you need to consider are corsages or something for the mothers and grandmothers to wear. Many mothers today opt for something other than a corsage. They prefer to carry a long stemmed flower down the aisle than to have something pinned to the dress that they just paid a fortune for and don't want pin holes in it. Grandmothers usually still go with the corsages. These flowers should vary in size and type of flowers. Your mothers should receive the most elaborate of the corsages you are offering. For example, you wouldn't give your grandmother orchids and your mother carnations. Unless, of course, that is what she requested. Orchids are a more expensive and glamorous flower than a carnation, and it would make sense to favor the mothers with the more glamorous flowers.

Roll Out the Carpet

Most florists should provide you with the aisle cloth—you know, the white carpet that is rolled down the aisle before the ceremony. Ask about the choices you have with aisle cloths. If you can, rent real cloth, not the plastic type. If you can't find the cloth type, then look for the aisle cloths that are heavy paper-type fabric, but that are still disposable.

Another important question to ask is whether the aisle cloth should be taped or pinned, and will the florist do that? I once had a florist who just dropped off the flowers and aisle cloth and then ran. I had never secured an aisle cloth before that day, and boy, did I learn a few things. Now I ask that question early on. Always make sure the aisle cloth is secured to the flooring. One bride didn't know she needed to secure the aisle cloth, and as she started down the aisle, the cloth rolled up under her gown. By the time she reached the end of the aisle, there was a huge white "thing" wrapped around her gown—not a very nice picture.

Petals and More

The flowers you choose to use at your ceremony site will depend on many, many factors. First, the almighty budget. Second, consider if the site is really in need of a lot of décor. Many churches are lovely just by themselves. Adding small amounts of flowers, such as some pew pieces, might be all you will need. Candles might be the only floral item you add. In Jewish ceremonies, it is popular to put flowers in the chuppa. It all depends on your site, your personal preference, and your budget.

Whatever you decide to do with flowers at the ceremony site, be sure those can be moved to the reception site. Whatever you choose, you will be spending some bucks here, and you might as well get some good use out of those dollars.

Centerpiece Ideas

For any type of reception besides a cake-and-punch reception, you will need to provide tables for your guests during the event. The layout of your facility, the time of day and style of the reception, the table size, and the number of guests you want to seat are all things you must consider before you decide what to use for centerpieces.

Simple or Sensational?

If you're on a tight budget but you still want something on each table, consider using simple votive candles in votive holders, some greenery, and maybe a sprinkle of glitter or confetti. The greenery adds a soft, natural touch to the table. The candlelight gives off a soft glow, and the confetti and glitter add some sparkle and a party atmosphere. You can rent the votives from your florist, and he also can provide the greenery. You probably can get friends to help set up the centerpieces for the day of the wedding, which helps reduce the labor cost in the florist's bill.

145

If you want something more elaborate, the sky is the limit. One bride rented beautiful five-point silver candelabra and asked the florist to place ivy and lilies and baby's breath intertwined along the stems. With tall white candles, it was a lovely setting for an hors d'oeuvres reception. While not too expensive, it was very elegant.

Some of the most elaborate centerpieces are floral arrangements created on pedestal stands. The stem of a pedestal stand extends up about three feet, and at the top is a section that can hold a large arrangement of flowers. These are very elegant yet practical because you don't have to peer around a centerpiece to be able to talk to the guest across the table. If your budget is wide open, then let the florist have full reign with the flowers. If money is a concern, go with a smaller, lower centerpiece, or do a combination high/low—some centerpieces tall, others short. This will save you some money and add drama to the room.

Other Table Ideas

Using other forms of decorations can add to the overall look of your tables. Most of the time, when the menu calls for hors d'oeuvres, the table decorations can be much simpler. Tables for hors d'oeuvres receptions usually are set only with cloths and centerpieces. Sometimes there may be champagne glasses present, but not always. So, if you want to add a little zest, consider using some form of favor that can double for added decorations.

For example, cluster together small vases with simple arrangements in each in the center of the table. This will give you the illusion of a "large centerpiece" when in fact, it is actually small. Then, when guests leave, they can each take a vase home with them. I coordinated a Christmas wedding where the centerpieces were actually wrapped Christmas presents stacked in the center of the table. Guests thought this was a cute idea, and when they were told to take one home with them, they found out the packages actually contained a Christmas ornament with the couple's name and wedding date printed on it. These two examples incorporate using the idea of a favor as your main centerpiece (more on favors in Chapter 16, "Do Yourself a Favor").

One of my most favorite centerpiece ideas is to have individual wedding cakes as the centerpiece. These cakes are your normal nine-inch, two-layer round cake size, but decorated like the wedding cake. Guests are provided plates and a cake knife after the dinner plates are cleared. After the couple cuts their cake, the guests are asked to do the same. Your guests can really get into this idea and have fun. And, you can go with a smaller wedding cake and have less waste.

Other ideas for centerpieces that are simple and cost-effective are colored ribbons down the center of the tables accented with either votive candles or tall candlesticks and some selections of greens.

Balloon bouquets on the tables are in order for the more informal reception. Balloons can create a party atmosphere and can cover a multitude of blemishes at the facility.

Even small things, such as using a decorative napkin fold or a flower placed inside a napkin, can add a nice touch to an otherwise simple table. If the caterer has choices of colored linens, ask to see samples. You might find something that coordinates nicely with your color scheme.

Making Beautiful Music

You must reserve wedding music early, both for the ceremony and the reception. Music completes your wedding atmosphere. Because it stays in the background, music is also one aspect of wedding planning that's easy to overlook, especially for the ceremony.

Waltzing Down the Aisle

Unless the couple comes from a musically inclined background, music is often a largely overlooked aspect of the wedding ceremony. If you use your imagination, however, the opportunities for unique musical touches are endless. For your ceremony, you might want to consider some of the more common choices: piano, organ, string group (either a trio or quartet), harp, violin, harp with violin, trumpet, or perhaps even a choir.

Several wonderful music pieces written solely for trumpet and organ are especially grand for processionals. "Trumpet Tune," by Purcell, and "Trumpet Voluntary," by Clarke, are two of my favorite pieces—both are quite majestic. The wedding march song from *The Sound of Music* is another magnificent piece for a processional and goes best with a long aisle. One bride wanted the organ and trumpet to play for her attendants' entrance, but she wanted only trumpets for her grand entrance. She hired three trumpeters who played a wonderful fanfare followed by a very majestic version of "Bridal Chorus"—it was fantastic! I can still hear all the guests saying "Ahh." I also worked with one bride on a tight budget who hired high school orchestra students to play for the ceremony rather than use the string quartet from the local union. The kids were thrilled to get some experience, were very inexpensive, and were quite good.

A choir adds a nice touch for the wedding service. One couple who were both members of a professional choir hired the group to sing several songs during the prelude and the lovely piece "One Hand, One Heart," from *West Side Story,* during the lighting of the unity candle. It was very moving, and it meant so much to that couple to have the choir and their friends be part of their service.

Wedding Woes

Try to use live musicians for your wedding ceremony. Couples think they can save money by using canned music—you know, your own CD player. I suppose you can, but I still remember the 14-year-old young man who was supposed to hit the Play button on the CD player and got so excited that he not only hit the Play button, but he also knocked over the candelabra, which burned a hole in the church's carpet. Not good.

I have worked with several couples who have sung to each other either before the service or during the service. One bride this summer surprised her groom at the altar after they had finished their exchange of vows. The soloist stood up as if to sing, and instead the bride, a music educator, started singing "When I Fall in Love." The congregation just melted in the pews. It was wonderful—so romantic and personal. The groom was totally surprised and delighted as well. But beware: Unless this sort of thing comes very easy to you, don't try this at home. Leave the singing to the professionals. You will be emotional enough on your wedding day; you don't want to have to worry about performing for 300 guests.

One bride I know had the honor of having several songs written for her as a wedding gift and played during the service. She listed that information on the program, and it was a very personal touch for her to remember.

Taped music is nice, but it can also be very risky. At a recent wedding, the young man running the tape machine missed his cue. He then got so excited that he jumped up, knocked over the music stand for the soloist, and turned on the microphone all in one fell swoop. The congregation found it humorous, but the bride and groom did not. When you deal with tapes and tape players, there is a possibility of problems—either human or mechanical.

When planning your ceremony music, remember that you can use a variety of songs as long as the officiant is comfortable with your selections. Depending on your officiant, he may have the final say about which music is acceptable and which isn't. Make the music mean something to you.

Visit the musician in charge of your ceremony music. If you're having the ceremony in a religious setting, that person will most likely be the Minister of Music, the Director of Music, or the organist or pianist. Talk with this person about your likes and dislikes and what you would like to hear on your wedding day. Ask for ideas as well. Many times, if you meet in the facility, the musician can play a few bars of a certain piece so that you can hear the music. If you don't have access to a musician who can accommodate you, visit your local music store and purchase some tapes of wedding music. I have several tapes I loan to brides so they can be more active in choosing their wedding music.

Some popular choices for ceremony music are …

➤ **Processionals.** "Bridal Chorus," by Lohengrin ("Here Comes the Bride"); "The Wedding March," from Mendelssohn's *A Midsummer Night's Dream;* "Rondo," the *Masterpiece Theatre* theme, by Mouret; "Prince of Denmark's March," by Clarke; "Fanfare," from *The Triumphant,* by Couperin; "Sarabande," from *Suite No. 11,* by Handel; "Theme from *Love Story,*" by Sigman and Lai; "Trumpet Tune," by Purcell; "Trumpet Voluntary," by Clarke; and "Water Music," by Handel.

➤ **Ceremony music.** "Jesu, Joy of Man's Desiring," by Bach; "Canon in D Minor," by Pachebel; "A Wedding Prayer," by Williams; "Wedding Song," by Stookey;

"One Hand, One Heart," from *West Side Story,* by Bernstein and Sondheim; "Somewhere," from *West Side Story,* by Bernstein and Sondheim; "Theme from *Romeo and Juliet,*" by Roto and Kusik; "Sunrise, Sunset," from *Fiddler on the Roof,* by Harnick and Bock; "Evergreen," by Barbara Streisand; "The Hawaiian Wedding Song," by Williams; "Theme from *Ice Castles,*" by Melissa Manchester; "On the Wings of Love," by Jeffrey Osborne; "The Hands of Time (Brian's Song)," by Michel LaGrand; and "The Lord's Prayer," by Malotte.

Party Music

Although certainly not mandatory, music is a nice addition to the reception. This can be very simple or very elaborate. A pianist playing soft background music is nice for the simple cake-and-punch reception, or you might choose to have a 20-piece orchestra in the ballroom playing the sounds of Glenn Miller for a formal dinner and dance reception. It goes back to your personal tastes and what style of wedding you want.

At one wedding I coordinated, the bride's name was Amy. During the evening, the groom had the band play "Once in Love with Amy." The couple danced around the ballroom to that tune, and everyone applauded during this very special moment for them. Another couple took ballroom dance lessons in order to have a wonderful first dance. They even went so far as to have that dance choreographed by a professional. It was great to see a young couple so very poised glide around the ballroom with their bends and dips. Fred and Ginger, eat your hearts out.

Bouquet Toss

The first gift registry was founded in 1901, much by mistake, at a store named China Hall in Rochester, Minnesota. A poor, stressed clerk (see, they even had stress back then) couldn't remember the local brides' china patterns and which pieces the townspeople had purchased for which bride. He decided to write each bride's name on an index card along with her china pattern and which pieces had been purchased for the couple. Somehow it caught on, and now we have gift registries all over the country.

Here are a few things to keep in mind when you discuss your reception music with the vendor:

➤ Ask for a tape of the musician or group if you're unfamiliar with the music.

➤ Check the contracts. How many breaks do the musicians require, and how often do they take those breaks? Do they have access to taped music to play during those breaks? It's nice for the guests to hear some soft music playing in the background rather than dead silence.

➤ Will they announce you or help with the garter and bouquet toss?

➤ How long will they play? Will they stay past their end time if you request them to do so, and how much will the extra time cost?

➤ What is their professional dress for the event? If you're lucky enough to see them perform before you book them, look at the poise and composure they have with the crowd. Your dance floor should be active most of the evening, which is usually a sign of a good reception. In order for that to happen, a band must be able to "read" the crowd. If a style of music isn't working, will they try something different? Again, check with family and friends who have used this particular musician or group before, and get those references.

➤ Ask if they have liability insurance. Many facilities require this, but a lot of bands and DJs do not carry it. It's probably a wise move to make sure the band has liability insurance.

➤ One thing you want to make perfectly clear is that you want all their equipment set up and ready to go long before the guests arrive. At one wedding reception, a wave of panic hit me when I entered the reception hall and noticed that something was missing: the band! The area where they were to be set up and ready to go was empty. The group was driving in from out of town, and the mother had paid some heavy change to book the musicians. We tried calling their office and got only a recording. Luckily, guests were having cocktails in another room and didn't notice the band moving in its equipment in cut-offs and T-shirts.

➤ Ask if the band offers a song list from which you can make selections.

➤ Ask about how cooperative they will be with the volume. Too many times, the music is so loud that the guests cannot carry on a conversation. The musicians also should be in tune (another pun, sorry) with the volume level during the reception. Take your guests' hearing into consideration: Some guests prefer to sit at their tables and chat with family and friends. If they cannot hear themselves over the music, it's too loud. You want the volume loud enough for those on the dance floor to appreciate, but not so loud as to make other guests shout to each other at their tables.

A DJ (short for disc jockey) is another avenue for your reception music. I've seen good DJs, and I've seen bad ones. Any form of music makers at your reception can make or break the party. Make sure you've seen a DJ's performance and understand what he will do and what he won't do. Read the contract carefully. Note how long he will play and how many breaks he will take. Check out whether he will need any extra electricity at the reception. Make sure he will be dressed appropriately as well.

Several years ago, I had a client who searched long and hard for a really good band for her daughter's wedding. She went all over the state listening to bands and finally found one she liked. She had all but signed the contract when she asked if they needed anything extra from the reception facility. It seems that this band had to have a certain type of electrical wiring, and the reception facility didn't have that type. It would have cost an extra $1,500 just to get the right wiring for this band. Needless to say, my client shopped elsewhere.

Music can add a wonderful aspect to both your ceremony and your reception. Make wise musical choices for both situations. Your musical choices can frame your wedding day and set the mood for all to enjoy.

The Least You Need to Know

➤ Before you sit down to discuss your floral needs, ask the florist to visit the ceremony and reception sites if she isn't already familiar with them.

➤ Allow the florist some freedom in designing what will work best for your budget and your overall expectations.

➤ Use favors that can double as centerpieces.

➤ Be sure to check with the mothers on the style of flower they will like.

➤ Check the musician contract carefully.

➤ Check on the musicians' dress code and whether they carry liability insurance.

➤ If at all possible, try to see the musicians at work before you put down a deposit.

Floral Worksheet

Company: _____

Address: _____

Telephone: _____

Type of flowers desired: _____

_____

Wedding colors: _____

Ceremony site flowers: _____

_____

Aisle cloth: _____

Secured by florist? _____

Floor plan for ceremony:

Floor plan for reception:

Ideas for reception flowers: _____

_____

Centerpieces: _____

_____

Musicians Worksheet

Company: _____

Telephone: _____

Address: _____

Contact: _____

Referred by: _____

Type of music (band, DJ, single instrument): _____

_____

Do they provide song list to choose from? _____

What is attire for reception? _____

How long will they play? _____

How many breaks will they take? _____

What are overtime charges? _____

Will they help with introductions and garter and bouquet toss?

_____

_____

Next appointment: _____

Sometimes some of the most special moments are those unspoken.

(Classic Contemporary Photography by Geno)

Notice the bold colors used for this wedding reception. Also notice the rose placed in the fold of each napkin. Nice touch!

(Colter Photography)

Notice the difference candlelight makes to this table. Everything, including people, looks better by candlelight.

(Colter Photography)

This is a new trend in head tables. The tables are long and used on both sides. Again, a lovely presentation.

(Colter Photography)

This gorgeous tent setting shows how tent poles can be used to incorporate added décor to the overall look of a reception.

(Gregeiger Co. UTD, Inc.)

This newlywed couple exits the ceremony amid a spray of bubbles. They look happy!

(Stephanie Hogue Photography)

Here's another example of "showering" the couple. Jennifer and Bryan chose pastel flower petals to be showered with as they exit the church.

(Colter Photography)

This flower girl isn't too sure about the job before her. But notice how darling she looks in her halo of baby's breath.

(Classic Contemporary Photography by Geno)

I'm not quite sure if this young lady is so excited to see the bride or is singing along with the soloist. At any rate, she's having a great time.

(Stephanie Hogue Photography)

Thanks, Mom. It was wonderful.

(Classic Contemporary Photography by Geno)

I've talked about private time for the couple before the action gets going. These pictures are a perfect example of a couple seeing each other for the very first time. Brian walks toward his lovely bride.

(Colter Photography)

Samantha isn't sure she's going to make it through this meeting.

(Colter Photography)

But, they do.
(Colter Photography)

This couple also chose to have some private time before the ceremony and photos. And to Jennifer's surprise, she receives a beautiful set of earrings from Bryan. He looks so proud.

(Colter Photography)

This dad is thinking, "Where did all the time go?" as he remembers his little girl.

(Colter Photography)

And this tells it all, too. Thanks, Daddy, and I love you.

(Colter Photography)

The toast to the happy couple. Samantha seems moved by the best man's speech.

(Colter Photography)

Her mom looks on during the toast, and you can just feel the emotion of the moment. This is what photojournalistic photography is all about.

(Colter Photography)

This lovely, breath-taking photo shows how to incorporate a mansion with a tented reception to make enough room for all the guests. Notice how the grounds have even been lit with pole lights.

(Gregeiger Co. UTD, Inc.)

This is actually the inside of a tent. Wow! Look at what the designer or florist has done with the tent poles and the main beam in the ceiling. This ceiling is also covered with fabric.

(Stephanie Hogue Photography)

*What a sendoff! Fireworks at the reception. (Make sure
you have the proper permit.)*

(Colter Photography)

*This is a beautiful Jewish ceremony performed under the chuppah. These
chuppahs can be simple or elegantly adorned, such as this one. Notice, too,
the use of fabric on the aisle poles. Instead of candles, the couple has
chosen to use flowers instead.*

(Colter Photography)

This beautifully decorated church gives off the essence of romance with the candlelight and tulle covering the aisle poles. This bride is wearing a cathedral-length train.

(Wyant Photography, Inc.)

The same couple at the reception, cutting their cake. Gina has removed her long train (it was detachable) so she can move freely around the ballroom. Notice the loose rose petals scattered around the cake table. Very nice touch.

(Wyant Photography, Inc.)

This head table shows the use of the unity candle (in the center of the flower arrangement) surrounded by the flowers from the altar at the church. Good use of dollars.

(Wyant Photography, Inc.)

As I said, sometimes the most precious photos are those no one knows are being taken. Wonder what these two are up to? People-watching, maybe?

(Colter Photography)

This couple takes their time lighting their unity candle. Notice their physical placement at the altar table. They have turned sideways so the congregation has a good view of them and the candle. Also note the flower girl and ring bearer peeking around to check out what's happening.

(Wyant Photography, Inc.)

While still a posed picture, this is another way to make the photography session fun. Notice how this photographer groups the wedding party so they're not all in a straight line.

(Wyant Photography, Inc.)

I talked about unusual settings for some of your photos. This gazebo makes a perfect background for Gretchen's photo with her bridesmaids.

(Wyant Photography, Inc.)

Another nice setting, away from the church, for some quiet photos of this couple.

(Wyant Photography, Inc.)

This formal, traditional photograph of Gina and Preston is taken off center so Gina's lovely train can be seen. Notice where she is holding her bouquet. It's held low to not distract from her gown.

(Wyant Photography, Inc.)

The wedding is over, but as it looks here, the party is just beginning. With their shoes off, this group is ready to rock.

(Classic Contemporary Photography by Geno)

Chapter 13

All Dressed Up and Somewhere to Go

In This Chapter

➤ Shopping for the wedding gown

➤ Dressing the bridesmaids

➤ Decking out the men in your wedding party

➤ Creative ideas for your wedding transportation

Finding the right gown for the bride and then trying to outfit the bridesmaids can sometimes seem like an insurmountable task. It doesn't have to be, though, if you take it one step at a time. This chapter will guide you down the aisles of bridal shops to help you find your dream gown and complementary dresses for the bridal party.

Also in this chapter, I'll be helping the men in your wedding party choose their attire, and I'll give you some creative ideas for wedding transportation.

Cinderella for a Day

Your wedding day is an opportunity for you to become a princess—to be the center of attention; to be oohed and ahhed at; and, of course, to wear the most magnificent dress you'll ever own: the dress of your dreams. Now, although the bride dons this dress for only one day of her life, it is important that it's just perfect. You don't want to look at those wedding photos a few years from now and proclaim, "Why in the world did I wear that?"

So it's crucial that you take the time to really figure out what you want. What flatters you the most? What sets the mood you want for the wedding? And, perhaps something several brides may not think about, is the dress comfortable? You don't want to be yanking up that strapless number over and over again while all eyes are on you.

It's also important to feel comfortable with the bridal salon and to be confident that they will act professionally. With all the stress of a wedding, you don't need to be worried on your wedding day that the dress hasn't shown up yet! So, here are several things to keep in mind when you begin gown shopping. But most of all, have fun!

Thinking Ahead

You should order your gown at least six months before the wedding. It doesn't take six months for your gown to arrive at the shop, but with delays in shipping, manufacturing problems, and alterations, it's best to be on the safe side. If you don't have six months lead time, make sure you mention that to the shop. Several bridal gown companies specialize in short order times.

Bouquet Toss

The traditional color of a bridal gown was not white until very recently. In ancient times, red was a favorite color, along with other brightly colored materials.

In the mid-nineteenth century, Empress Eugenie, wife of Napoleon III, broke the medieval tradition of wearing a brightly colored wedding gown and chose white.

In the Victorian period in this country, brides from affluent families began wearing white gowns to show that they could afford to have a special dress they would wear only one time. Most women simply wore the best dress they had at the time. A white gown did not come to represent purity until the twentieth century.

By Appointment Only

Make sure you check with the bridal shops to see if you need appointments before your visit. This makes you appear more serious about buying, and if they know you're coming, they can give you the time and attention you deserve. If the shop doesn't accept appointments, ask for the best time to shop. Saturdays, for example, are often very busy days for bridal shops; try to shop on another day of the week.

Oh, It's So You!

When shopping for your wedding gown, look at many different styles of dresses. You might be really surprised to find that a gown style you thought would not complement you really does. You'll have several options in terms of style, cut, fabric, and adornments. Your first time, try on a few different styles to get a feel for what works for you. Perhaps you look best with off-the-shoulder, or you realize you're too petite for a train. Or, the dress you fell in love with in that magazine makes you look like a marshmallow. If you're not familiar with the different types of silk, ask the sales person—and that person should be very knowledgeable because that's what she's there for!

Some advice: Shop with an open mind. Just because you have your heart set on a sheath gown with a detachable train, don't be afraid to try on the gown with the flowing skirt and cowl neckline. And even if you don't like it on the hanger or on the model, that doesn't mean it won't look fabulous on you. Remember how fun the game of dress-up was when you were a kid? Well, this is just like it (except that the gown will be made to fit), so relax and have a good time!

A second (or third) opinion is always a good idea. Many mothers dream of the day they can take their daughters wedding-dress shopping. So, take one or two people with you when you shop. Your mom or one or two trusted friends can offer plenty of advice. But do not go armed with your entire wedding party—too many people giving you advice will only cause you more stress. Too many opinions also make it harder for you to choose the dress that's right for you.

And don't think all stores are the same—shop around. You might even find the same or similar dress elsewhere but realize you like the service or location of the shop better. It's also a good idea to get referrals from recent brides.

For help in shopping wisely, turn to the "Wedding Gown and Bridesmaids' Dresses Worksheet" at the end of this chapter.

Dress the Part

If you don't dress up for this wonderful occasion, at least take a pair of dress shoes with you. Have your hair fixed appropriately, and add a little makeup. You want to look your best, and you want to get a realistic picture of how you will look on your wedding day in the gown. Somehow, trying on a bridal gown wearing your Nikes and your hair in a ponytail just doesn't seem to paint the appropriate picture.

Don't Veil the Truth

It's wise to wait until you've decided on a gown before you begin picking out your veil. You wouldn't want an unflattering veil to overpower the beauty of the dress. The salesperson might suggest that you try on a simple veil with the gown of your choice to provide you with the whole picture, but refrain from choosing a style until you're sure of the wedding gown—different styles of gowns complement different styles of veils.

You might be surprised at all of the options you have with a veil—different weights of fabric, choices of trimmings, and, of course, length. All these decisions will be based not only on what works best for you, but also what works best with the gown.

You have the following choices in veil lengths:

➤ **Fingertip veil.** Just brushes the shoulders and frames the face.

➤ **Elbow-length veil.** Brushes the elbows.

➤ **Chapel-length veil.** Measures three yards long (nine feet).

➤ **Cathedral-length veil.** Measures four yards long (12 feet).

If your gown doesn't have a long train (or a train at all), you might want to consider having a longer veil to act as a train. Try on different styles to be sure that you get the best match for both your gown and your hairstyle.

Bouquet Toss

Before the sixteenth century, veils were worn by unmarried women as a sign of modesty, and by married women to show that they were submissive to their husbands. My, how things change.

A natural component of the veil is the headpiece, from simple clips, to headbands, to pillbox hats. Be sure to think about how you'd like to wear your hair on your wedding day—you don't want to choose a headpiece that looks good only with your hair down, when you imagine yourself walking down the aisle with a French twist.

The Glass Slippers

You might think that shoes are not something you need to devote much time to—who's going to see them anyway? But think about how many hours you're going to be on your feet! I can't emphasize this enough: Make sure the shoes are comfortable! The last thing you need is a pair of shoes that make your feet hurt. If your feet are complaining, you won't relax and enjoy the festivities.

Brides often choose a lovely pair of formal shoes for the ceremony and then slip on a pair of ballet slippers for the reception. Their feet are exceptionally appreciative.

Also popular are tennis shoes trimmed with ribbons and lace to dress them up. These can be purchased at many bridal shops or through catalogs and can help the bride dance all night.

The Final Touches

Sometimes it's the little things that make the difference—the sparkle of a necklace, the elegance of gloves, the charm of a matching clutch. Take the time to consider these accessories.

Jewelry is an accessory that can add to your total look. Don't overload yourself, though, especially if your gown is heavily beaded. A pair of pretty earrings and a simple pearl necklace may be all that you need. You should remove your watch and any other everyday jewelry as well.

You are going to be royalty for a day, so you have the right to don white gloves, if you wish. Sometimes a pair of long silk gloves are the perfect touch to a very simple gown. (And if you're wondering what you'll do with the ring at the ceremony, the bridal shop can remove some stitching in the finger of the glove so you can have the ring placed properly, on your finger itself.)

These days, more brides are opting to carry a small bag as well. How often they actually keep it on them is another story, but it might be nice to have a place for your lipstick. This might not be something you want to break the bank on—perhaps choose a purse you can use again.

Wedding Woes

It's not a wise move to order your gown from a shop advertising that it's going out of business. If you can buy the gown off the rack, that's fine. But don't put down a deposit and allow the store to order your gown. One bride I worked with learned this lesson the hard way. The shop called and said that the gown was in. When the bride went to get her gown, the shop had "lost" the gown and couldn't reorder. What really happened was that the shop had sold that gown to another customer for more money.

Underneath It All

What goes underneath your gown is just as important as all your other accessories. The type of bra and slip you choose to wear with your gown should be well thought-out. Most bridal shops carry these undergarments. First, you want a bra that is comfortable and that gives you the support you need with your particular gown. The slip helps give you the proper shape, whether your gown is a sheath or a southern belle–style gown. If your gown is a slim sheath, you might decide not to wear a slip. Make sure, however, that you cannot see panty lines through your gown—you should show smile lines, but not panty lines!

Service with a Smile

If you know others who have used a certain shop, ask those brides how they were treated. Were all their questions answered satisfactorily? How did the gown look when it was ready to be picked up or when it arrived at the ceremony site? Were the sleeves stuffed with tissue? Was a *bodice form* used? Was the train tied up or draped over the hanger?

Nuptial Notes

A **bodice form** is a piece of cardboard shaped like a woman's upper body that the shop places in the bodice of your gown to keep it wrinkle-free and looking fresh. This protects the gown during travel time from the shop to your home or ceremony site.

All the Hustle and Bustle

Ask the shop how the gown's train will be bustled. Bustling the train means that either hooks and eyes or buttons are sewn onto the back of the gown at appropriate places. When the buttons are looped, the train is pulled up, or bustled, so that you can move more freely during the reception. Bustling your gown is very important, so be sure to get answers to these questions.

These may appear to be little things, but they can make a difference in whether your gown looks freshly pressed or as if you slept in it. Not a pretty sight.

A Little Nip Here, a Little Tuck There ...

Be sure to ask about alterations! Are they included? If not, how much should you expect to pay? This can become a major expense when ordering your bridal gown. Manufacturers all use a different set of guidelines for measurements. While you might wear a size 8 in ready-to-wear women's clothing, formal wear has a different set of measurement guidelines. Let the bridal shop explain how a particular manufacturer determines sizes.

Do not order a gown two sizes too small because you expect to lose that much weight before the wedding. Bad idea. If you want to lose weight before your wedding (and many brides do), explain that to the shop so that they are aware, but order the gown using your present measurements. It's always possible to have a dress taken in, but letting it out can be more difficult—and sometimes impossible.

If It Was Good Enough for Mom ...

Sally Lorensen Conant, Ph.D., president of Orange Restoration Labs in Orange, Connecticut, offers the following advice and ideas if you're considering wearing a family gown—either your mother's, your grandmother's, your sister's, or even a friend's gown:

For the bride who values tradition and sentiment, a family gown may be just right. Family gowns come in all sizes and shapes, and they can be fitted to all sizes and shapes. In fact, we know a bridal shop that can make a gown as many as 12 sizes larger! Always make the decision to wear a family gown, whether it belongs to your mother or your favorite aunt or even a close family friend, based on the meaning the gown has for you and whether the style suits you—not on the way it fits or its condition. A specialist can restore even a yellowed, badly stained gown to the true color, and a talented dressmaker can reshape almost any gown to your size.

You can also update a gown by changing the sleeves, the neckline, or the shape of the skirt. Three sisters in one family remodeled their mother's gown so extensively that it looked completely different at each of the three weddings. Some brides add lace and beading such as pearls, sequins, or crystals, but these days brides more often choose to wear a family gown because they like the simplicity of the cut and the beauty of the fabric. Simply cut, unembellished gowns today are often the most expensive gowns on the market, and a bride may look just as elegant in a family gown at far less cost.

Wedding Woes

Alterations can be very expensive; always know up front what the shop will charge for alterations. Your best bet is to try to remain approximately the size you were when you ordered your gown. If you're expecting a large weight loss, either have your gown made locally or wait until you're closer to the desired weight before you order.

See Reverse for Care

Whether you choose a gown off the rack, have one ordered, or decide to wear Mama's gown, Sally Lorensen Conant again offers this advice:

Teddy's Tips

Several companies offer gown restoration services, which can make your mother's or grandmother's yellowed gown beautiful again. Call the Wedding Gown Specialists Association at 1-800-501-5005 for a cleaner/ preservation specialist in your area.

Beware the unserviceable gown! Before you actually purchase a dress, look at the care label. Federal law requires manufacturers to put labels into clothing describing the proper care for the garment. Some labels actually say "Do Not Wash" and "Do Not Dry Clean." Unless you have absolutely no interest in what happens to your gown after the wedding, better pass up a dress with this label.

Also look carefully at the decorations on the gown. Something like dried rosebuds will not survive cleaning, no matter what the care label says, and the gown will have to be taken apart before it can be cleaned. Are the beads sewn onto the gown, or are they glued? Some glues dissolve in water, and others dissolve in dry cleaning, so either way you lose. Beads that are sewn can be a problem, too. Some manufacturers knot the thread very infrequently so that when one thread breaks, many, many beads fall off. Others use beads that melt in the dry-cleaning process. You can test for loose beads by pulling at one or two of them, but without special chemicals, you can't very well test the bead's serviceability. That makes it even more important to read the care label; the manufacturer has to stand behind the recommended care. If there is no label, better ask the shop about the care recommended by the manufacturer.

Pretty Maids All in a Row

When shopping for your bridesmaids' gowns, try to take only your honor attendant and/or your mother or a close friend. Do not—I repeat, do not—take your whole wedding party with you. Most bridal shops cringe when they see an entire wedding party march through the door. If you're asking only one or two friends to be in the wedding, then you can take your whole party; otherwise, it's best to take only a select one or two. (If you have a variety of shapes and sizes among the girls, try to take along two of the bridesmaids with varying figures. If you have a very tall, athletically built attendant, but only bring along the very petite one, you won't know if the dress will look flattering on someone six feet tall with broad shoulders.)

It's the bride's responsibility to choose what the attendants will wear. You should take into consideration their physical size and coloring, and you don't want to force them into bankruptcy, but the final choice is yours. There is a lot of pressure these days to choose something the bridesmaids can wear again, but you shouldn't sacrifice the look you want for your wedding. I've also heard many bridesmaids say they don't feel comfortable wearing the dress elsewhere—they feel they will *look* like bridesmaids.

You also need to make sure that the style and color of their dresses complements your gown. You don't want to have your six bridesmaids dressed more elaborately than you.

Horror stories of brides and bridesmaids getting into real shouting matches while deciding on the attendants' dresses abound in the wedding world. It doesn't have to be that way. I've worked with several brides in the past couple years who have said to their bridesmaids, "Wear a black dress; no satin or sequins, but other than that, I don't care." When the first bride told me this, I was a little skeptical. The final picture, however, was rather pleasing. Each girl got to pick a dress that complemented her figure, and because each chose her own dress, it was probably something she would wear again. I've also had brides purchase material and then have their bridesmaids choose their own patterns. So, although they dressed alike in color and fabric, the dress styles were individualized. Again, each girl got the dress she wanted and would most likely wear it again.

Try to choose a dress with a reasonable price tag as well. If your attendants are providing their own transportation to your hometown, buying you a gift, and paying to stay in a hotel (although it would be nice if you could either pay for their hotel or find them a room in Aunt Laura's home), along with all the other expenses that come with being in a wedding party, their calculators will be running overtime. Help them out by keeping the cost of the dress manageable.

Dressed to Kill: Formal Wear for Men

The groom and his men want to look just as handsome as the bride and her attendants want to look beautiful. Take some time to look through bridal magazines to get a feel for what's available for the men in your wedding party. (Be sure to use the "Tuxedo Worksheet" at the end of this chapter.) There are hundreds of tuxedo styles, different ties, shirts, vests, and colors from which to choose. The sky is the limit with tuxedo choices.

The groom may choose the traditional cutaway coat with gray-striped trousers and an ascot. If your wedding leans more toward semiformal or informal, a nice dark suit and a white or pastel shirt is always a good choice.

Going with the Flow

Select the style and brand of tuxedo that will complement the wedding theme, the time of day, and what the bridesmaids are wearing. If the bridesmaids are in very casual street-length dresses, you wouldn't want the groomsmen dressed in a formal black tie and tails. The salespeople at the tux shop should be able to help you determine just what style you need and what will go well with the wedding theme.

Accent with Color

Prints, gold and silver threads on black vests, along with accents in ties and cummerbunds are appearing more frequently these days. Of course, the white tie is still considered very formal and is a most appropriate look for a formal wedding after 6 o'clock in the evening. Many times, for a hint of color to coordinate with your bridesmaids, the groom might choose to have colored handkerchiefs in the men's breast pockets.

Right Down to Their Feet

Make sure that the men have formal shoes. You don't want them dressed to the hilt in a wonderful tuxedo, yet wearing cowboy boots or tennis shoes. They need to have a pair of black or gray (depending on the color of tuxedo) leather or patent leather dress shoes. Also, white socks just don't complement the ensemble for someone wearing a dark suit or tuxedo! Make sure that the groomsmen have black socks to go with their formal shoes.

Bouquet Toss

One ancient tradition was to dress the bridesmaids and groomsmen like the bride and groom so that the evil demons would be confused if they tried to put a curse on the couple.

Getting the Suit on Time

The men should order their formal wear about two to three months before the wedding. Look in the Yellow Pages under "Wedding Services and Supplies" or "Formal Wear" for listings of retailers that offer tuxedos (formal wear) for rent. You also can purchase tuxedos, but they are expensive; unless you plan to use one extensively, it's cheaper to rent a tuxedo when you need it.

Buying in Bulk

Many stores offer some kind of special or discount on tuxedo rentals: "Rent six tuxedos, get the groom's free," or maybe, "Rent your tuxedos from us, and you receive your limousine rental free." Always ask about specials.

Your rented tuxedo is a package deal. In other words, you will receive the jacket, trousers, choice of shirt, tie, vest or cummerbund, studs, and cuff links for one price.

Shoes may be rented also, but that's usually an extra charge. Sometimes colored handkerchiefs are included to add color to the outfit (they go in the breast pocket, not the back pocket).

The Perfect Fit

Alterations are usually kept to a minimum. Jacket sleeve length and pant length are always altered, but unless you have a specific concern, shops try not to get bogged down with alterations.

Long-Distance Shopping

If you have out-of-town men in your wedding party, then the task of getting them fitted is relatively simple. When you go to the shop to select your formal wear, give the names of the men who need to be fitted to the shop. They will provide postcards with the brand name and style number of the tuxedo included. Send those postcards to your out-of-town men, and have them take the cards to their local tux shops. There, they will be measured and can try on the same brand of jacket to check for fitting. That shop will also take other measurements to ensure a correct fitting.

Teddy's Tips

It's a good idea to carry collar extenders in your emergency kit in case the shirt is too tight around the neck. This little contraption can add an inch or so to make your life—and breathing—a little easier.

Then, have your men return the cards to the local tux shop to have their tuxedo orders placed. When the men arrive in town for the wedding, have them go to the tux shop and try on their tuxedo completely (or, at least the jacket and trousers). Last-minute alterations can be made if something doesn't fit properly.

Arriving in Style

The mode of transportation you plan to use for your wedding day is one little detail that's easy to overlook. With a little planning, however, this item can add a unique flair to your special day. The "Special Transportation Worksheet" at the end of this chapter can help you in this area.

Many couples use special transportation to take them from the ceremony to the reception. Other couples use special forms of transportation from the home to the ceremony, and some couples use special types of transportation to take them from the reception to their wedding night destination. It's a personal choice; be creative, but stay within your budget.

That Luxurious Limousine

The most common form of transportation is, you guessed it, the limousine. Elegant and classy, the limousine can make you feel like a movie star. When choosing a limo company, be sure to ask for references from family and friends.

Most companies offer either hourly prices or package prices. Ask what services are included. Will the driver be uniformed? Nothing looks tackier than a beautiful bride and a handsome groom exiting the church to an awaiting white limo with the driver decked out in jeans, a dirty T-shirt, and tennis shoes. Ugh! I have seen it happen, so be sure to ask the right questions so that it doesn't happen to you.

In most states, the limo company employees cannot furnish champagne or wine unless they have a liquor license. If you purchase the liquor, however, they usually are willing to serve it. With any luck, they will even use some lovely crystal stemmed glasses.

Make sure you get all the specifics in writing: pick-up time, where you are to be delivered, and any extra services you require. I recall one nightmare story that drives home the importance of using reputable limousine companies recommended by friends and family who have had positive experiences. This particular driver turned to the bride as I closed the car door and said, "Hey, babe, where are we headed?" Now mind you, I had just reminded him where he was to take the couple, but I guess it was just too much for him to comprehend. Anyway, the bride was upset but told the driver where the reception was being held. The driver didn't have a clue how to get to the reception, got lost, had to stop for gas, and was an hour late in getting the couple to the reception. To top it all off, he had the audacity to walk into the reception, approach the mother of the bride, and demand more money because he had gone into overtime! Do you think I've ever hired this bozo again? I don't think so. Make sure you get referrals from people you trust. Don't let something like this happen to you.

If you need to have your luggage taken from the ceremony site and transferred to a vehicle at the reception, get those specifics in writing now so that you don't have to worry about that at the wedding. You want to get everything in order before the big day.

Absolute Elegance

If a limo isn't a favorite of yours or you want something a little classier, then a Rolls Royce might be what the doctor ordered. These fine, elegant, classic cars are pure heaven to ride in and add a smart touch of class to your get-away. Most Rolls Royces can be rented from limo companies or under their own company in larger cities. They will be more expensive than your limo but, if that is a priority of yours and it's in the budget, then go for it.

Another mode of nontraditional transportation is the classic car. You might even be able to borrow a convertible, vintage ride from a friend. Most cities also have car clubs and sometimes will rent a car for wedding transportation.

This couple has chosen a classic convertible for their grand exit.

(Colter Photography)

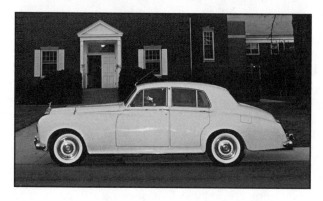

The luxury of the classic Rolls Royce.

(Colter Photography)

This Won't Turn into a Pumpkin!

If a limousine isn't in your plans, there are other options you can consider. Many cities have horse-drawn carriages that can transport you on your big day. I worked with one bride who was having an outdoor wedding and whose dream was to arrive at the ceremony site in a horse-drawn carriage just as the processional was beginning to play. Guests turned their heads to witness the bride arrive in a white carriage pulled by two white horses. It was lovely, and she was extremely pleased. That's also the only time in my business career that I've had to cue a horse.

When looking for information on horse-drawn carriages, look under "Wedding Services" or "Carriages" (in larger cities) in your Yellow Pages. Make sure the company carries liability insurance—this is very important.

Expect to pay some big bucks for this luxury. The reason it's costly goes back to the liability insurance. Ask about uniformed drivers. Ask what happens to your deposit if Mother Nature doesn't cooperate and it rains. Ask your questions now, and avoid disappointment later.

If a limo or Rolls Royce isn't your cup of tea, a horse and carriage are always a fun way to escape.

(Stephanie Hogue Photography)

Be Creative

Perhaps my trophy for the most unique mode of wedding transportation I have ever witnessed goes to a couple I worked with several years ago. They had a beautiful garden wedding followed by a lovely garden reception. The home was in the country, and we were surrounded by trees, flowers, and the beauty of nature. When I asked them if they were going to leave from the reception in any special form, they assured me that they had nothing in mind and would just leave in their car. When the time came, the bride's brother appeared with a small Ford tractor (yes, I said tractor) that had a box on the back for hauling. The couple took one look at the tractor, hopped on board, and off they rode into the sunset (or the field, or wherever their car was parked). The picture that scene created was fantastic and still remains in my mind today.

Parents of one bride surprised another couple with a helicopter ride from the reception to the airport. So be creative, and if possible, try to tie in the season, location, and your interests.

Transporting the Whole Gang

If you have a large wedding party and would like to transport everyone in one vehicle (whether you join them or not), you have a couple choices. Some cities boast trolley cars that you can rent for special events. These are trackless but still remind you of simpler times. You usually can rent these for a half day or a full day, depending on your locale. Couples sometimes use them to transport the entire wedding party from the ceremony to the reception. You can decorate these cars to coordinate with your wedding colors or theme and have a lot of fun.

Over the years, I've coordinated some larger weddings in which the couple rented buses for their wedding party. The buses not only transported the wedding party from the ceremony to the reception, but they also shuttled family members and some out-of-town guests. The buses returned to the reception site later and took the guests back to their cars. If your budget allows, you can go one step further and have the bus pick up the out-of-town guests at the hotel, deliver them to the ceremony site, take them to the reception, and finally deliver them safely back to their hotel. Wow! What a deal. No worry about getting lost in a strange city or drinking too much at the reception—just a lot of happy, well-cared-for guests.

One wedding I coordinated had a groom from New Jersey and a bride from Indiana who expanded on the bus idea. The wedding was held in Indiana, so the groom's family rented a Turner Coach to transport 60 relatives and close friends to the wedding. They had a wonderful time on the trip. Each guest paid for his or her share of the bus ride, and although it probably wasn't cheaper than driving a personal car, it was much cheaper than flying—and more relaxing and enjoyable!

Use your imagination. Make your grand exit in style, but make it in *your* style. As always, remember to ask many questions of the various vendors and to get referrals.

The Least You Need to Know

➤ Try to allow at least six months for ordering and receiving your wedding gown. If you don't have that much time, you may find that it will cost you a bit more.

➤ Take only your mother or a friend or two with you to shop for your gown. Too many opinions can make your decision all the more difficult.

➤ Consider using a family gown.

➤ When choosing bridesmaids' dresses, think about the attendants' physical attributes and coloring, as well as what they can reasonably afford.

➤ The groom's formal wear should complement the style of wedding you're planning as well as the bridal gown.

➤ Be creative when deciding on the transportation you will use for your wedding day. Use your imagination and have fun with this decision.

Wedding Gown and Bridesmaids' Dresses Worksheet

Shops to visit: _____

_____

Referred by: _____

_____

Date of appointments: _____

_____

Contact at shop: _____

Telephone: _____

Style of gown: _____

_____

Color selection: _____

Budgeted amount for gown and veil: _____

Budgeted amount for accessories

    Bra: _____

    Slip: _____

    Shoes: _____

    Jewelry: _____

Deposit paid (date): _____

Payments to be made (dates): _____

_____

Bridesmaids' dresses

    Color choices: _____

    Style of dresses: _____

    Cost of dresses: _____

    Cost of alterations: _____

    Number of attendants: _____

Attendants' names, phone numbers, and addresses:

1. _____

_____

_____

_____

2. _____

_____

_____

_____

3. _____

_____

_____

_____

4. _____

_____

_____

_____

(Add more paper if needed)

Next appointment: _____

_____

Questions to ask: _____

_____

_____

_____

_____

Tuxedo Worksheet

Name of store: _____

Address: _____

Telephone: _____

Salesperson: _____

Price: _____

Style number: _____

Color: _____

Tie/cummerbund/vest/shirt color: _____

Accessories

    Shoes: _____

    Gloves: _____

    Hats: _____

    Other: _____

Deposit made: _____

Special Transportation Worksheet

Mode of transportation desired: _____

Contact: _____

Telephone: _____

Referred by: _____

Contract used: _____

Contract/deposit returned (date): _____

Hours needed (time of day): _____

Special instructions/directions sent: _____

Chapter 14

Pretty as a Picture— Photographers and Videographers

In This Chapter

➤ Understanding wedding photography

➤ Finding the right videographer

➤ Making sense of photographer contracts

In this chapter we take a look at the photography and video industry—what's out there and what choices you have. (Yes, despite everything you hear, *you* are in control and make the final choice—I'm writing this book to help you make *good* choices.) These two elements of your wedding day are so important. Don't take shortcuts here if they are a high priority for you. Shop wisely for these vendors.

Focusing on Your Photography

Photography is an expensive undertaking for most couples. You want good pictures that capture your special day, but that means you're going to have to spend some time investigating your choices now and to allow for enough money in your budget to accomplish that goal.

So Many Questions, So Little Time

When you meet with the photographer, you need to consider several items. The first thing you should look at is the quality of the photographer's work. Does the photographer's work capture the moment? Look through the display albums. Do the pictures express the romance of the day? What catches your eye? Are they straight shots? Do the pictures tell a story? Find out whether the photographer will take candid shots; many photographers will not. Is the photographer available on your wedding date? What is the fee? What kinds of packages does he offer?

Make Sure That What You See Is What You Get

Ask what percentage of the photographer's work is in wedding photography. Is her business mostly weddings, or is she primarily a studio photographer? It takes a certain personality to take wedding pictures, so you want to be sure to hire an experienced wedding photographer.

As you're looking over the work displayed in the studio, be sure to ask whose work you're viewing. If Mr. Smith took the pictures they are showing you, but Ms. Jones will be the photographer shooting your wedding, ask to see Ms. Jones's work.

If it's a large studio, make sure you know who will be photographing your wedding. One couple I worked with a few years ago was very excited because they had booked one of the biggest studios in town for their wedding. I knew that the studio contracted out some of its photography work to other photographers, but the couple didn't know this. When I asked who was going to take pictures at their wedding, they responded that Mr. Smith, the owner, was going to shoot the wedding. I asked if they were sure about that, and they were very surprised that I asked this question. When they checked with the studio, they were shocked and disappointed to learn that Mr. Smith was not going to photograph the wedding pictures, but instead their wedding had been contracted out to someone they had not met. Had they read their contract more carefully, they would have discovered that fact sooner.

Teddy's Tips

Be sure to find out what kind of contract the photographer uses. Does the contract include a time limit? You want to avoid having to pay overtime to your photographer; overtime can add up to big money very quickly.

Teddy's Tips

Make sure you examine the work of the photographer who will be taking your wedding photographs. Looking at the work of another photographer from that studio won't help you decide whether the photographer you are considering is right for the job.

Do You Have That Warm, Fuzzy Feeling?

One of the most important questions you have to ask is whether you both feel comfortable with this photographer. Be honest with yourselves. You will spend a lot of time on your wedding day with this person; if you don't like the person, for whatever reason, it will show in your pictures. Over the years, I have watched brides who were so obviously annoyed by their photographer that the only things that came across in the finished product were clenched teeth and forced smiles. Not good! It's important to have a good rapport with your photographer.

What's in a Picture?

You might encounter several different styles of wedding photography from which you will have to choose. The type of wedding photography that a particular photographer offers depends on his ability, experience, and personal choice, but you'll be better off if you at least know the differences and can understand the terminology.

Teddy's Tips

Always take care of your support staff—photographer, videographer, DJ or band, and coordinators—by offering them food and a special place at the reception for them to regroup.

Soft Focus

When we were married, I remember fondly the photographer pulling out these wonderfully romantic pictures from his samples and waving them tantalizingly in front of my eyes. They were dream-like and romantic with soft lighting. That type of photography is called *soft focus*. The photographer uses a special lens to give a romantic look to the pictures. You wouldn't want your entire album in this style, however, because after a few shots, the romantic look loses its effectiveness.

Portraiture

Portraiture is probably one of the most common types of photography, although you might not know it by this name. This refers to the formal posed pictures at the ceremony site and reception. There isn't much spontaneity here, but the pictures can be almost perfect, depending on the photographer. The time element here is what you need to understand. Yes, your pictures can be quite lovely, but if it's going to take the photographer five hours to accomplish that task, maybe you should think of other alternatives.

Natural Light

This type of photography does not use artificial light. In other words, no flash is used with the camera. The photographer takes what light is available naturally and uses that to create the image. When done well, a *natural light* photograph reminds you of a fine work of art, but it's very difficult to arrange.

Photojournalistic

Wedding photography done in the *photojournalistic* style takes its technique from the news media. The photographer, through pictures, tells the story of your wedding on film. Instead of posing pictures trying to create a mood, the photographer follows the people and mood of the event and captures it on film as it happens. This can be a fantastic way to show emotions, highlights of the day that have special meaning, the people involved, and anything special you want to include. Examples of "capture the moment" photography are located in several places throughout this book. It is becoming more popular with couples all over the country, as well as the mixing of color photos with black-and-white images.

In one wedding I coordinated, the groom's mother had died just six months before the wedding. He wanted to do something special in her honor at the service. When the parents were to be seated, the groom appeared in the back of the church and walked by his father's side down the aisle. They went to the altar rail and lit a candle in memory of his mother. It was a very touching moment, and one which the photographer really couldn't pose. By using the photojournalistic approach, the photographer got a wonderful shot to capture this special moment.

Contracts

It's very important to understand the kind of contract the photographer uses and exactly what the price includes. Make sure you understand this. Does the contract include albums? Does it include a charge for the proofs?

As I mentioned, one very important feature to consider is whether the contract includes a time limit. When you buy a package, is there a time limit on how long the photographer is available? Suppose your wedding is at 5 P.M. You don't want to see each other before the service, so the bride has some pictures taken with the bridesmaids and family. The groom has similar shots taken with his groomsmen, ushers, and family. The majority of the pictures, however, must be taken after the service. Then, of course, you want the photographer to go to the reception and get some shots there: the cutting of the cake, the toast, your first dance, and so on.

If your contract has a four-hour time limit and you start pictures at 4 P.M., that means that at 8 P.M., the photographer either is finished shooting your wedding or goes into overtime. That's what you want to avoid, if at all possible. I've been quoted $150 per hour overtime for photographers in the Midwest—that's a lot of money. So check whether the contract contains a time limit clause. It may be cheaper for you in the long run to get a package with more time than you think you'll need just to save you from paying overtime.

When All Is Said and Done

Good wedding photography is meant to last a lifetime. You want to choose a photographer who can help you capture on film all the wonderful emotions of your big day.

You want someone who treats you with respect and sensitivity, and you want all this without even noticing that the photographer is in the room. Use the "Photography Worksheet" at the end of this chapter to determine your photographic needs.

Hiring a Videographer

After you have hired a competent photographer to shoot the still pictures for your wedding, you also might want to consider booking a videographer. Videotaping by an experienced videographer can add so much life to your wedding memories that this is fast becoming a very popular wedding component. Some couples are even opting for a professional video in lieu of professional photography. With technology today, it's possible to pull still frames from a video or add animation to help create the video of your dreams.

See Samples

When you check out a video company, always ask to see a demo tape. This should give you an idea of the quality of work the company provides. When you view this tape, look for clarity both in film quality and in the coverage of events. Does the tape flow smoothly from one portion of the wedding to the next? Does the videographer use fade-outs?

Make sure you understand whether the tape will be edited or unedited. Edited is what you would most likely prefer. One couple didn't check these details and ended up with 12 hours of unedited tape. Can you imagine inviting friends over to see your 12-hour wedding video? Ask to see a recent tape (not just the demo that will be the best one ever shot).

Home Video Quality

The biggest complaint I hear from brides who asked Uncle Henry to tape their wedding is, "I thought it would be just like TV." Well, it's not. For a videotape to have some of the major components of a TV show, you will need at least two cameras—and three would be better.

Ask the video company whether it can provide the groom with a wireless microphone to pick up the vows segment of the ceremony. Ask about including special effects, such as incorporating your baby pictures into the video or using animation. Ask whether the videographer will attend the rehearsal to get a feel for placement at the ceremony site and

Wedding Woes

Always check with the officiant to make sure you're permitted to have your ceremony videotaped. That's your responsibility, not the video company's. Nothing is more embarrassing than having the video company all set and ready to go when the officiant announces that his church or synagogue does not permit videotaping.

Teddy's Tips

This is the time in your wedding planning when you might want to consider visiting some retail establishments in your area to register for wedding gifts. Unless you don't care whether you get 42 sets of glasses or 16 toasters, get yourself down to the local department store or national home store and register. Usually the store will have someone assigned to help couples register.

to meet the officiant. For help with this part of your wedding planning, turn to the "Videography Worksheet" at the end of this chapter.

Get Me the Soundtrack!

Is there music that will be added to your edited video? Will you have a choice in the selection of music? Most videographers consider themselves artists and in that regard, do not like having you pick the music. Some videographers, however, will ask a couple to select a few meaningful songs to include, and then fill in with what they consider appropriate.

The Package Deal

Just as you would with any other aspect of planning your wedding, ask questions about price and what is available to you. Can you order extra tapes? Approximately how long after the wedding will you receive the tape? Does the videographer use a contract? (Most do.) Is there a time limit on his contract? Does he charge for overtime? What do the videographers wear for the wedding?

The Least You Need to Know

➤ Make sure you feel comfortable with the photographer who will be taking your wedding pictures. You will be spending a significant amount of time together and need to have a good rapport.

➤ Be sure you view the photographer's finished product.

➤ Ask the officiant if your wedding may be videotaped.

➤ Ask to see a demo tape of a videographer's work before you make a commitment.

Photography Worksheet

Photographer: _____

Address: _____

Telephone: _____

Referred by: _____

Type of photography (portraiture, candid, photojournalistic, soft focus, natural light):

_____

_____

Deposit: _____

Package plan (including time limit, overtime charges, charge for proofs, number of pictures, albums, and so on): _____

_____

Next appointment: _____

_____

Videography Worksheet

Company: _____

Address: _____

Telephone: _____

Contact: _____

Referred by: _____

Type of video requested (edited or unedited): _____

Attends rehearsal: _____

Number of cameras needed: _____

Music selection: _____

Provides cordless microphone for groom: _____

Special effects used: Baby pictures? Credits? Animation? Fade in or out?

_____

_____

_____

Come to my Wedding
or Heaven help you.

Bring a gift.

Chapter 15

Extra! Extra! Read All About It!

In This Chapter

➤ Getting your money's worth in your invitation order

➤ Putting the invitation package together

➤ Using a "save the date" card

➤ Sending a wedding newsletter to friends

➤ Adding welcome letters for out-of-town guests

➤ Designing a wedding program

Isn't it exciting when you open your mailbox and find a wedding invitation? You can usually tell it's for a wedding right off the bat—the envelope is a different size and shape than the others in the pile of mail, the quality paper is usually notably nicer, and sometimes it's even a different color than that of the same old white envelopes you see in there every day.

And stand out it should—the invitation is the first hint your guests will get of what your wedding will be like. In this chapter, I'll tell you all about invitations, from how to get them to how to put them together. Plus, I'm going to add a little more to the paper trail by showing you how to put together a "save the date" card, a wedding newsletter, welcome letters, and design a wedding program.

Taking Stock of Your Invitations

I've learned a lot about invitations over the past few years, and I now offer invitations and accessories to brides at a discount. Rule 1: Never pay full retail price for invitations. I can hear the invitation companies screaming right now, but there is so much competition out there for your invitation order that you should never have to pay sticker price. You can always get something at a discount.

Nuptial Notes

A typical wedding invitation "packet" might include the invitation itself, reception card, response card and return envelope, an inner envelope containing all the contents, and an outer envelope, which is addressed.

Teddy's Tips

If you're having invitations engraved, be sure to allow at least six weeks for the delivery of the order.

You can find selections for your wedding invitations at many stores and bridal shops. Most times, if you open the Yellow Pages and look under "Invitations" or "Wedding Services," you can find a whole range of retailers that offer invitations. Many bridal consultants and bridal salons offer invitations as well. Other resources are card shops and party-goods stores.

Your wedding invitation is the first thing about your wedding your guests will see. It sets the tone for the wedding and the reception to follow. It also gives the guests the first glimpse of the type and formality of your wedding. Whether it's an engraved, ivory-colored, formal invitation, or a pair of kissing frogs (there really is such an item), your invitation tells your guests what they can expect in terms of the mood of the big event.

Turn to the "Invitations Worksheet" at the end of this chapter for help with invitations.

Selecting Your Invitations

You have a few things to consider when choosing your invitations—whether you want them engraved, what type of paper you like, and what size and shape you want the invitation to be. It's best that you familiarize yourself with some of the terminology of printing invitations before you go shopping. Here's a primer to give you a head start.

Putting Your Stamp on It

Engraved invitations involve a process in which the paper is stamped with a mold, leaving an indentation in the paper. The ink is added to fill in the indentation, and then it's dried. If you look on the back of an engraved invitation, you will see indentations. The stamp is sent back to you as a keepsake.

Just keep in mind that it takes six to eight weeks to order engraved invitations. Also be prepared for sticker shock—engraved invitations are much more expensive than other printed types. Engraved invitations are considered to be the most formal and elegant type, so if this is the message you want to send about your wedding, make sure you budget appropriately.

Rise to the Occasion

A newer technology, *thermography,* is more popular today than engraving. This is the opposite of engraving. In this process, the words are written out in glue, and the ink color is sprinkled over the glue. Then it's heated, so the lettering is raised. If you run your fingers over the invitation, you can feel the lettering. Thermography is much less expensive than engraving and still has an elegant look.

The Paper Chase

After you decide which type of printing you want, you'll need to find the proper paper. (There are certain types of paper you can't engrave.) When you look through all those books of invitations, remember that the paper is the only thing that can't be changed. Everything else that goes with the invitation is fill-in-the-blank. You can change the script, the ink color, and the wording, and some companies will even change the format. Don't think that just because the invitations you like are shown in navy ink and you have your heart set on gold ink that you have to find other invitations. Chances are, you can change the ink color.

Feel the paper quality. Is it heavy enough for your tastes? A good, cotton bond paper is the best choice. There are all kinds of papers out there; from plain linen bond to vellum. It all boils down to what you have to spend and the tone you want to set.

Pure Poetry

Wording your wedding invitation can be a simple task, or it can be very complicated. Located in the front of most invitation books (from which you will select your invitations) are wording suggestions for almost every known circumstance. You can find the traditional, formal wedding invitation issued by the bride's parents to the wording used when Uncle Fred is sending the invitations for his niece's wedding. From those samples and from the samples you see on the following pages, you should have the help you need to make the wording for your wedding invitation an easy task. Most times, salespeople are standing by to help with details that are complex or unusual.

Teddy's Tips

Never—I repeat, never—include a list of the stores where you're registered within your wedding invitation. You can spread the word through family and friends, but it should not go out with the invitation.

Those Little Cards

A wedding invitation wouldn't be complete without those additional little cards and stamped envelopes. Often, reception cards and reply cards are included in the wedding invitation packet. If many guests are coming from out of town, a map with directions to the ceremony and reception is enclosed. Also, if you are having a large wedding, you might want to consider "within the ribbon" cards.

Nuptial Notes

Within the ribbon cards are those cards enclosed with the invitation that give guests special seating "within the ribbon" or in a reserved spot. Within the ribbon cards are usually used for very large and very formal weddings where many guests are expected and seating special family members is a must.

Wedding Woes

Be careful about the wording on your invitation if your wedding falls around a mealtime. For clarity, list on the reception card what type of reception this will be: "Hors d'Oeuvres Reception" or "Dinner Reception." That way, guests know what type of food service to expect.

Now, Let's Party!

Because the wedding invitation focuses on the ceremony, guests often need to be instructed as to where the reception is being held. That's where reception cards come in handy. Reception cards are cards enclosed with the invitation that invite the guest to the wedding reception, stating where it is and perhaps what kind of reception it is. For example, if you're having an hors-d'oeuvres-and-cocktail reception, your card may read, "Please join us directly following the ceremony at the country club for hors d'oeuvres and cocktails."

Sometimes, guests are invited only to the ceremony and not the reception. Usually, however, guests are invited to both. Most formal invitations include a reception card enclosure.

RSVP

The response card and matching self-addressed envelope is always stamped. It asks for the guests to reply to the wedding host by a certain date. It is a very important piece of the wedding packet. It needs to be worded so that guests understand you need it mailed back so you know who is going to attend. Using the old RSVP format (guests respond by sending a note on personal stationery) doesn't cut it anymore. Most couples say:

> Please let us know if you can share in our celebration.
>
> Name _____

Map It Out

Map and direction cards are common in the wedding packet today because so many of your guests could be from out of town. The least-expensive way to do these cards is to print out one sheet on your handy PC and then make copies on nice paper.

Order! Order!

You should order your invitations at least three months before the wedding, except for engraved invitations, which take much longer to produce (see the preceding section). That will give you one month for the order to be delivered (plenty of time) and one month for you to address them and get them in the mail one month before the wedding.

At holiday times or other busy times of the year, you may need to order your invitations four months in advance. Just be sure that everything is solidly booked with the ceremony site and the reception facility before you place your order.

When ordering your invitations, be sure to check with the store about what will happen if there is a mistake in the order. Do they guarantee their work? To ensure that your invitations will be correct, I recommend working face-to-face instead of discussing your invitation order over the phone.

Teddy's Tips

Always order 25 more invitations and enclosures than you think you will need. It's much cheaper to order the extra 25 than to have to order more later.

Return to Sender (!)

Make sure you take the finished invitation to the post office and have it weighed to determine the correct postage. You don't want all your invitations to come back stamped, "Return for postage."

One bride I worked with recently took her invitations to the post office three different times to have them weighed. Each time, the invitation was under one ounce. The day she took all 250 invitations, with postage, to the post office to mail them, the clerk informed her that they were oversized and would need additional postage. I don't know why she wasn't given the correct information on her three previous visits, but when I checked the book from which she had ordered her invitations, a disclaimer on the page declared that this type of invitation was oversized and would require additional postage. The moral of this story is that just because the invitation weighs less than one ounce doesn't necessarily mean that it won't require additional postage.

Printed Accessories

Invitation companies offer all sorts of extra accessories to complement your wedding invitations, such as informal notes, thank-you notes, napkins, at-home cards, scrolls, place cards, post-it notes for favors, and matches.

Informal Notes and Thank-You Notes

Informal notes and thank-you notes are the same size as your reception or response card's. The informal card and envelope can be used for notes or thank-you notes almost any time you need to send a short note. Thank-you notes are just used as thank-you notes.

Napkins

Many couples order cocktail napkins to be used at the bar and/or on the cake table. Try mixing your color scheme a little here to add variety to your reception.

One suggestion I make to couples is to not print the wedding date on the napkins. If you leave the date off your napkins, for example, you can use them after the wedding in your new home. You might consider printing just your names or initials on the napkins.

I worked with one bride who wanted something different for her napkins. She wanted to use only a large initial of her new last name. It took a special dye cut to make the initial (which she had to pay for), so she ordered not only napkins but also informal notes to use for thank-yous and some larger stationery. She made good use of the special dye cut and had some unique stationery to show for it.

Bouquet Toss

An at-home card was used more in the mid-century when couples took extended honeymoons and guests would be told that "After January 8, Mr. and Mrs. Smith will be at home," meaning you could visit after January 8. Today, this information may appear on the back of the wedding program.

Scrolls

Scrolls are small pieces of paper, usually a fine paper, with a verse or message from the couple printed on them. These scrolls can be handed out at the ceremony or saved and used as a favor at the reception.

Place Cards

Place cards are another little extra that can make your wedding more unique. Actually, place cards are used two different ways. The true place card is an individual card with the guest's name written on it and then placed at that guest's place setting at the table. I've had mothers or aunts make these cards by taking the plain white card and adding dried flowers or strips of ribbon to them to add color to the table.

A table assignment card is many times referred to as a place card, but that's not its function. This little card can be plain or enclosed in an envelope. It either stands or lays on a table outside of the banquet room and contains the name of the guest and his table number. In other words, he is being assigned a table for the wedding reception.

You can chose to do one or both, but please remember that these are small details that take a lot of time and patience and need to be worked out in advance. They make for a more formal wedding and can be quite a lovely addition.

Really Personalize It!

By now you've covered the biggies, and the dollars are starting to add up. You still want your wedding to have a uniqueness, but how can you make your wedding unique when you're on a tight budget? If you have no budget (yes, Virginia, there really are brides without a budget), what kind of ideas can you incorporate to give your wedding some personality?

Here are several ways to incorporate certain paper accents to help make your wedding more unique.

Mark Your Calendars Now, Please

We all know how scattered our society has become and how busy we all seem to be. If your families and friends are coming from the four corners of the globe (don't laugh—I've had weddings bring in families and friends from all over the world), you might try a "save the date" card to let guests know of the upcoming event.

This can be as simple as a postcard with the couple's name, wedding date, and place. You can also do it in the form of a short letter. Its main purpose is to announce the wedding date. Put simply, it might say:

We've finally set the date, so please put it on your calendars. We want you to be able to share this wonderful weekend with us.

Saturday, May 20, 2001—New York, NY

Sally Winters and Tom Fox—you can visit our Web site at www.wearelove.com.

As I said, a postcard will do. Sometimes it's nice to give a heads-up for the guests. One of my recent couples took this idea one step further and sent out Valentine's Day cards to everyone. They had become engaged the end of January and decided that Valentine's Day was the perfect time to share their great news.

Simple programs with ribbons and only the couple's first names.

(Colter Photography)

Start Spreadin' the News

Another relative of the "save the date" card is the wedding newsletter. Now this is where you can create your own flavor and entice the guest's curiosity. You might send one out early in the planning process to let guests know some of the activities you have lined up and to set a tentative agenda for the weekend. You might wait and send it only to the wedding party and close family and friends, especially those who will be coming from a distance. You can also do two separate newsletters: one to guests in general and one to the wedding party members and family.

Give the guests the low-down on the weekend activities and what the dress is for the rehearsal dinner or the Sunday morning brunch. Be as helpful and sensitive to their needs as possible. Make the letters fun, relaxed, and again, unique to the two of you. Remember, all these people are coming from all over to share with you one of the most important days of your life. So make the newsletters sound like the two of you.

You also can provide the directions to the hotel, check-in time, and information on the climate (someone coming from Florida to Wisconsin in February might not be prepared for the cooler temperatures). Again, spell out the activities involved and what the dress is for each.

For the newsletter to just the wedding party, you might take this opportunity to introduce your wedding party, if all have not met. "The maid of honor is Amy Wright, Janet's best friend since first grade. Tom's best man is Jim Smith; he and Tom are fraternity brothers and shared an apartment in New York." Also in this letter, make sure you tell when the rehearsal is and that you need everyone to be there on time. Give a map and written directions from the hotel where they will be staying.

Your old friend the PC and a nice printer can do this feat for you very inexpensively. Postage will be the expensive part.

Here's an example of a recent newsletter that went to the wedding party, all the family members, and a few close friends. The rest of the guests received a shorter version in their welcome baskets that talked about those activities available to the guests (golf, shopping, ceremony, reception, and brunch). (See Chapter 16, "Do Yourself a Favor," for more info on welcome baskets.)

We've started the countdown: We have less than four weeks before the big day. We are so excited you will be with us. We thought we'd give you some updates on activities and times and, of course, directions. April in Iowa can be quite pleasant. You might need a light jacket for evening, but otherwise, you should be fine. No winter coats unless you hear we got hit with a blizzard!

Thursday, April 6: Early check-in at Hyatt

Meet in the Grill (lower level of hotel) for informal get-together at 8 P.M. Casual dress.

Friday, April 7 (the day before!)

Bridesmaids luncheon at 12:30 P.M., third floor of Hyatt, Room D. Dresses/pantsuits.

Guys to play golf at 11:30 A.M.—see John Smith for sign-up sheet, Room 1215.

Shopping in mall attached to hotel via walkway.

Historical museum across from the hotel; very interesting if you're a history buff.

Rehearsal at Century Church, 1256 N. Meridian St. (for wedding party, readers, immediate family); meet in lobby at 5:30 P.M. for transportation. Rehearsal is at 6:00 P.M.

Rehearsal dinner: Canopy Club at 7:30 P.M.; 3500 N. Meridian Street—see map. Dressy attire. Those attending this event should have received an invitation from John's parents.

Saturday, April 8

The day! It's here at last!

Ladies in wedding party meet in Suite 1245 for hair and makeup at 9:30 A.M. Breakfast breads, juice, and coffee served. Come with clean hair, clean face, and a smile.

Men in wedding party meet in Suite 1247 at 12:00 P.M. sharp for pictures. Please be on time.

Leave for church (all) at 2:00 P.M. Limos will pick us up outside the lobby entrance.

2:30 P.M.	Begin pictures at church
4:00 P.M.	Pictures finished (if we're on time)
	Ushers need to be ready to greet guests
4:30 P.M.	Here comes the bride ...

Following the ceremony, we will be releasing the rows and greeting guests at each pew. When we finish, we will make our grand exit to the limo and meet you at the reception.

Let the party begin!

Sunday, April 9

12:00 P.M. Champagne brunch in the Porch Room. Everyone is invited, and we hope you come by and say hi.

The hotel has extended our guests' check-out time until 3:00 P.M.

If you have any questions or concerns—anything that we can help make your time with us go smoother—please call our bridal consultant, Teddy Lenderman. She is staying at the Hyatt also, in Room 1009. Please call on her for assistance.

Have a safe trip home, and thank you again for taking the time to spend with us on our wedding weekend.

Love,
Susie and John

One bride and groom even used the following newsletter to send to the men in the wedding party about getting their measurements for the tuxedos. It was titled "How Do You Measure Up?" which I thought was quite clever and yet got the point across.

BRIDAL UPDATE

Susie and Todd—October 2, 1999

To all Attendants, Ushers, Father of the Bride, and Father of the Groom:

How Do You Measure Up?

I hope this note finds you all excited about joining us in the festivities during our wedding weekend. We are in need of your tuxedo measurements as soon as possible. The tuxedo rental company requested that you have your measurements taken by another tux shop and then phone or fax them in. They have found that measurements from tailors don't always provide a proper fit. And, of course, "looking good is half the battle!" Right?

Please phone or fax your measurements to:

Smith's Tuxedo Shop
102 N. 8th St.
Des Moines, IA 56409
320-234-5566
320-234-5568 (fax)

Mention the Miller/Stewart wedding.

Your tux may be picked up any time on Friday. The shop requests that you allow 15 to 20 minutes to try on the tux prior to leaving the shop. That way, if any of you look like you are ready for a flood, it can be fixed then.

We can't wait to see all of you. Please call with questions: 306-555-7896.

Love,
"The Bride" Susie

When the Masses Arrive

Now, when guests check into the hotel, have a scaled-down copy of the weekend activities for everyone. List the activity and time, dress, directions, or shuttle information, and make sure everyone checking in gets a copy. You might even put some copies in the hospitality suite, if you are using one. You also can enclose a copy in their welcome baskets, if you are including them.

For guests not staying at the hotel, have some copies available at central locations (the rehearsal) so that people can get the information they need. Every wedding is different, so there are lots of ways to get the news out.

And remember, make these letters personal, unique to you, and fun (hey, this is a wedding celebration, not a funeral). Do try to use some humor, and remember who is writing the letter—you, the bride and groom!

Teddy's Tips

I have had my name added to the welcome letter several times, and it does take pressure off the couple or the parents. One groom even put the information on his rehearsal dinner invitations because he didn't want his bride or himself to have to deal with questions.

Wedding Woes

Be sure to stress to the men in your wedding party how important it is to try on their tuxedos *before* the wedding day!

Just Follow Along, Please

Wedding programs make a nice addition to your wedding service. They can be simple or elaborate. The whole purpose of a wedding program is to enable the guests to participate in the ceremony by displaying the order of the service and identifying the members of the wedding party. It's something like a playbill at the theater.

Guests do enjoy seeing who the cast members are. Sometimes the couple will list titles next to the wedding party member's name, such as "friend of the bride," "cousin of the groom," or whatever is appropriate. Other couples have listed each attendant's hometown. It's interesting sometimes to see just how far your wedding party has come to be part of this day. Use the "Programs Worksheet" at the end of this chapter to help you create your program.

Use Your Imagination

Some couples write notes of thanks or appreciation to their parents and guests in the program. Other couples list their new address and telephone number on the back of the program. Some programs even explain a part of the service that's out of the ordinary. One couple married on the bride's parents' thirtieth wedding anniversary in the same church. The groom's parents had celebrated their thirty-fifth wedding anniversary during that same year. In the program, the couple wrote a short letter to their parents, congratulating them and thanking them for providing good role models for a long and happy marriage.

Here's a nice addition. Try programs for the reception. Similar to the wedding program, the reception program lets the guests know the order of events at the reception. Very classy.

(Classic Contemporary Photography by Geno)

Another couple who had been to "hundreds" of weddings, as they told me, decided to put some wedding trivia in their programs. This way, they reasoned, their guests would have something to do besides listen to music or make grocery lists while waiting for the procession to begin. It was a clever program, and the trivia actually tied in some of the customs they were carrying out in their service. Make these programs as unique as the two of you.

Keep It Simple ... or Go to Extremes!

Many brides try to coordinate their programs with their invitations. The trick here is to order blank stock to match your invitation paper when you order your invitations. Then take this paper to a local printer to have your program produced. It's much cheaper than having the invitation company produce your program, and you have more control over the outcome.

Programs can be as simple as a single sheet of colored paper printed on a computer and duplicated. Roll it up and tie it with a coordinating ribbon, and you have a simple, attractive, and inexpensive presentation. For an elaborate look, have your programs printed on several sheets of paper covered with a heavy outer paper, emboss or engrave monograms on the front, and then tie the paper with coordinating ribbons.

One of the most elaborate wedding programs is a missal. This is used in a Catholic service and includes, verbatim, everything the priest says. This type of program is especially nice when the majority of your guests are not of your faith. At a Greek Orthodox wedding I coordinated, the couple was very considerate of the fact that many of their guests were not Greek Orthodox. They included in the program explanations of each of the three parts of the worship service. This gave all the guests insight into the meaning of the service and made it much more enjoyable. This type of program is more costly simply because of its length, but you still can produce it economically.

At one of my Jewish weddings, the bride and groom did the same thing as the Greek Orthodox couple did. They incorporated terms used in the Jewish ceremony (read in both Hebrew and English) and explained why that part or that word was so important to the ceremony. That way, their non-Jewish friends could really understand the tradition and beauty behind the ceremony. The couple even spelled out the Hebrew words phonetically—yes, that did help.

Formal invitation issued by the bride's parents.

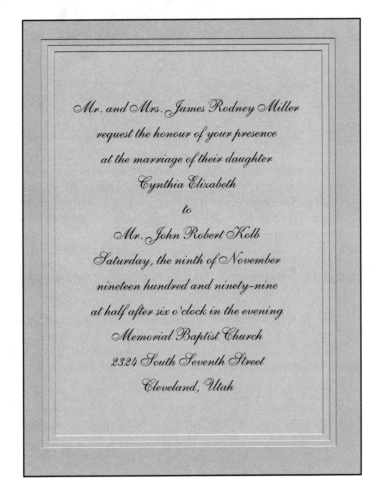

Mr. and Mrs. James Rodney Miller
request the honour of your presence
at the marriage of their daughter
Cynthia Elizabeth
to
Mr. John Robert Kolb
Saturday, the ninth of November
nineteen hundred and ninety-nine
at half after six o'clock in the evening
Memorial Baptist Church
2324 South Seventh Street
Cleveland, Utah

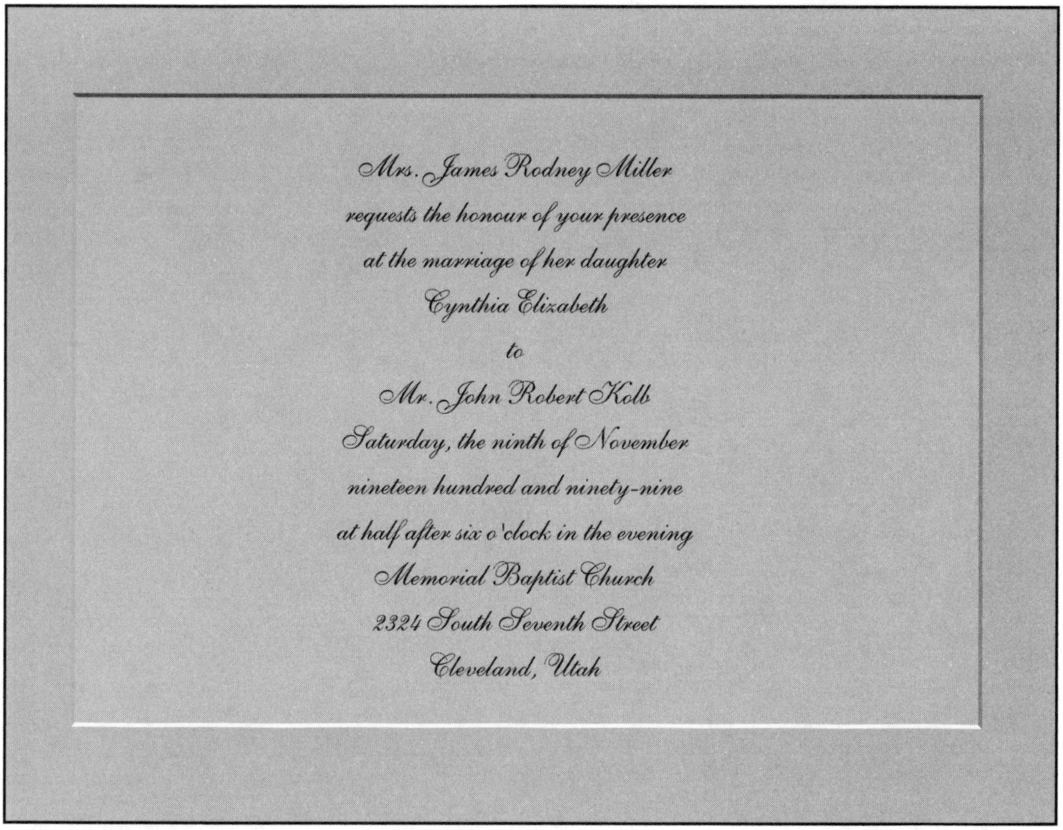

Mrs. James Rodney Miller

requests the honour of your presence

at the marriage of her daughter

Cynthia Elizabeth

to

Mr. John Robert Kolb

Saturday, the ninth of November

nineteen hundred and ninety-nine

at half after six o'clock in the evening

Memorial Baptist Church

2324 South Seventh Street

Cleveland, Utah

Formal invitation issued by the bride's widowed mother.

Mr. and Mrs. James Rodney Miller
request the honour of your presence
at the marriage of his daughter
Cynthia Elizabeth
to
Mr. John Robert Kolb
Saturday, the ninth of November
nineteen hundred and ninety-nine
at half after six o'clock in the evening
Memorial Baptist Church
2324 South Seventh Street
Cleveland, Utah

Formal invitation issued by the bride's father and stepmother.

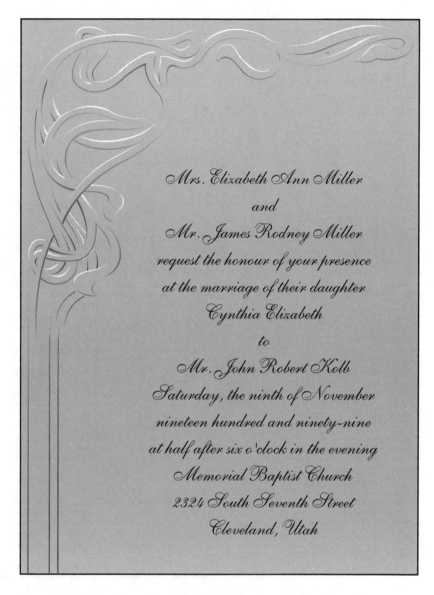

Mrs. Elizabeth Ann Miller
and
Mr. James Rodney Miller
request the honour of your presence
at the marriage of their daughter
Cynthia Elizabeth
to
Mr. John Robert Kolb
Saturday, the ninth of November
nineteen hundred and ninety-nine
at half after six o'clock in the evening
Memorial Baptist Church
2324 South Seventh Street
Cleveland, Utah

Formal invitation issued by the bride's parents, who are divorced.

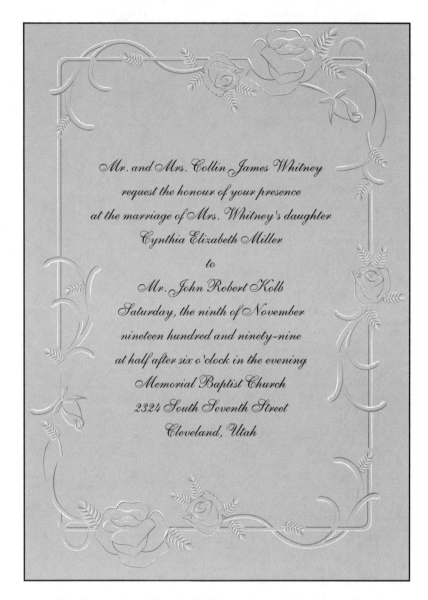

Mr. and Mrs. Collin James Whitney
request the honour of your presence
at the marriage of Mrs. Whitney's daughter
Cynthia Elizabeth Miller
to
Mr. John Robert Kolb
Saturday, the ninth of November
nineteen hundred and ninety-nine
at half after six o'clock in the evening
Memorial Baptist Church
2324 South Seventh Street
Cleveland, Utah

Formal invitation issued by the bride's mother, who is divorced and remarried.

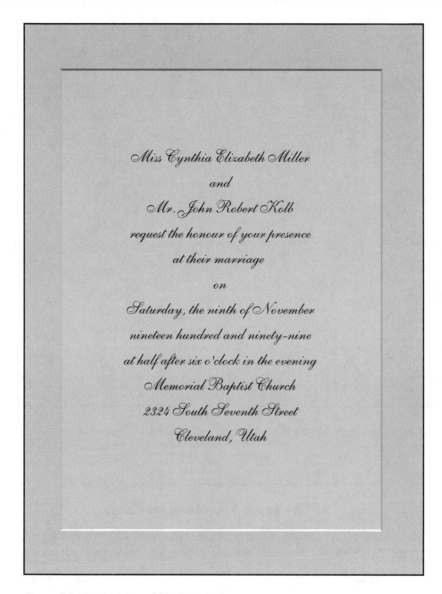

Miss Cynthia Elizabeth Miller

and

Mr. John Robert Kolb

request the honour of your presence

at their marriage

on

Saturday, the ninth of November

nineteen hundred and ninety-nine

at half after six o'clock in the evening

Memorial Baptist Church

2324 South Seventh Street

Cleveland, Utah

Formal invitation issued by the couple.

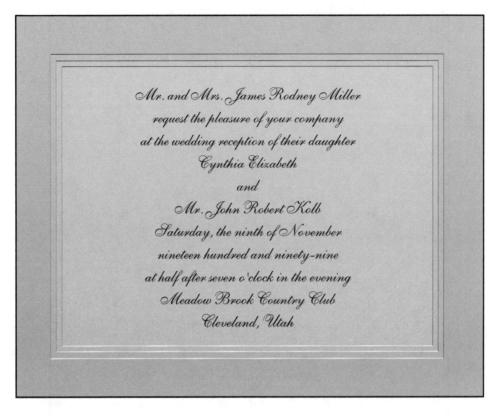

Mr. and Mrs. James Rodney Miller
request the pleasure of your company
at the wedding reception of their daughter
Cynthia Elizabeth
and
Mr. John Robert Kolb
Saturday, the ninth of November
nineteen hundred and ninety-nine
at half after seven o'clock in the evening
Meadow Brook Country Club
Cleveland, Utah

Formal invitation issued by the bride's parents to the wedding reception only. This ceremony is private.

The Least You Need to Know

➤ Always ask about getting a discount on invitations; you should never pay full price. Always order 25 more invitations than you think you will need.

➤ Consider sending a "save the date" card if your guests are scattered across the country and you think an advance notice would help.

➤ Use newsletters to keep your guests, wedding party, and family members informed about the wedding plans.

➤ Think about incorporating a wedding program into your ceremony.

Invitations Worksheet

Company: _____

Contact: _____

Telephone: _____

Discount available: _____

Paper size: _____

Color ink: _____

Number needed: _____

Traditional vs. contemporary: _____

Enclosures

    Reception cards: _____

    Response cards: _____

    Maps: _____

    Within the ribbon cards: _____

Accessories

    Napkins: _____

        Sizes: _____

    Toast glasses: _____

    Place cards: _____

    Programs: _____

    Matches: _____

    Cake knife: _____

    Scrolls: _____

    Favor ribbons: _____

    Thank-you notes: _____

    Cake boxes or bags: _____

Programs Worksheet

Type of program desired: _____

Method of producing:

❑ Self   ❑ Printer   ❑ Invitation company

Contact: _____

_____

_____

Telephone: _____

Deadline for production (date): _____

Deposit paid (date): _____

Suggested wording: _____

_____

_____

_____

Chapter 16

Do Yourself a Favor

In This Chapter

➤ Researching new ways to use favors

➤ Tips and hints on where to look for favor ideas

➤ How to incorporate cameras at your reception

➤ Gifts for your attendants

In this chapter, I will talk about the use of favors at your wedding to help continue to keep your wedding unique and make your guests feel special. I'll offer some advice on ideas to use for favors and how to create your own ideas. I'll also talk about how and what to give your wedding party members. I'll also share some wonderful ways to incorporate welcome baskets (even on a tight budget) into your wedding package. Read on and let your imagination run wild.

Favoring Your Friends

Favors are making a big comeback. A *favor* is a little gift you give your guests as a thank-you for attending your wedding. You can select expensive and elaborate favors or very inexpensive and simple favors. The idea is not to dazzle your guests with great favors, but to make them feel special and appreciated and to add a special touch to your wedding. For help in planning favors, use the "Favors Worksheet" at the end of this chapter.

Gayle O'Donnell, owner of Do Me a Favor!, in Renton, Washington, specializes in wedding favors (actually, favors for any type of function). She also operates The Last

Detail Special Event Planning, which has been in business since 1992. Gayle is also the Washington State Coordinator for the Association of Bridal Consultants. She has this to say:

Wedding favors have become the way of putting a mark of individuality on a bride's day, while at the same time offering a token of gratitude for those in attendance at the wedding. They have grown in popularity as brides have moved away from the standard offering of almonds in tulle netting to much more creative items that carry out a theme or signify a characteristic, occupation, or hobby of the bride and groom. In today's weddings, brides are interested in expressing their individuality, and favors are the perfect vehicle for this. Do Me a Favor! markets itself as a company with themes as its specialty. Examples of ideas created to express themes are ...

➤ *A bride and groom who had just graduated from the Dentistry School at the University of Washington had chocolate toothpaste tubes with real toothbrushes imprinted with their names and wedding date, attractively packaged and placed at each guest's place setting.*

➤ *For a garden wedding, guests received miniature galvanized watering cans filled with pastel Dutch mints that complemented the wedding color scheme. A tag tied to the handle was printed with matching colors to thank guests for coming.*

➤ *A Christmas wedding was the perfect opportunity for one couple to have their engagement photo placed in a framed tree ornament with a Christmas motif. Their names and wedding date were printed on the back of the ornament. These were hung on a tree near the entrance of the reception, and an announcement was made asking each guest to take an ornament from the tree when they left. These could also be placed at each place setting for a dinner reception.*

➤ *Do a play on the geographical surroundings of the wedding. For example, many weddings in the Pacific Northwest have a Northwest theme to promote the natural surroundings and products. Some items used have been live fir trees in a tube with a printed enclosure, chocolate apples, sea shells, salmon wrapped in colored foil, or imprinted coffee mugs with individual serving packets of the famous Seattle-based coffee companies. Other couples have presented the female guests at their receptions with small silver coffee scoops filled with white chocolate-covered espresso beans. As a gift for the men at these same weddings, a chocolate personalized cigar is always a hit.*

➤ *A couple who met in aeronautical school had miniature airplanes with their names and wedding date painted on the wings.*

You are likely seeing with these examples that there are no rules around what you give as favors. The key is to be creative and make sure the favor helps complete whatever look and feel you are trying to create with your wedding.

The guests will appreciate edible items, so it's hard to go wrong with chocolate truffles, enclosed in an attractive box with ribbon and personalization. The key, no matter what you choose to do, is to try to give your guests something that makes them feel pampered and appreciated. Pricing for wedding favors can run the gamut from very inexpensive, sometimes under a $1, to more elaborate offerings, depending on the budget for the wedding. Whatever is chosen, make sure it is something the guests will have a use for once they leave your wedding, if you are going with a nonedible item. Some examples would include candles, a small picture frame (which can double as your place card holder), or decorative soaps.

Wedding Woes

Make sure you have enough favors to go around. Nothing would be worse than having more guests than favors and having to decide who gets one and who doesn't.

Millie and Michael chose to use M&Ms to help create their signature on their wedding.

(Colter Photography)

Candy is an elegant, although not as costly, favor idea, as mentioned previously. Many candy makers use a mold that says "Thank you for sharing our joy"; the chocolate bar is then wrapped in clear paper and tied with a coordinating ribbon. Place these chocolates at each guest's setting to add to the table decoration, or place them in a pretty basket or on a large silver tray near the exit. Guests then can each take one as they leave.

Here are some other simple favor ideas:

- ➤ Individual votive candles
- ➤ Candy bars wrapped with verses
- ➤ Golf tees imprinted with the wedding date or your initials
- ➤ A single silk rose tied with a ribbon and placed at every female's plate
- ➤ A small tulle bag containing rose petals or potpourri
- ➤ A scroll printed with your favorite verse or poem, and tied with a ribbon or enclosed within a gold ring
- ➤ Seedlings that guests can plant and nurture to maturity to represent the growth of the marriage
- ➤ Squeeze water bottles (for your exercise friends)

You can go wild with seasonal favors during the holidays. For Christmas weddings, another idea is to make individual wreaths with ribbons and maybe a bell for each guest to take home.

Another favor idea: brass bells. These can be given out as guests leave the ceremony or placed on tables at the reception. What a wonderful way to greet the couple.

(Colter Photography)

Another rather innovative idea for more established couples is to make a donation to a favorite charity and then to leave a nicely calligraphied card at each place setting, which lets the guest know that a donation was made in his or her honor. The card may read, "A donation from Jenny and Matt has been made in your name to Habitat for Humanity."

Here are some additional tips to get you thinking about possible favor ideas:

➤ Purchase small wicker baskets (check out some of the wholesale houses), and place a small arrangement of silk flowers, assorted candies, or small decorative soaps inside.

➤ Cluster your favors to make the table centerpiece. For example, small individual pots with flowers or plants arranged in a circle in the center of the table make a lovely focal point. You can even drape some tulle around the base of the circle or tie some ribbons around the pots. As guests leave, ask that they each take a pot with them.

➤ Check craft stores in February for heart-shaped items and ideas. A mug with a heart and your initials makes a nice favor. A heart-shaped magnet for the refrigerator or heart-shaped candies also make small, inexpensive favors.

➤ If your wedding has a theme, try to stick to the theme when you plan for favors. A Mexican wedding theme, for example, could have small sombreros or piñatas for favors. For a Hawaiian wedding theme, floral leis were handed out as guests arrived at the reception. This was a fun way to say, "Glad you're here."

Wedding Woes

When ordering candy through the mail, be sure you know when it will be delivered so that you can arrange for someone to be at home to receive it. What an ugly mess it is to find 300 candy bars melted all over your front porch because no one was there to accept the package. Not a pretty site.

Smile, You're on Candid Camera!

One fun way to help capture your special day from many different angles is to provide disposable wedding cameras at every table at the reception. (You can now purchase these cameras in almost any color combination, including white lace boxes, tuxedo boxes, and holiday boxes.) It's usually wise to include a little note of explanation with the cameras to let your guests know that they are provided for their use.

Some brides wrap the cameras like gifts (to complement the wedding colors) and use them as part of the decorations. You can purchase as many cameras as your budget will allow. Some couples put cameras at every table, while others spread them out to every other table. Make sure there are instructions as to where guests are to deposit the used cameras. Many times a large basket at the exit is sufficient.

Attending to Your Attendants

The gifts you choose to give to your attendants (a nice way of saying, "Thanks for putting up with my irrational behavior for the past six months") need to be custom-designed for your wedding party. I'm not saying go out and have something custom-designed for each and every member of your wedding party. I just mean that you should try to make the gift truly special, not just another mug or fake string of pearls. Do you know how many sets of fake pearls the average 24-year-old woman accumulates? Probably more than you or I would dare to count, and certainly enough to open her own jewelry store. So, when it comes time to look for gifts for your attendants, think about who they are and what they like. Nothing is carved in stone that says you must buy them all the same thing. I know that's usually easier, but with a little planning, you can come up with some unique gift ideas for these special friends.

Have fun selecting these gifts. For the sports nut, how about a new racquet or a membership to a health club? For the traveler, an overnight bag and travel alarm clock are good ideas. For the new home owner, consider wind chimes, a brass door knocker, or a stained-glass sun catcher. Books are also great personal ideas.

What about a gift certificate? One bride knew her matron of honor was on a very tight budget, so for her gift, the bride gave her a gift certificate to her favorite restaurant. Do you have any collectors in your wedding party? How about a glass piece, a Hummel figurine, or maybe a Precious Moments figurine?

Bouquet Toss

The idea of a bridal shower goes back many centuries to the Netherlands when a poor Dutch miller fell in love with a rich maid. The maid's father disapproved of the marriage and refused to provide a dowry. The miller's friends got together and "showered" the couple with items that would help them establish a household. Thus, the bridal shower was born.

Any item that you can have engraved or monogrammed is just that much more personal. Beer steins, basketballs, footballs, and Swiss Army knives are some ideas for the men. For the women, try picture frames or lingerie. (I gave all six of my bridesmaids different types of lingerie according to their personalities—some slips, some bras, some teddies.) Of course, you can always give jewelry, especially if you want them to wear the same necklace or earrings for the wedding. I've known some brides who have given their attendants the hose and shoes they needed for the wedding; others have given them gloves to wear. One bride chose a different book for each of her bridesmaids according to their individual tastes, and then wrote a personal message on the inside cover.

You don't have to spend an arm and a leg on gifts for your wedding party, but you need to offer at least a token for supporting you on this special day.

Some other wedding party gift ideas include the following:

For men:

➤ Cuff links

➤ Monogrammed wallet

➤ Engraved money clip

➤ Travel kit

➤ Engraved calculator

➤ Basketballs

➤ Footballs

For women:

➤ Jewelry box

➤ Basket with soaps or perfumes

➤ Charm bracelet

➤ Bud vase

➤ Music box

➤ Lingerie

For children:

➤ Mug with name

➤ Charm bracelet

➤ Games (checkers, chess, backgammon)

➤ Stereo headset

➤ Classic edition of Mark Twain

➤ T-shirt ("I was a ring bearer in Matt and Cathy's wedding")

➤ Stuffed animal (for the young child)

For either sex:

➤ Anything monogrammed in crystal or pewter

➤ Silver picture frame

➤ Personalized stationery

➤ Candle holder

➤ Pen and pencil set

➤ Bar set

➤ Crystal ice bucket

Bouquet Toss

Bridal showers are wonderful parties given in the bride's honor. Friends and relatives "shower" the bride with gifts for her new married life. Gifts can be either for personal use or for her new household. Anyone can offer to host a shower in the bride's honor, but generally speaking, the bride's mother or sisters probably should not be the hostesses. Aunts, and certainly a good friend or the mother of a good friend, may host a bridal shower.

Bridal showers come in all types these days. You may find a kitchen shower appealing, or maybe a linen and lingerie shower (think about those lovely teddies and nightgowns) would be a real plus. You also could opt for a couples' shower so that the guys can get in on the act, too. Couples can bring items that the bride and groom each can use.

Welcome One and All!

With our society so scattered and family and friends all over the world, weddings have become more than just a way to spend a couple of hours on a Saturday afternoon. With that in mind, the idea of the welcome basket was born. Since guests come from all over, it's nice to offer them some goodies when they check into the hotel.

Welcome baskets or packages can come in all sizes and shapes. Even the tightest budget can accommodate a welcome basket for a few family members. The ideas for a welcome basket are endless and can only be limited by your budget or imagination. A lot of "baskets" are really fancy bags (you know, the color kind you find in craft stores). You can fill them with anything you want, but some necessary items should include a note from the couple, an itinerary of the weekend, a map showing ceremony site and reception site on it, emergency phone numbers, and a small gift item. Some of these might include something to eat (cheese and crackers with a small cutting knife), a bottle of wine or soft drinks, some fruit, or homemade cookies. Several couples have "welcome bag parties" where they invite friends over to help stuff these bags. If your budget will allow, do one for every hotel room reserved for your wedding. The hotel should be able to give you a printout of all the guests who have reserved a room under your block. If your budget won't allow for that many, then be sure to include any parents who are coming in from out of town, or other close family members and the wedding party. It's just a delightful way to say, "Glad you're here—have a great weekend."

These lovely boxes of truffles await guests. These boxes are tied with paper ribbons and dried roses. For this wedding they will be placed at each place setting.

(Colter Photography)

In a welcome package, include an agenda or itinerary of all the activities for the weekend. On the agenda, make sure you include the time, place, and date of the event; the dress for the event (casual, dressy, black tie); the hosts for the event ("David's parents are hosting the wedding breakfast"); a shuttle schedule or transportation schedule from the hotel or home to the event; the phone number of the event site (in case of emergencies); and a map of the area with the events marked (numbers work well, such as "#7 on map is wedding site"). Also in the package, include something to eat (maybe some homemade cookies, a small basket of fresh fruit, or some chocolates beautifully wrapped to coordinate with the wedding colors).

If you want to splurge, you also can include champagne or wine with a couple wine glasses or some plastic wine or champagne glasses. In every basket, be sure to include a personal note from you both welcoming your guests and thanking them for being with you on your wedding weekend.

The Least You Need to Know

➤ Say thank you to your guests for helping make your day so special by presenting them with favors. Favors do not have to be expensive; something as simple as a bag of Hershey kisses at each place can be a nice touch.

➤ Providing disposable cameras at the reception is another way to add to the festivities and capture the moments on film.

➤ Try to choose gifts for your attendants that have some special or personal meaning. If possible, have the gifts personalized.

➤ If budget will allow, try to do some welcome baskets for those out-of-town guests.

Favors Worksheet

Ideas: _____

_____

_____

_____

_____

_____

_____

_____

_____

Cost per person: _____

Contact: _____

Telephone: _____

Making the Most of Your Dollars

I've talked about budgets (I know—still not your favorite subject), and I've discussed questions to ask vendors to make sure you're getting what you pay for. Let's get some serious work done in this chapter and trim up that budget (in ways no one will recognize) and talk a little about contracts and agreements (I know, I know, more of that boring stuff, but nonetheless, *very* important).

Saving Your Pennies for Priorities

So far, I've suggested some questions for you to ask the vendors you're considering using. I've told you what to expect from these vendors, and you've started spending some of those precious wedding budget dollars. Before you blink and all those dollars have disappeared, it's time to look at ways you can trim some costs from your wedding bill.

Smart wedding shopping techniques begin with having patience and not being an impulsive buyer. Time is your friend when you're in the wedding market. As you shop with the various vendors, give yourself the time you need to make sure you're getting the best product for the best price. A lot depends on the importance you place on each. If that certain photographer is very important to you, figure out a way to incorporate his fee into your plans. One bride I worked with found the perfect gown for her wedding—the gown was an original and very expensive. Her parents told her she had a choice: the gown or a dinner-and-dance reception. She chose the gown; it was a higher priority for her. It doesn't matter what your cousin Shelly did for her wedding. This is your wedding, and you need to decide which items are most important to you.

Teddy's Tips

Don't ever be afraid to ask if an item can be discounted or rented. What more can someone say than "No"? Many times, you will find yourself pleasantly surprised by the answer. Just because you've never heard of doing it this way doesn't mean that it can't be done. Ask if the florist has suggestions on how something can be done less expensively.

One couple on a limited budget decided they wanted their money to go toward the reception. Both sets of parents were divorced and remarried and not on the best speaking terms. So, they decided one way to cut costs, keep tensions in check, and still have the reception they wanted was to have a small, private ceremony for only immediate family. We found a darling chapel on a university campus, which held about 40 guests. The chapel didn't cost anything since they were alumni. The florist used some floral pieces that were later transferred to the reception site. They chose not to use programs, again because of the small guest list. Yet the ceremony was still very meaningful and lovely. The reception was wonderful, just what they had envisioned. Again, you need to decide what is best for you and go with your dreams, not the dreams of someone else.

The following sections give you some ideas of specific ways you can cut wedding expenses and stretch your wedding dollars.

Finding Ways to Cut Your Floral Bill

There are several ways to cut costs in the floral department. I will touch on several of the easiest ways. Keep in mind that just because this is a wedding, does not necessarily mean you have to use great gardens of flowers. Sometimes, less is best. Read on for more floral cutting tips.

It's All About Sharing

Check with the church to see if another wedding is scheduled on the same day as yours. If so, ask the other couple about sharing the expense for ceremony site flowers. The florist can make arrangements in neutral shades of white or ivory and can add colored ribbon to make each arrangement more coordinated with that wedding's specific colors. You could luck out and find a couple who shares your color scheme. This can save you half the floral bill for the ceremony site. A good friend of mine learned that the church was booked for another wedding the same day as hers. Karen called the other bride, they met with the florist, and they were able to split the bill in half. Each bride had truly beautiful church flowers at only half the cost.

At the ceremony, have the pew markers designed to double as centerpieces at the reception. I recommend this frequently to brides, and they all love the idea of having wonderful pew markers and equally wonderful centerpieces. Transporting the pew markers can be a problem, but it's nothing that your florist and wedding coordinator can't handle.

For that matter, transport any flowers you use at the ceremony to the reception. Why spend all that money on flowers for guests to enjoy for only 30 minutes? Again, your florist and wedding coordinator can take care of this detail, or you can ask a trusted friend.

Au Naturel

If you're being married in the spring or summer, you can eliminate the cost of a large, expensive bridal bouquet by gathering wildflowers the morning of your wedding and tying them with a lovely ribbon to coordinate with your colors. You need to be careful that the flowers you're gathering will be open and blooming when you go pick them so they'll look perfect when you walk down the aisle. With this in mind, you might want to make sure that you've located a good spot for flowers ahead of time.

Apprentices Wanted

If you live in a large metropolitan area, check to see if there is a local floral design school. Many times, students at these trade schools will gladly produce your wedding flowers for the cost of materials so that they can gain the experience and a letter of recommendation.

Save Bucks Covering Blemishes

If your reception facility needs some "plastic surgery" to cover flaws in the room (marks on walls, exposed pipes, ugly pictures that cannot be removed), use balloons instead of flowers or greenery. The balloons are cheaper, will cover more, add a festive party look, and can be assembled the morning of the wedding.

Keep It Simple

Select flowers grown locally, and use only flowers in season. Instead of carrying a bouquet of roses, you can carry a single rose or a small floral arrangement on a family Bible or prayer book.

Some of the prettiest arrangements I've seen in churches have been assorted greenery mixed with candles. There were no flowers present, just an assortment of greens, palms, ferns, and plants, intertwined with votive candles. This type of arrangement should be less expensive than using all flowers.

Flowers for Rent

Check with your florist about the possibility of renting centerpieces. One couple on a tight budget had 20 tables to decorate for the reception. They found a florist whose daughter had recently married, and he rented his daughter's silk arrangements to them. The arrangements were lovely, and no one was the wiser.

Dressing for Less

If you are a very talented sewer or have access to a good seamstress, make your gown and veil. You can save some big bucks here. I've had brides find wonderful seamstresses who produced the gown they had always wanted for a fraction of the price they would have paid in a bridal shop. Just be sure to examine other gowns produced by this seamstress before you secure her services.

Here are some additional ideas to help you save money on your wedding attire:

➤ Check out the bridal discount stores, but be very careful! If you can buy a dress off the rack at one of these stores, you probably will come away with a bargain. If the store must order a gown for you, be sure that you understand the terms completely. With many stores of this type, the gown that arrives in the box is what you take home—rips, tears, stains, and all. The store usually will not send it back if it's damaged—it's yours! Just be sure you know what you're agreeing to.

➤ Look for a ready-to-wear tea-length gown that requires very little alteration.

➤ Look for sales at the bridal shops. You can often find truly lovely gowns on the sale rack for one-third to one-half off the original price.

➤ Consider wearing your mother's gown (see Chapter 13, "All Dressed Up and Somewhere to Go"). Many times, these gowns from days gone by are actually back in style or will blend with the theme of your wedding. My sister, Kim, wanted to wear our mother's gown for her garden wedding. (Mother had also had a garden wedding.) The seamstress had to take a tuck here and there, but otherwise, it was perfect for Kim. Instead of wearing a veil as our mother had, Kim wore a garden hat with fresh flowers and veiling. My dad said there was a huge lump in his throat as he walked Kim down the aisle and thought about his bride of 30 years.

➤ Consider wearing your grandmother's gown. A friend of mine used a Victorian theme for her wedding and wore her grandmother's gown. She even wore the high-buttoned shoes to match. Even if you can't physically get into the gown, see what can be done to remake it. You might be surprised at what a good seamstress can accomplish.

➤ Don't overlook resale shops. These stores are springing up all over the place in the Midwest. Many gowns that have been worn only one time end up here. You can pick up a lovely gown for a fraction of its original cost.

➤ Order your bridesmaids' dresses from national catalogs. One bride ordered all seven of her bridesmaids' gowns from a catalog and saved half of what she would have paid in a shop.

➤ Rent your gown and your bridesmaids' dresses. This is a great idea when you don't have a lot of planning time for your wedding.

➤ Borrow shoes from a friend, or buy inexpensive ballet slippers. I wore white slippers that cost only $2.95, and no one knew the difference.

➤ With tuxedos, always look for package deals, such as, "Rent five, get the groom's tux free."

➤ Try to rent the tuxedos from stores that have a local warehouse. Then if there are problems, you stand a much better chance at getting the problem resolved.

By taking some time to think carefully about what is important to you and your groom, you can prioritize those items where you want to spend the bucks. And, as I've shown already, there are many ways to trim dollars from your expense sheet to get the best use of your wedding bucks!

Wedding Woes

All bridal discount stores are not created equal. Try to buy off the rack, because ordering from these establishments can be risky. Before you put down a deposit, make sure you understand what you're buying and what the store will do about flaws or mistakes.

Regulating Your Reception Expenses

If you're trying to watch your reception dollars, plan your reception for some other time than mealtime. You can save quite a bit of money by having a morning or early afternoon wedding and reception. Because the wedding doesn't fall within a mealtime (that is, 6 P.M.), you can get away with serving simple hors d'oeuvres or cake and punch.

Here are some additional ideas to help you pinch those reception pennies:

➤ Watch for sales on liquor or paper goods. Ask about discounts when buying by the case.

➤ Use paper products instead of renting crystal or china.

➤ Use carafes of wine on the tables rather than bottles. Open wine bottles can be wasted, especially if the guests at a table do not drink alcohol.

➤ Rent a champagne fountain instead of using champagne bottles on the tables, or have individual glasses of champagne served to guests.

➤ Instead of offering an open bar, limit your guests' choices to only wine and/or beer, or serve a champagne punch instead of other liquor.

➤ Use only house brands of liquor. Most of your guests will not notice, and the cost difference between house brands and premiums is tremendous.

➤ Check local vocational schools for students or recent graduates in food service or decorating who would be willing to produce the food or decorations for your reception in exchange for the experience and the exposure. Many times, those just starting out will offer their services at a discount for a reference. You gotta start somewhere!

➤ Cut down the size of your guest list. Remember, the cost of the reception equals about 35 percent of your total budget. If you can't feed a crowd of 500 a sit-down dinner, try to cut that number to what you can handle. You can even do two receptions. Immediately following the service, have the cake and punch at the church social hall for the larger crowd. Then, later that day, offer your close friends and family the dinner-and-dancing reception.

➤ If you're having a do-it-yourself reception, take all the offers you can from family and friends who volunteer to bring in items. Although this is risky because someone might not follow through on a promise (yes, it does happen), it can save you many dollars.

➤ Borrow as many items as you can. Don't rent or go out and buy a brand-new punch bowl, cake servers, or toasting glasses. Some friend or family member who has married recently might have these items. Ask to borrow them.

➤ If you need extra help with serving, check with a local sorority or fraternity. Many times, for a donation to their philanthropy project, these groups will send several people to help serve your reception.

"Think before you spend" is a wise statement to keep in mind as you plan your wedding. There are lots of ways to cut costs and still have the wedding of your dreams.

Managing Your Music Dollars

Music can add some large expenses to your wedding, but if you do your homework, there are a couple of tricks you can use.

Check into using local high school or college student musicians instead of paying union wages for experienced musicians. The students are often thrilled with the extra money and the added experience. Be sure to listen to them perform so you know what you are hiring. Like any other musical vendor, make sure they understand what they are expected to wear and how long you need them to play.

Here are some more ways to save some dollars with your music funds:

➤ Ask a reliable friend who has some experience and understanding of what makes a good DJ to play some CDs for you at the reception. He'll need a good sound system.

➤ Hire the musicians for a minimum amount of time.

One couple wanted a string quartet to play for their service and part of their reception. They couldn't afford to have the group for more than two hours, so they used them for the ceremony and then used them for an hour during the beginning of the reception. The crowd loved the soft music for the opening of the reception. When the musicians left, the couple had a friend play CDs for dancing music.

Economizing on Those Extras

As I mentioned earlier, borrow any items you can. Don't buy a ring bearer's pillow, cake servers, or toasting glasses. Unless you get these items as gifts, there is little reason to spend extra money on them.

Here are a couple more simple ways to trim costs:

➤ Don't have a date stamped on your wedding napkins. That way, you can use the extras in your new home after the wedding.

➤ Have the ring pillow made. It's fairly simple and will mean even more to you.

One bride asked her grandmother to make some of the extras for her wedding. The grandmother felt so much more a part of the planning. She made the ring bearer's pillow, the bride's two garters (one to throw, one to keep), crocheted hankies for each bridesmaid to carry, and a table cover for the cake table with the couple's initials embroidered on it. She also crocheted pew bows for the ceremony. It meant so much to the bride that her grandmother was part of the wedding preparations, and the grandmother was so proud.

Another Christmas bride (married on December 26) made all the favors for the wedding. They were grapevine wreath ornaments with bells and Christmas ribbons. It also helped add color to the reception tables.

Paring Photography Costs

Hire a professional photographer to shoot the formal wedding pictures, and then have a trusted friend who has some skill with a camera take the candid shots at the reception.

Check out colleges and trade schools for an advanced photography student to shoot your wedding for a set fee and then give you the negatives for processing.

These are some ways to keep a little cash in your wallet. Check out wedding magazines and Web sites for articles on saving on costs. Another source is *The Complete Idiot's Guide to Budgeting for Your Wedding,* by Sue Winner.

Contracts and Agreements

During the course of your wedding planning, you will most likely be required to sign several contracts or agreements with the various vendors you're hiring. If you're not accustomed to a contract and its terminology, take someone with you who is familiar with the legal mumbo jumbo.

Most contracts are written by an attorney who wasn't hired to make legal jargon understandable to the uninitiated. If you aren't sure what the contract means, if you need a point clarified, or if you want to be sure you understand what is required of you, ask the vendor to explain the contract in lay terms. If you're still not sure what it means, ask to take the contract out of the store to share with your family, with your attorney, or with someone else who can help you. Most vendors don't have a problem letting you take the contract—if they do, maybe you should wonder why. The contract is for both your protection and that of the vendor's. Although it can be confusing, it does have a legitimate purpose during the wedding planning.

Wedding Woes

Never—I repeat, never—sign anything, whether a contract, agreement, or letter of intent, if you do not completely understand its meaning.

One couple I know didn't check their contract with the band. There was a requirement listed that stated the band must be fed a meal. It didn't say what the meal was to be; just that they were to be provided food during the evening. The band was not provided with anything and the couple got a surprise—the final billing from the band included a check to a local restaurant. When they called to question, they were told they had asked for food during the reception and their request denied so after the wedding, they got something to eat and billed the couple. Always read the fine print.

Always keep your contracts in a safe, easily accessible place. When you need to look at your contracts, you won't want to spend hours trying to find them.

The Least You Need to Know

➤ There are many ways to cut costs from your wedding budget.

➤ Never be afraid to ask for discounts or to inquire about renting items instead of buying them.

➤ Always make sure you understand what you're signing when you put your signature on a contract or agreement. If you don't understand the document, find someone who can explain it to you before you sign on the dotted line.

Part 5

Help! My Family Is Driving Me Nuts!!

Even if you're already well into the wedding planning stages, when you stumble on this part of the book, do yourself a favor. Stop! Read Part 5 from start to finish. It can make all the difference in your emotional state for the remainder of your planning. If you've turned to this part before you've begun any actual planning, you're taking a good first step toward having as stress-free a wedding as possible.

Part 5 deals with the emotional side of this whole wedding thing. It examines what goes on emotionally—and mostly subconsciously—with some of the people around you as the process unfolds. I'll talk about marriage as a rite of passage and why some decisions are so emotional for those involved. Then I'll offer some practical tips that might help smooth things over. I'll also examine the wedding stress factor (what's normal and what's not), how to work with divorced parents and blended families, and where you can turn for help.

So strap yourself in tight and get ready for the roller-coaster ride!

And in This Corner ...

A marriage is a rite of passage. A marriage can be a very stressful event even under the best of circumstances. Understanding what goes on emotionally during this process can help curtail unnecessary emotional turmoil from invading your wedding bliss.

Let's start off with a true story of how not understanding that marriage is a rite of passage affected my own wedding.

This Could Happen to You!

On April 9, 1970 (yes, this really happened before many of you were born), my husband-to-be asked my father for my hand in marriage. Back in 1970, this ritual was still considered proper etiquette.

I will never forget that day as long as I live. Daddy and Floyd were in the living room for the longest time. When they finally emerged, my dad had the biggest smile on his face. He hugged me and told me how happy he was for me. My mother was working in the den. She taught school and, as was usual on a Sunday evening, was grading papers. When Daddy went into the den to tell her the big news, there was silence. Lots of silence. I mean absolute silence. The kind of silence that cuts right through you. This was not a good sign. Dad left the den, still grinning from ear to ear. (Hey, being one of four children, my marriage meant one less mouth to feed—just joking, Daddy.) As he walked out, my mother just looked up at me from her chair and said, "Why?"

"Why what?" I said.

"Why are you marrying him?"

"Because I love him."

"That's not a reason," she said. "It will never work. You're too different."

Teddy's Tips

Several books on the bridal market now deal with the emotional side of marriage—it's about time!

And she started to cry. She cried from April 9 until December 27, the day my best friend Karen hosted a lovely bridal shower for me. I think it was then that my mother realized that her oldest daughter was going to get married with or without her consent. She stopped crying, and Floyd and I were married on January 30, 1971.

I was totally unprepared for the confusing emotions my mother and I were about to experience. I didn't know that something as wonderful as making plans for my wedding could cause so much stress in a relatively normal family. None of the wedding planning books I bought mentioned anything about the emotional side of getting married.

I remember wondering why, if this was supposed to be the happiest time in my life, I was feeling so miserable. I would ask my mother a question or ask her opinion about some detail, and she would respond by crying. She would look at me and start crying. It began to feel more like I was planning my funeral instead of my wedding.

Mother did little to help with the wedding plans. It was a combination of me being organized and her being reluctant even to acknowledge that the upcoming wedding was really going to take place. I think she believed that if she didn't help, things might not have gotten done and there would have been no wedding.

It wasn't so much that my mother objected to Floyd. We had dated for more than three years, we were both college graduates, and Floyd was established in business. We didn't sit down and talk about "it" because neither one of us knew what was really going on. It wasn't until I started working with couples that I put two and two together and figured out what was happening. Some good research on the subject proved I was on the right track. In the end, all turned out for the best, but it certainly was a bumpy road and one I wasn't expecting. Mother's reluctance was actually due to the fact that she didn't want to believe she was old enough to have a daughter of marrying age. One of her babies was old enough to leave the nest. That is a traumatic moment in a mother's life, as I now know from personal experience. I now claim a 26-year-old college graduate out on his own.

By the way, as this book goes to press, Floyd and I are celebrating our twenty-eighth wedding anniversary.

Marriage: A Rite of Passage

Over the years, I've had brides and their mothers explode into major battles in my office. I've had brides and mothers burst into tears. I've had mothers so upset with their bride-to-be daughters that they've walked out in the middle of a consultation. This mother-daughter tension is not a pleasant experience, and you won't see much written about it in wedding planners. You and your mother may experience some of this emotional tension, so it's something you both need to understand. I know that if you can understand why all this is happening, then maybe, just maybe, you will find some peace in what can be a very hectic and stressful time in your life. Gaining the knowledge and understanding of why these emotions are exploding might make your wedding planning go a little more smoothly.

Brides and their mothers sometimes disagree on many topics during the wedding planning stages, even the choice of mate. This was something I didn't understand at 23 years of age but that I have come to understand through my work with brides and their families: Marriage is a rite of passage. You're passing from one part of your life into a new part; you're leaving the primary role of child and taking on the new role of spouse. This universal rite demonstrates to a community that one of its own is old enough, responsible enough, and mature enough to take a mate.

There are three basic rites of passage: birth, marriage, and death. Of these three, marriage is the only one you choose. With this rite of passage comes a whole slew of emotions. These emotions are what fuel that roller-coaster ride you and your mother—and perhaps other members of the family—find yourselves on during the planning process.

The Emotional Roller Coaster—What to Expect

Let's talk about your emotions for a minute. Keep in mind that most of what goes on with your emotions during this time is subconscious. You don't know why you feel the way you do; it's just how you feel. Right now you're engaged to a wonderful person. You're excited; you're scared; you're happy; you worry about how well your in-laws will like you; you wonder whether your parents will get along—all kinds of things are running through your head. Now throw in the fact that your mother insists on beef for the entrée and that you and your fiancé both want chicken, or that she thinks pink is a terrible color for the bridesmaids' dresses while you've had your heart set on pink for years. You have the makings for some major fireworks, but what's really going on here? Is it about beef and chicken? Is it about the 10 different shades of pink you want to incorporate? I doubt it. It's about the bonds between parent and child, it's about power and control, and it's about growing up.

Mother and Me

At this point in your life, you may be torn between yearning for independence and yet not being ready to leave the nest. You want to make your own choices and decisions, but you might be reluctant to give up the security of having someone take care of you.

Your mother also might be feeling torn. She has reared you to be an independent person, but she's not really ready to lose her baby. She wants you to be strong, but she wants to make sure you make the right decisions (which often translates into the decisions *she* would make). Your mother is afraid that the marriage will break the bonds between the two of you, and that makes her sad. So, while she might be perfectly willing to argue over beef or chicken, or your choice of colors, you can be fairly certain that's not really what she's upset about. She's afraid the marriage will change your relationship with her. She's afraid your new spouse will replace her, and you won't need her anymore.

She's also afraid of the aging process—you getting married means she's getting older. Again, she's afraid of losing her baby. She's afraid of many things, most of which she can't explain to you, nor does she understand. She wants to be your friend and let you have your way, but in doing so, she loses some of her control. Her mothering abilities are on display now, and she wants a great report card to show when all is said and done.

There is also the flip side to moms. One bride shared with me her story. She found her mother pulling away rather than becoming overly involved in the wedding plans. This was partly because the mother had read so many articles and heard so many complaints about overbearing mothers taking over the wedding that she went overboard the opposite way. Many times, she didn't offer any opinions and only said "That's nice, dear," when told about details. She offered little help with any of the plans. The mother never even discussed anything besides a general dollar figure, so the bride ended up feeling like her mother couldn't have cared less that her daughter was getting married. In reality, the mother was trying too hard to let her daughter make her own decisions.

Don't be too hard on her. Had I understood what I know now about what my mother was really experiencing, I think we could have talked some and made each other feel so much better. Try not to let these subconscious emotional issues get in the way of your planning, fun, and excitement.

Daddy's Little Girl

Much is written about the prewedding tension between mother and daughter. But what about daughter and dad? Where does he fit into the plan?

Fathers are generally very interesting creatures when it comes to making plans for their daughter's big day. Your dad is proud of the woman you've become, and he wants only the very best for you. On the other hand, he may be somewhat jealous of your groom, the man who is going to take you away. Dad has been your protector; now he's giving up that role, and he does so with a little sadness. It doesn't matter how he feels about your groom; his little girl is growing up.

Dad also might feel left out of all the planning stages. At times, it does seem like a solely mother-daughter planning frenzy—kind of like a marathon of planning. If he seems grumpy or on edge from time to time, he might just want to be part of the process, too (other than writer of the checks), but he just doesn't know how to ask. When you ask if he would like to help, he may gruffly tell you that you and your mother are doing just fine with the planning, but he might not tell you that he feels better just that you had extended the offer.

Ask your dad how, or if, he wants to be involved in the wedding planning. If he gives the go-ahead, offer him some task that he will feel comfortable handling. Ask him to arrange for the limos for the day, or ask him to talk with the bartender about the brands of liquor you plan to serve.

Always try to keep your dad informed about the decisions you've made. Try to ask his advice and counsel. This will make him feel close to you and needed. It wouldn't hurt to give him some extra hugs along the way, either.

Mama's Baby Boy

So you think this chapter is just for the bride and her family? Well, as a future mother of two grooms, I'm here to tell you that the emotional stress happens to the males, too. While it has always been associated with the female gender, grooms, along with their fathers, and of course, the mothers, all go through the same rite of passage as the bride and her family.

The best advice I can offer grooms is to get involved with the wedding plans (it's your wedding, too) and keep those lines of communication open with your family. Where you will pick up the stress and the emotions is from your mom. She is the ill-fated "mother-in-law," and we all know that mothers-in-law are just these horrible creatures who prey on defenseless brides. I don't think so. You and your family are also experiencing the same emotions as your bride and her family. But because you are the man, it's just not talked about as much.

Your mom is thinking the same things as your fiancé's mom: Is she good enough for him, will she like us, should I ask if I can help? To help ease the tension and break the ice, involve your folks as much as they want to be involved and where they can be involved. If nothing else, keep them informed as to what is happening and where. You might suggest to your bride to ask your mom for her opinion on an item. Does she think you need to use a monogram or have the napkins printed with your names? If you ask simple questions and for opinion only, then you can take the advice or leave it. But the point is, you've asked and that's what matters.

When parents feel left out is when there is no communication taking place (and sometimes this happens for a reason) but most times keeping those lines of communication open can save everyone lots of heartache. (P.S.: Be sure to tell your mom you love her. That gesture always helps.)

Who's in Control Here?

One point of battle that might creep into your plans is the "Who's in charge?" theme. See this wedding as your wedding, and rightly so—it should be. You know what you want and don't want for this day. You've taken every precaution to check out references with vendors. You've read articles, been to bridal shows, and interviewed tons of vendors. You know exactly what you want this day to include, down to the last piece of wedding cake.

The only problem is that your mother might not have read the part that says you're in charge. Your mother wants to be in charge, too. Your mother might hold the checkbook, and the checkbook might have strings attached. It's her one last chance to show her stuff. Your mother may be having a tough time giving up her dominant role. She has taken care of you for all these years and made decisions with your best interests at heart. How could you not want her to make all the arrangements for your wedding, whether you like them or not? Control, power, whatever you want to call it—that's what this is all about. She's afraid of losing her power.

Another factor that might determine what kind of a role your mother wants to have in your wedding is how much control she had over her own wedding. So many times, the mother who had a small, simple wedding wants to create through her daughter the wedding she never had. She wants the control she didn't have. Your invitations will be the ones she didn't have. Your gown will be the one she wanted. Your entrée choice will be beef because her own mother, or her circumstances at the time, did not allow her to serve the food she really wanted to serve. If your mother wants to make this the big production she never had, yet you have a small, simple wedding in mind, you might have some big problems. If you can't go along with your mother's desire to have the wedding of the year, then be prepared for the fireworks—I can guarantee you that they'll be there.

If this sounds like what you're going through, or what you think might happen, try talking to your mother.

Teddy's Tips

In this part of the wedding process, patience is indeed a true virtue. Compromise and don't sweat the small stuff.

Sit down with her in a quiet setting; talk calmly and rationally about the wedding plans you have been planning. In your most adult, mature voice, let her know (very delicately) that this is your wedding, and while you want her help, it needs to be for items you as a couple want included. You'll find more practical tips later in this chapter.

Tension Between Parents

Something else that I have come to recognize (often on sight) is tension caused by two sets of parents vying for the couple's allegiance. You're no longer dealing with just your parents. All of a sudden, you've got another set of parents to worry about. The groom might want his parents' names on the invitation because they're paying for the liquor at the reception. The bride's mother, however, might refuse, saying that tradition dictates that only the bride's parents' names appear on the invitation.

Well, dear reader, your parents are battling out (subconsciously) their fear of losing your loyalty. How many times have you heard married friends say, "Oh, our parents are driving us nuts. They both want us to spend Christmas with them. How can we choose?" Well, you have to make a stand, and the sooner the better. It's nothing more than a power struggle over you, the new couple on the block. Your parents are arguing over who will have more control over you after the wedding. They want to make sure you still have allegiance to them. You as a couple need to have a heart-to-heart talk early on and decide what limits you will set. Your primary allegiance needs to be to each other.

Just remember that your parents aren't creating all this turmoil intentionally. Often, they don't understand why they behave like they do. Once you understand what's going on, you can learn to work around it or work with it. How I wish someone would have told me some of this back in 1970. It certainly would have made my life a lot easier just understanding what my mother was experiencing. I know if we could have talked openly about the emotions we were both experiencing and the fears we shared, she and I would have had an easier time with my whole wedding process.

Wedding Woes

It's best to decide very early what limits you will set as a couple regarding the expectations of your respective parents. Floyd and I agreed before we were married that I would handle concerns/problems with my parents, and he would deal with his. So far (28 years), it has worked out very nicely.

Practical Tips

The closer your wedding day gets, the thicker the tension. Hey, I said I would tell you why it's probably happening—I didn't say you'd stop arguing with your parents! Okay, now what? Well, let's talk about it. Here are some practical ideas that might help:

➤ Work on your attitude. Attitude makes all the difference in the world. Don't think of this wedding as solely your property—think of it more as a family affair. It's still your wedding, don't get me wrong, but if you can focus your attention away from yourself, you might be more open to others' suggestions and be willing to compromise.

➤ Remember, above all else, it's the marriage, not the wedding, that's really important. Which gowns are worn, flowers are carried, and entrées are eaten doesn't matter in the end. What matters is the marriage between two people who care, trust, love, and like each other enough to spend the rest of their earthly lives together. That's Commitment folks, with a capital C.

➤ Put all the cards on the table. Know what you're dealing with and whom. As a united front, you as a couple should approach your families with your wedding desires. See what they are willing to contribute, and take it from there. At least you'll know where you stand. Trying to second-guess your parents is not only time-consuming, but it's also not at all practical. Many couples would rather know what amount of money they have to work with than to guess at what they think they might be working with. You need to know what's what.

The same philosophy applies to the marriage in general. If your parents are opposed to the marriage, listen to their views and explain your position. In my situation, my mother made it quite clear that she did not approve of the wedding. I listened to her opinions, explained my feelings, and kept moving forward. I knew almost from day one the resistance I was up against.

➤ Decide which items about the wedding you must have control over and which items you could turn over to your mother or other family members. Don't let her feel left out. You want to prevent your mother from feeling insecure, if possible. Insecurity sometimes leads to irrational behavior, and you sure don't need that now. The same advice goes for your partner's mother. One of the fastest ways to make an enemy of your future mother-in-law is to keep her guessing about the wedding plans. Unless she's helping financially, she doesn't have a real decision-making role, but asking her opinion, her advice, and which colors she likes best will help make your relationship stronger and make her feel more a part of the process. Keep her informed, and ask for advice.

➤ If you and your mother have a huge argument and you hang up the phone or slam the door on her, take a deep breath, count to 100, and call back or walk back in the room. It might be

Teddy's Tips

Make time for your physical needs; eat right, exercise, and get enough sleep. You can't possibly keep up with the physical drain of wedding planning, plus all the raging emotions, if you're exhausted.

very hard to do, but it will help you in the long haul. Explain that it's the wedding stress that has you bummed out, not her. Try to start fresh. Forgive and forget. In 10 years, no one will remember.

➤ Send your mother a card or flowers, and tell her you love her. Mothers love that mushy stuff—and please, make it sincere. So many times, mothers act the way they do just because they're mothers. (It's in the contracts we sign when our babies are born—really, it is.) If she feels appreciated and loved, and still knows you care about her, that will go a long way toward mending fences.

➤ Try to get enough rest and exercise, and eat properly during the wedding planning. Stress depletes the body's reserves. If you aren't physically able to handle all the ups and downs, you will be more stressed.

Wedding Woes

Be patient with each other. This is normally a stressful time, just given the nature of all that goes on. Don't let a relatively small item ruin the fun and excitement of planning for one of the most important days of your life. If you argue, take a deep breath and count to 10 or 100—or even to 1,000, if necessary—and start over.

Above all, try to stay calm and be patient. Keep the lines of communication open. Always be willing to listen. Good luck!

The Least You Need to Know

➤ Just understanding that arguments naturally happen during this planning process (and that those arguments are normal) might make this time easier to get through.

➤ Marriage is one of the basic rites of passage. You're leaving a familiar role and assuming a new role, and it's normal to experience uncertainty and tension on this journey.

➤ Try to take into consideration the emotions your parents are experiencing. They don't understand, at least consciously, why they're acting as they are.

➤ If you get into an argument with a family member, take a deep breath, count to 10, and try to start over.

➤ Remember that in the end, it's the marriage that counts, not the wedding—they are very different. Don't get so lost in planning the details of the wedding that you forget about the marriage.

Chapter 19

I Think I'm Losing My Mind

In This Chapter

➤ Understanding normal wedding stress

➤ Finding ways to control the stress

➤ Dealing with divorced parents and blended families

➤ Getting help if you need it

Stress—it's an everyday word in our society. There is good stress; there is bad stress. And, no matter how hard and how well you plan, there is stress during your wedding planning months. In this chapter, I'll start off talking about what's normal wedding stress and what isn't. We'll talk about divorced and blended families (they're out there everywhere), and I'll give you some sage advice on how to deal with the stress caused by the happiest day of your life.

Is This Normal?

"I'm stressed to the limit. I just can't take any more." During the wedding planning stages, you'll find yourself saying this more times than you can count. You'll be saying it to family members, to friends, to yourself, and even to perfect strangers.

Yes, by their very nature, weddings are stress-producing events. The escalation of your emotions stemming from the added burdens and worries associated with wedding planning can cause prewedding stress. This is an emotional time. Much of the stress comes from all the details you have to be involved with, along with a sense of not having control over all that's going on. You might feel pulled in many directions as well; you have too many advice-givers and not enough supporters. At times, you might even wish that you had just chosen to elope. Relax—all these feelings and emotions are in the normal range of wedding stress.

You might be angry one minute and feel relaxed and energized the next. You might be smiling, and then suddenly you burst into tears. You and your partner might fight over little things—after all, your partner might feel overwhelmed with the planning as well and might not want to be included in it. You may feel as though you haven't a friend in the world. Just understand that all these feelings and emotions (the ups and the downs) often accompany this time in your life.

Not every couple experiences prewedding stress. I've talked with some couples and their families who thoroughly enjoyed the wedding planning process. However, if you're like the majority of harried brides in the months before the wedding, you're likely to feel some added anxiety. Let's look at some of the reasons for this stress.

It Costs What?

Think back to Chapter 3, "Simple or Extravagant—Setting Your Budget," when I talked about the budget and helped you determine what's important to you as a couple and how much you have to spend. Remember when I suggested that you try to stick to that budget? Well, one very good reason for sticking to a budget is to help prevent all the negative emotions that can accompany spending more money than you've allotted.

Going over your budget is one of the biggest stress factors in wedding planning. It's like extending the limit on your credit cards; it's like running a tab for every friend and distant relative at the local pub. It just keeps adding up. You buy something here and something there. You order your flowers, and when the estimate comes, it's twice your budget. Instead of getting the violinist for the prelude music, you've decided to add a string quartet. How much more can three little musicians be?

What started out as a simple affair has now escalated into a complex and expensive event. Your wedding costs may resemble the national debt, and the price tag keeps right on climbing. Then there are all the little extras: garter, guest book, welcome packages at the hotel, parking fees—the list goes on and on. Not expecting the add-on costs and not getting an accurate estimate for a service can leave you drained both financially and emotionally. This is why keeping your expectations reasonable and setting realistic goals is so important.

Friends and family can get rather edgy when dealing with money matters. Your dad just doesn't understand why everything costs so much or why you're having the quartet instead of just the violinist. Add in a family crisis, and you have the ingredients for a stress-filled event. One couple, who was paying for the wedding themselves, had carefully budgeted what they expected to pay for their outdoor wedding. Down to the last penny, everything was right on track. Unfortunately, their new puppy picked up the parvovirus and spent nine days at the vet's with IVs and medication. Suddenly, the couple had an $850 expense they had not planned on.

Emergencies and crises happen; that's just part of life. Take into consideration normal living expenses during your wedding planning, but also try to set aside some money for surprises.

Too Much Advice from Too Many People

When you become engaged, it's like you're suddenly wearing a sign that says, "Advice Needed Here!" You're deluged with all kinds of advice from all kinds of people. In Chapter 1, "Your First Step Toward the Altar—Getting Started," I suggested that you seek advice from those who had recently married; this is always a good idea, but be prepared for a lot more than you bargained for from other advice-givers.

All of a sudden, you get to hear the details of every wedding horror story, the details of every wedding planning detail problem, and countless hours of "I did it this way." You will be filled to the limit with too much advice. Here's a scene that just might happen to you.

Scene: Coffee shop. You run into a friend you have not talked with for several months.

"Oh, Sally, good to see you."

"Say, Cindy, I heard you're getting married."

"Yes. Jim and I finally set the date."

"Well, tell me about your plans."

"Oh, we just want a simple wedding, nothing too fancy."

"Where did you get your gown?"

"At Bitsy's Bridal Boutique."

Silence. Then, "Bitsy's Bridal Boutique?"

"Yes, why?"

Wedding Woes

Don't get bogged down with too much advice from the advice addicts. Yes, they might have your best interests at heart, but if you've done your homework, you should be fine.

"Oh, nothing, it's just that they ruined Jane Owen's gown. Ruined it, I tell you. They didn't hem the dress, left a huge hole in the side seam, and then, would you believe it, the gown came back with a big pink stain on the front. They said they didn't do it, but who else did? I tell you, Cindy, you're a fool to work with them."

At this point in the conversation, you're sweating and your pulse is beginning to beat rapidly. You're starting to breathe heavily and your head is spinning. And you're wondering, "Did I do enough homework on Bitsy's Bridal Boutique? I checked with other friends who used them; they seemed happy with the outcome. So far, they're completely on schedule. Have I made a big mistake? I don't want pink stains on my wedding gown."

Get a grip! Do a reality check! You've just experienced what I fondly refer to as listening to the "advice addict." If it happened, the advice addict knows it—this person knows why it happened, knows whom it happened to, and knows what to do about

239

it. Take what that person has to say with a big grain of salt. Although you do need advice from many friends—especially those recently married—you eventually will reach a saturation point. You will become the proverbial sponge that can no longer soak up any more advice. Your cup will begin to overflow.

Relax! Take a deep breath. Let the advice addict's message go in one ear and out the other. Use what you can, and discard the rest.

This, too, shall pass.

Trying to Please Everyone

Another potential point of certain stress is trying to please everyone. "Everyone" means the entire Western Hemisphere. "Everyone" means both sets of parents, grand-parents, aunts, uncles, cousins, second cousins, second cousins two times removed, all your friends, and your boss (you probably do still have to work for a living).

I've talked about this being *your* wedding. Don't lose sight of that now. You can't pos-sibly please everyone. There will be someone, somewhere, who doesn't agree with what you're doing, the way in which you're doing it, or what you're serving, wearing, saying, singing, playing, or handing out. With weddings, it's just a given—you can never please everyone.

If you've done your homework, then just go with the flow. Worry about what you as a couple feel is necessary and what you want to include. Do take into consideration your family and their desires or wishes, but the bottom line here is that this is still *your* wedding. You will drive yourself nuts if you try to meet the demands of the en-tire family.

If you run into resistance with family members, be calm, be tactful, be diplomatic, and be firm. Don't alter your plans just to please someone else unless you can make the change without compromising your basic desires.

One bride wanted a very simple floral design for her wedding ceremony site. Her mother insisted that the church had to be filled to the ceiling with flowers and can-dles. Not wanting to call in the fire department, the bride made her point with the florist and thought the matter was completed, but the mother changed the flower order and did not tell her daughter. When the flowers were delivered and were being set up in the church, the bride noticed a change in the order. She was upset, to say the least, but she calmed down enough to talk with the florist. They worked out the details. She let her mom have some additional floral pieces, deciding she could live with some extra flowers, but she sent back the six sets of candelabra. She wasn't par-ticularly partial to the idea of the sprinkler system going off in the middle of "The Wedding March."

Divorced and Blended Families

Where do I begin on this topic? Divorce happens. It happens frequently in this coun-try. It might have happened to your parents or your partner's parents or someone in your family. With divorce and remarriage of parents come blended families—you know, "yours, mine, and (sometimes) ours." If your parents are divorced and have remarried, you have a stepparent and probably some stepbrothers or stepsisters and extended aunts and uncles and grandparents. This is what we, in the wedding industry, refer to as a blended family. And the sheer numbers added to your family tree can provide plenty of additional stress.

Divorced family members don't automatically bring any additional problems to your wedding planning. If the divorce was particularly nasty, however, and the parties involved are still relatively hostile, you have the potential for some wedding fireworks. Some extra precautions could be in order.

I've been hired in several situations because there were less-than-amicable divorced members in the family and the hiring party wanted me to help keep the peace. I know from firsthand experience how Matt Dillon must have felt back in Dodge City in the 1800s. With the divorce rate so high in this country, you might encounter this problem. If you're faced with divorced family members— particularly parents—you need to proceed with caution.

Teddy's Tips

If your parents are divorced and not on friendly terms, never assume that they will put aside their differences long enough for you to walk down the aisle. Always use caution, courtesy, and compassion when you discuss your wedding plans with them and how you see their individual roles.

When Divorced Parents Are Talking

Perhaps your parents have been divorced for many years and are on good speaking terms with each other and you. Both have remarried, and you feel comfortable with the stepparents. When you announce your engagement and sit down to discuss plans, be sure to include both sets of parents—that is, both sets of your parents and your partner's parents. If there is physical distance separating all of you, make sure you keep both parties informed as to what you discuss and decide, and ask for opinions from all sides. Never put the two sides at odds with each other. Don't compare them to each other. Please don't say to your mother, "Well, Daddy's wife is going to take me to see Vera Wang about designing my gown." (FYI: Vera Wang is a big-time designer who creates some fantastic gowns with hefty price tags.) You'll only create a distance between parties that doesn't need to be there.

I know what it feels like to be a negotiator. I've been asked many times to make a stepmother who feels left out and wants to be included feel good about being involved in the wedding. It's not easy. So many times, just a matter of having more open communication between the parents is all that's needed. You must make very sure that all your communication between your divorced parents is accurate and complete. Don't expect them to assume anything.

As for finances with divorced parents, let me offer this tip: Open a checking account to be used solely for wedding expenses. Have each contributor (your mother, your father, and so on) contribute equal amounts of money to the account. As the wedding bills are paid, each party contributes additional equal amounts to cover other costs. Any money left over might be given to the couple for a nest egg. This helps greatly in alleviating the "But I paid for this" syndrome.

It's also helpful to chart out who is going to be responsible for each aspect of the wedding expenses. Take a piece of paper and make several columns. One column is for the item and the others are for each set of contributors (you, your father, your mother, and so on). Then, go through the list and decide who will be responsible for what. Now you've got it in black and white. Give each contributor a copy of the plan.

What I just described is the ultimate situation when dealing with divorced families. Unfortunately, there are more situations where we pray for peace among the parents just long enough to get through the day.

When Divorced Parents Aren't Talking

If your divorced parents want nothing to do with one another, accept that fact and work around it. For seating purposes, your mother should be seated in the first row and your father in the second. I have had brides request that their divorced parents be seated together in the first row. It's truly an unselfish act for divorced parents to put aside their anger and support their child, and it's not too much for a child to ask.

I know of one wedding that had an unusual twist to the divorced parents' situation. The groom's parents had been divorced for many years and were both remarried, but they were still not speaking to each other. As the mothers (all three) were being seated, the young usher seating the groom's stepmother and father seated them in the first pew, where the groom's mother and stepfather were to sit. When the groom's mother realized what had happened, she demanded that they be moved. Not wanting to cause any more of a scene than there already was, a friend suggested that certainly for 30 minutes they could all sit together in the same pew, for the son's sake. Reluctantly, they did. They managed to control their frustration with each other long enough to get through the service.

One wedding many years ago involved a wonderful couple who had extensively planned their wedding. We had spent time covering all the little details. The bride's parents were divorced, and her mother had remarried. When we had finished the final consultation a few days before the wedding, I asked the bride if there was anything else I should know. She paused and replied, "Have I mentioned that my father hasn't spoken to us in five years?" Well, no, I hadn't picked up on that. I asked her who was going to escort her down the aisle, and she informed me that she had asked her brother. So, that's the way we practiced at the rehearsal.

I received a late phone call after the rehearsal was over. The bride was very upset and crying. Her father had called her and demanded that he be the one to walk her down the aisle. She didn't know what to do. We talked about options and decided that she should probably let him do the honors. He showed up right before the ceremony, appropriately dressed in a tuxedo. He was very uncomfortable standing in the church lobby. When the processional began, his daughter came up to him and took his arm. They marched down the aisle, and before she left him at the altar to go to her groom, she reached over and gave him a hug and a kiss. Here was a family who had not spoken to each other in five years. And with this one simple act, the ice had been broken. Since then, the other two sisters have married, and their dad has been at each of their weddings. While I'm sure that those parents are still not best buddies, they have put aside their differences long enough to give their children happy, peaceful wedding days.

Each wedding with divorced families has a different set of circumstances that must be addressed. You have to be sensitive, to a point, to the wishes of your divorced parents. Be supportive and try to be understanding. If you're faced with dealing with divorced parents and family members during your wedding, try to accommodate their requests. For example, don't put your mother at the same table with your father and his 22-year-old new wife. Even if they get along great, the fact that your new stepmother is younger than you might wear a bit on your mom. Use some common sense when dealing with divorced parents. They are still your parents. Hang in there, keep your chin up, and move forward.

Teddy's Tips

For additional help in dealing with divorced family members, you might find some helpful suggestions in *Planning a Wedding with Divorced Parents*, by Cindy Moore and Tricia Windom.

Where to Get Help

All right, I'll admit it. Sometimes these delicate issues can cause some hairy situations. What do you do if you need some objective help and guidance? Several options are open to you.

The Officiant

One of the best places to gather some strength and advice is from your minister, priest, or rabbi. These trained professionals deal with all kinds of stressful situations, including parents who hate each other and who are going to be forced to spend three hours in the same room together at your wedding.

If you're experiencing some difficulties with your wedding planning due to the circumstances of the divorced members of your family, make an appointment with your minister, priest, or rabbi. He should be familiar with your family situation. Explain what has happened and how you're feeling, and ask for some guidance. Sometimes, by just expressing our concerns, fears, and uncertainties, we feel better, even if the situation hasn't changed. You still might be faced with the same problems as before, but just being able to vent your feelings and have your concerns heard can reduce the stress level. Sometimes, too, if you get your fears out in the open, they aren't as frightening as they first seemed.

Your family might need a counseling session. If your family will have nothing to do with counseling, then go yourself. If your partner will attend with you, that's great. At least you should feel better and will be better prepared to handle the other pressures of the wedding planning.

Bridal Consultant

Many consultants feel that through our experiences, we should at least have earned our Ph.D. in human behavior. Given how close I am to the individual situations that arise with families, there are many times when I've felt as though I could easily hang out a shingle, "Dr. T.M. Lenderman." I've learned many things about human beings and what we can do if pushed hard enough.

Sometimes, if you're having some difficulties coping with the stress of accommodating divorced family members, your bridal consultant can be a great help. She probably has seen the same situation several times before. If nothing else, discussing how you can rearrange the reception tables so that your two sets of parents and their new partners won't be seated next to each other will at least get the frustration off your chest. Besides, she might have an idea or two you haven't thought of to help resolve the problem.

The more experience your bridal consultant has, the better off you are as far as dealing with divorced families. For one wedding I'll never forget, the couple hired four armed guards and stationed them at the church doors and at the reception to keep out an unwanted guest. As sad as it was, the unwanted guest was the groom's mother. I don't believe I've ever been more nervous and anxious at a wedding. The mother had threatened to come to the church and blow us all away. Now, I've been in delicate situations before with divorced parents and angry parents, but this one left me sweating bullets (pun intended). She was angry with her son for inviting her ex-husband to the wedding. She didn't show up, but the fear from that day still sends cold chills down my spine.

Trusted Family Member or Friend

If you aren't comfortable discussing your problems relating to your divorced parents with an officiant or bridal consultant, seek out a trusted family member or a good friend.

If you choose a family member, be very certain that you can trust him or her to be discreet and not share what you have confided. What you don't need is one side of the family against the other side over the fact that you shared your concerns with Aunt Marilyn, and she told Cousin Helen, and Helen told your sister Jane, and so on. No, you don't need that. What you need is someone who is reliable and is also a good listener.

The same policy applies to a friend you may confide in. Make sure that your friend will keep what you share in confidence. You need to express your feelings, and you need to know that it's okay to be feeling these things.

These challenges don't need to dampen your wedding planning or your wedding day. You know your family. If your partner's parents are experiencing difficulties in dealing with divorced players, let your partner handle it. Just use some common courtesy, tact, and diplomacy. Keep your sense of humor, and make the best of the situation. Remember, no family is perfect. You just have to work with the cards you're dealt and keep your chin up!

Prenuptial Agreements

In our society today, we're faced daily with decisions that can be very difficult to make. In this decade, the prenuptial agreement has reared its ugly head, and more couples are being faced with this decision before they marry. This can add more stress than either of you thought possible. This is especially true when a family business is involved whose wealth has reached a point where a future divorce between the couple could be disastrous for the rest of the family. I know it's hard to think about this at a time when you're madly in love and think that nothing will ever part you, but sometimes, signing off on a prenuptial agreement is the only way you can say, "I do." Some source books that you can find at your library include *Don't Get Married Until You Read This,* by David Saltman and Harry Schaffner; and *Premarital Agreements: When, Why and How to Write Them,* by Joseph P. Zwack.

The Least You Need to Know

➤ Don't be surprised if you feel overwhelmed and stressed during the planning stages of your wedding. These are normal reactions to this often hectic and emotion-filled time.

➤ Keep in mind that lots of folks out there are just waiting to give you some advice, whether or not you ask for it. Take what you can use, and let go of the rest.

➤ When working with divorced family members, be considerate of their feelings. Never compare the parents to each other.

➤ If your parents are divorced, it's especially important to try to work out potential financial problems before they happen. You might want to open a joint checking account, have each parent contribute equally to the account, and pay all your wedding bills from that account.

➤ If the situation demands, get some outside help. Many times, you will feel better just by talking to an objective listener about what you're feeling.

Part 6

Special Weddings

Every wedding is a special wedding. Ask any bride-to-be, and she'll tell you just how special her wedding will be. What I'm referring to here, however, are weddings that take on a special flair or a unique idea, or that follow a theme.

Part 6 talks about all these "special weddings." I'll introduce you to theme weddings, including seasonal, outdoor, military, and Victorian weddings. You'll find out what a weekend wedding consists of and how to plan one. I'll also tell you what a destination wedding is and offer some ideas for where you might want to hold one.

Chapter 20

What's in a Theme?

In This Chapter

➤ Considering a theme wedding

➤ Discovering ideas for seasonal, outdoor, military, and Victorian weddings

➤ Utilizing practical tips to help you plan a theme wedding

Weddings with themes are big these days. Brides and grooms want to create a unique atmosphere for their big day and are choosing themes around which they can build this atmosphere. Couples often select a wedding theme based on a particular season or date. Or, maybe they have a favorite special interest, such as golfing or sailing, so they build their wedding around that theme to make their big event a true statement of who they are.

Seasonal Weddings

A seasonal wedding is one that takes place near a certain holiday or during a certain season of the year. Examples of holidays around which you might choose to hold your wedding include Christmas, New Year's Day, Valentine's Day, Halloween, and the Fourth of July. Each seasonal wedding can have as many or as few themed parts as you want. Have fun thinking up new ways to celebrate the season and your wedding.

Weddings around Christmas or on New Year's Day are popular. I've been involved with weddings for both these occasions and have found them to be delightful.

Christmas Weddings

Christmas weddings, in particular, can be wonderfully romantic. I don't know if it's the season, the snow (at least, here in the Midwest), the decorations, or the soft glow of all the candles. The season itself just seems filled with more love, hope, and peace, and those sentiments tend to shine through weddings held during this time. Most facilities and churches decorate for the holiday, which can add a special and lovely touch to your wedding festivities (and actually save you money on decorations).

Wedding Woes

If you hold your wedding in a Catholic church, be sure to check on exactly when the church will be decorated for the season. Some Catholic churches are decorated late. Even if your wedding is on December 20, don't assume that the church will already be decorated. A Catholic church cannot be decorated before the last Sunday in Advent. When in doubt, ask the priest.

Usually, the church is filled with wonderful Christmas decor, which can mean less work for you and a break for your budget. Candles are especially nice during the holidays, adding to the warmth and glow of the season. Lots of red ribbon and Christmas greens with pinecones are a natural touch, and poinsettias, the flower of Christmas, usually abound. One beautiful Christmas wedding I attended had the church filled with 500 white poinsettias. If you're thinking of being married at Christmas, you might want to shop for a decorated facility.

Here are some additional touches to consider for a Christmas wedding:

➤ Think about having your musicians play Christmas carols as prelude music or having a children's choir caroling among your guests, either down the aisles before the service at church or between the tables at the reception. Print Christmas song sheets on parchment paper, tie them with a red velvet ribbon, and leave them at each place.

➤ Give guests a program tied with a plaid Christmas ribbon. Leave a small wreath tied with Christmas ribbon at each place setting. Have ornaments printed with your names and wedding date, and hang them on a large Christmas tree at the reception. As your guests leave the reception, they can take an ornament to hang on their own trees.

➤ Dress your bridesmaids in traditional black velvet tops and plaid Christmas skirts. Bouquets could contain silver bells or other ornaments among the flowers.

➤ Use touches of gold with red accents in the bouquets or centerpieces. Use different-sized "presents" tied up with festive ribbons and stacked in the middle of the table for centerpieces. Or, small pine trees individually decorated with tiny Christmas ornaments could adorn each table at the reception.

➤ Drape white lights and garland around posts or in front of the cake or the head table to give off a warm glow.

➤ Carry a white muff instead of a bouquet; pin silk poinsettias onto the muff for color. Serve hot mulled cider as guests arrive at the reception, and add Christmas cookies to the dessert table.

New Year's Eve or New Year's Day Weddings

You can create a special atmosphere planning a New Year's wedding, whether on New Year's Eve or New Year's Day.

For the New Year's Eve wedding, the obvious is to have noisemakers and confetti for your guests. Here are some additional ideas for New Year's weddings:

➤ In the center of the dance floor, have a huge sack of balloons tied up, ready to release at the stroke of midnight.

➤ Have guests make New Year's resolutions at their tables, seal them in envelopes, and leave them in a basket by the door. Mail those out later in January to your guests as a reminder of the resolution and of your wedding.

➤ Consider providing a big-screen TV or several smaller TVs spaced around the reception room for the football buffs, or consider providing a separate room with a TV so that die-hard fans can get a glimpse of the games. This idea works best if your reception is small and informal. While probably not high on your list of things to offer for your wedding reception, this does allow for mingling and some fun for your guests.

Valentine's Day Weddings

Valentine's Day is a romantic holiday; add a wedding to the day, and you have the setting for some special happenings. Here are some ideas to consider for a Valentine's Day wedding:

➤ Consider a gown in a pale shade of pink, or wear a traditional white gown and dress your bridesmaids in varying shades of pink or the traditional Valentine's Day red velvet.

➤ Use heart-shaped everything at the wedding and reception. You can rent a heart-shaped candelabrum from the florist, and you probably can find unity candles with hearts on them and even a guest book in the shape of a heart. Have two intertwined hearts printed on the front of your programs. Use heart-shaped chocolate mints at the reception. You can even buy heart-shaped napkins—really, you can.

➤ Go with a red, pink, and white color scheme. Rich red tablecloths, touches of pink in the flowers, and white linen napkins can give a striking appearance to

251

your reception. Add white votive candles and red or pink rose petals sprinkled on the tables, and you have pure romance.

➤ Have place cards or table numbers written on heart-shaped cards. Obviously, don't forget the heart-shaped wedding cake. Top it off with a hand-blown glass figurine of two hearts. Gifts for your bridesmaids may include heart-shaped jewelry either to wear at the wedding or for their personal enjoyment.

➤ Have your florist send a balloon bouquet—heart-shaped, of course—to your bride or groom on the morning of your wedding. Write a love poem, and attach it with a pretty ribbon. What a romantic way to start the day!

Fourth of July Weddings

Talk about fireworks! As the ceremony ends and the officiant pronounces you husband and wife, what's more appropriate than a fireworks display? (Try not to catch the facility on fire.) Here are some more Fourth of July theme ideas:

➤ It's July, so why not plan for an outdoor reception with red, white, and blue tablecloths?

➤ Lead off the processional with a 1776 traditional drum and fife core. Consider using the "1812 Overture" for the recessional. How majestic!

➤ Have your gown and those of your wedding party made in an eighteenth-century style.

➤ Top off the cake with sparklers, and give children some sparklers to enjoy (with adult supervision).

➤ Right before you and your partner exit, gather the entire reception out on the lawn and have a fireworks display to bring your wonderful day to a dramatic end.

Halloween Weddings

It might sound a bit weird, but a Halloween wedding can be a real treat. One of the more outstanding weddings I've been involved with recently took place on Halloween night. The bridesmaids were dressed in black-sequined dresses, complete with sequined shoes. The bride chose a white-sequined gown with a detachable train. It was elegant! The couple used lots of gold accents throughout the decorations at the church and at the reception.

We carried out the Halloween theme more fully at the reception site. When the bridal party was announced, each female attendant carried a hand-held mask (you know, the kind you see at a masquerade ball). The masks were lovely: Some were beaded; some were covered in a moiré ribbon fabric; some were sequined. The men in the wedding party each wore a half face mask. As each couple was introduced, they entered the ballroom, bowed and curtsied to the audience, and removed their masks. The bride and groom each had very elaborately designed masks. It was fun, and certainly a unique idea.

Other Halloween weddings have held more to the tradition of Halloween and have asked guests to come in costume. Some of the traditional Halloween elements have been included, such as candy apples as part of the food, a black-and-orange color scheme, fall leaves, baskets of nuts and berries, corn stalks and pumpkins nestled together, and so on. For favors, have Halloween treat bags prepared and left at each place setting for your guests with a note from you and your partner.

Go with the Flow of the Season

Whatever your ideas for a seasonal wedding, don't try to go against the grain. If you choose to marry in December, for example, and you know the facilities will be decorated for Christmas, it makes no sense to take down all the decorations and put up something else.

One couple, planning for their December wedding, rented a church that was fully (and most beautifully) decorated for the holiday season. Every pew had a gorgeous red pew bow. Garland had been hung, and a huge Christmas tree was aglow with white lights. The bride had chosen peach and blue for her colors, and she removed only the center aisle red pew markers and left all the other Christmas decorations in place. Those peach dresses in December looked a little out of place with all the Christmas decorations. Just use some common sense.

Outdoor and Garden Weddings

Outdoor and garden weddings are probably the most difficult to plan and the most risky to carry out. For some reason, people seem to feel that if they opt for an outdoor wedding in Grandma's lovely garden, it somehow will be easier and cheaper than renting a facility and a reception hall. Nothing could be further from the truth.

The Unpredictable Mother Nature

The only place in this country where it's not too risky to plan an outdoor wedding is California, where Mother Nature usually cooperates—aside from the occasional earthquake or mud slide.

Teddy's Tips

Choosing an outdoor wedding does not mean it will necessarily be cheaper or less elaborate than an indoor wedding. A great deal depends on your geographic location. If you live in a climate such as California, where the weather is not a major risk factor, then an outdoor wedding is an easier task. If your wedding will be in the Northeast, however, be prepared for a sudden rain storm, a chilling cold front, or a sticky heat wave.

Ah, Mother Nature. "It's not nice to fool Mother Nature." Well, trust me, you can't. I know—I've tried. She will do what she will do, and there's nothing you can do about it. If bad weather crashes your outdoor wedding, you might be in for some big trouble.

The first thing to consider when scheduling an outdoor wedding is to have a back-up plan. Ask yourself where the events will take place if the weather doesn't cooperate. This is an important agenda item. Never assume that it wouldn't dare rain on your parade.

Mother Nature sometimes can be downright mean. One of my most outstanding wedding memories is a lovely outdoor wedding that was held in a nature preserve. The couple owned property adjoining the preserve, and more than anything, they wanted to be married by the lake. We decided to have tents put up as our back-up plan. The tents arrived on Friday morning. The rain started Friday night. It rained so much that it washed out half the road leading to the property. The wedding was scheduled for 7:00 on Sunday evening. We had water everywhere—I mean everywhere. I don't think that even Noah himself encountered more water. The tents had bowed at the top from too much water. Two of the uprights came completely out of the ground. We had standing water in some places. You could literally float an air mattress inside the tents. It was a mess!

Bouquet Toss

Superstition says that if it does rain on your wedding day, it's a sign of good fortune.

When the wedding day arrived, it sprinkled and the clouds were dark and ominous, but at least it didn't rain. Right before the service, the minister came up to me with a look of panic on his face and asked, "Teddy, what should I do if it starts raining during the ceremony?" I looked him right in the eye and said, "If they're little drops, read fast. If they're big drops, read faster." At that point, there's nothing else you can do.

Not only is it possible that you could have rain or cold to contend with, but you also might run into excessive heat at an outdoor wedding. One June wedding I coordinated drove home the problems that heat can cause. June weather is normally fairly nice and mild in Indiana, but for this wedding, the thermometer kept right on climbing. After it hit 103 degrees, I stopped looking. The wedding reception was held in tents.

Do you know how hot tents can get with temperatures in the 100s? The musicians were sweating profusely. I was sweating profusely. The guests were dying on the vine. They couldn't dance because they were afraid of heatstroke. Some guests actually had "water" in their shoes. That's hot, folks, any way you look at it—and it was very uncomfortable for everyone.

Dealing with outdoor weddings can be made a little easier if you have the budget. Tents can be floored so the water level won't cause your guests discomfort. Flooring for tents is very expensive. That's one reason why selecting the right site for your tent needs to be left to the professionals. Tents can also be heated (remember in the movie *Father of the Bride*) or cooled. Both heaters and air-conditioners will heat or cool a tent but not as effectively as being indoors. They, too, are expensive but, as we say in this business, nothing is impossible.

Rule 1 for outdoor weddings: Always have a back-up plan for all the events of the day, including the ceremony.

What You'll Need

Another hard fact of life with outdoor weddings is that you have to bring everything you'll need to the outdoors; you must be completely self-sufficient. For example, your caterer doesn't want to find out that she can't use the water in the well for cooking because it hasn't been tested. Depending on the size of your crowd, you might have to rent Port-O-Potties, lighting, tables, linens to go on the tables, markers to guide the guests, a guest book stand, chairs, a valet parking staff (or at least help with traffic control), plus the normal wedding items: food, drink, and music.

You also want to make sure that you have the bug population under control in the area. Have a professional outfit come to the site several weeks before the event to determine what you need to have controlled. Always let the professionals deal with insecticides. Most companies will spray early in the week and then again later, closer to the exact date. Just because you don't see bugs when you're out in the woods doesn't mean they don't see you. It's a pretty scary sight to see your lovely white wedding cake covered with a black trail of ants marching up the side.

Let's Get Physical

Okay, so you still want to have an outdoor wedding. Pay close attention to the physical site. Look for uneven places on the ground. Where will the wedding party enter? Wearing high heels on soft ground is not pleasant and might even ruin your shoes.

The physical placement of your ceremony is extremely important. It helps if you can see the site at the time of day you plan for your wedding. For example, you and your partner do not want to be facing west at 4:00 on a September afternoon—you will be blinded by the sun. Likewise, you don't want your guests facing into the sun, for the same reason. Therefore, check lighting, sunshine, and sun position so you know what you're up against.

If your wedding is at night, then you need to make sure you have sufficient lighting for your guests to safely move around the site. That includes wandering off to the Port-O-Potties (hopefully away from the main site), to traveling to the parking area and walkways in general. You need to be very careful you provide all reasonable lighting possible. That's your responsibility as the host of this once-in-a-lifetime event. You don't want Aunt Tilly to fall and break a leg. That would put a damper on your day, not to mention hers.

This is proof that a wedding can take place anywhere. Notice the rocks in a circle around the wedding party. Also notice that this couple knew they could not be heard above the winds of Mother Nature and brought in a sound system.

(Stephanie Hogue Photography)

My sister opted for an outdoor wedding and was married in our grandmother's garden. We had put the chairs out that morning. It was a beautiful, sunny June day. The ceremony was scheduled for 2:00 in the afternoon. As the guests were escorted to their chairs, you could tell immediately which chairs had picked up the heat of the day. One quick sit, and the guests popped up. Those chairs were hot! Be sure to pay attention to all the little details.

Because you'll have to make up your aisle at your outdoor wedding, try to fashion something that fits with your theme. At a July outdoor wedding held several years ago in a city park, the bride and her father arrived in a horse-drawn carriage as the processional began. She had made an aisle of clusters of balloons to coordinate with her colors, anchored by rocks covered with wrapping paper. The balloons gently blew in the breeze, and as the string quartet broke into "Trumpet Voluntary," the bride stepped out of her carriage and marched radiantly down the aisle to meet her groom. It was a lovely entrance.

You should decide on one focal point for the service so that your guests can focus their attention toward one area. Try for something natural: a grouping of trees, a fountain, or the head of a garden. You're outside, so you don't want to compete with Mother Nature—just enhance her.

Here's a nontraditional site made more beautiful by the flower-covered arch and the aisle posts topped with flowers. Note the path of petals that's been laid to enhance the aisle.

(Stephanie Hogue Photography)

Park It Here, My Dear

As I mentioned earlier, depending on your property and the size of your guest list, parking can be a major problem. Wherever you schedule the outdoor wedding, make doubly sure that you have adequate parking facilities and attendants. What you don't want or need is someone parking sideways and blocking another car, either the next door neighbor's or a guest's. (You're in big trouble if that person turns out to be your neighbor, who wasn't invited.) Valet parking is a great idea, if the logistics can be worked out.

Another solution is to run a shuttle from a local parking lot (for example, a school or a church) to the site. (Make sure that you check with local authorities in case you need a special permit.) Then hire a company to operate a van or bus.

If you're planning an outdoor wedding, make sure that the neighbors know what's taking place. You want to keep on good terms with them.

Teddy's Tips

Valet parking is a wonderful service, and if you have a tight area to put lots of cars, it's a good idea to get help with the parking.

A Different Kind of Train Track

One more thing to think about is your gown. If you're going to be outside, you probably don't want to haul around a gown with a long train on it: It will only get dirty and pick up every available grass clipping, leaf, and bug in the general vicinity. A tea-length gown or a gown without a train might be a better choice.

Tears over Melting Tiers

When choosing your menu for your outdoor wedding, keep in mind that it is going to be outside. You know, among nature—the birds, the bees, the bugs. And the heat. Hire a reputable caterer to guide you to a menu that will hold up under the warm-weather sun. Most caterers have cooling units and stove units to keep items hot or cold. But nothing can keep cold items truly cold, for long periods of time, in a summer heat wave. Rely on your caterer's advice. It could mean the difference between a great honeymoon or food poisoning.

You need to be somewhat of a risk-taker to take on and enjoy an outdoor wedding. If you're someone who likes to feel in control of a situation, I suggest that you stick with a more conservative plan and stay indoors. Outdoor weddings can be beautiful, but they certainly are not for the faint of heart.

Military Weddings

The biggest differences between a military wedding and a civilian wedding are the invitation, the uniformed attendants or the couple, and the arch of swords (or sabers) at the end of the service. Everything else is the same.

The wording on the invitation needs to be written precisely according to standard etiquette, your branch of service, and your rank. Be sure to check with your bridal consultant or the stationery store expert for the correct military wording on your invitations. There are many different correct forms to use.

Bouquet Toss

The tradition of the arch of swords at the end of the wedding started in 1909, when an officer bridegroom and his attendants raised their swords to toast the bride. The idea caught on and has been formalized to be part of military tradition.

Here's what happens at the end of the ceremony: All commissioned officers present form two lines opposite each other outside the church or right inside the foyer. As the couple exits, the head usher commands "Draw swords" (Naval officers) or "Draw sabers" (Army, Air Force, and Marine officers). Then, using their right hands, the officers draw out their swords or sabers to form an arch. The couple passes underneath the arch, and the officers return their swords or sabers to their sheaths.

Dress can be your dress uniform or full-dress uniform, including medals or merely ribbons. Badges also may be worn. Men or women in uniform do not wear flowers, corsages, or boutonnieres.

If the groom is a member or graduate of one of the academies, you may display its flag in the church along with the American flag. One wedding with a military theme that I coordinated used white braid rope for pew markers. The couple had the florist add some greenery, creating a very nice setting. That same rope braiding was used at the reception hall on the stairways and at the entrance. Even the cake was draped with "rope" icing to coordinate with the overall picture.

Victorian Weddings

A Victorian wedding refers to the Victorian period in England when Queen Victoria ruled (1837–1901). It was during her reign that many of the customs we now think of as Victorian were established. A Victorian wedding makes us think of softness, beauty, lace, ribbons, and flowers.

Bouquet Toss

Another Victorian touch for your wedding cake is to have the baker enclose small charms in the top layer of your cake. Attached to the charms are ribbons. Gather your bridesmaids around you, and have them each take a ribbon and pull out one of the charms. According to tradition, the charms will tell the bridesmaid of her future, love, hope, and good luck, as well as who is next to marry and who will be the old maid.

For the bridal gown, shop for a dress that features a high neckline, puffed sleeves, and a form-fitting bodice with a fitted waistline. Several patterns on the market duplicate the Victorian look if you can't find one ready-made.

Bouquets in the Victorian period were small clusters of flowers held together by a silver, ivory, or gold holder called a *Tussy Mussy*. These are making a comeback in the Midwest. Many mothers, instead of having corsages pinned to their dresses, are choosing to carry a Tussy Mussy with their flowers. You can incorporate old pieces of lace and ribbon in the bouquets, and the bridesmaids can wear lace and ribbon in their hair. If their dresses have the appropriate neckline, you could have each brides-maid wear a ribbon with an antique broach pinned on it—that's very Victorian. For pew markers, use long pieces of lace and ribbons interspersed with pink roses and ivy.

Make your centerpieces full and romantic, with roses and lots of baby's breath. One added touch is to sprinkle rose petals around the table. Some florists will give you these petals. They have to pull off the outside petals of roses anyway (they tell me that the outside petals are not of high enough quality), and they just throw them away. This can make a very nice touch.

Teddy's Tips

Finding some books at the library on a particular theme you've cho-sen for your wedding can help, as can searching the Internet (see Chapter 1, "Your First Step Toward the Altar—Getting Started").

Chair bows are another nice touch for Victorian wed-dings. Tie large bows of lace and ribbon with rosebuds and baby's breath to the back of your chairs at the re-ception. If you have a large floral budget, tie bows to all the guest chairs. If you're on a tighter budget, tie bows only to the wedding party's chairs, or maybe every other chair. It's a wonderful sight to enter a re-ception hall and see all the ribbon and flowers accent-ing the table and chairs.

To complete the Victorian look, consider placing a single baby rosebud tied with a thin ribbon at every female guest's place setting.

You can develop any type of wedding theme as much as you want. You might use only a hint of a theme, or you might go all out and make it a truly thematic wedding, from start to finish. The choice is yours.

The Least You Need to Know

➤ Seasonal weddings are a natural idea if you want to give your wedding a theme. You can have some fun picking a date to plan your wedding around.

➤ Outdoor weddings can be beautiful and fun, but they are risky. Always have a back-up plan.

➤ Military weddings differ from civilian weddings only in the way in which the invitations are worded, the presence of uniformed attendants, and the arch of swords or sabers.

➤ Victorian weddings can be wonderfully romantic with the addition of lace, flowers, and candles.

Chapter 21

Hey! What Are You Doing This Weekend?

In This Chapter

➤ Learning about weekend weddings

➤ Including activities for your guests

➤ Going over some practical tips

➤ Understanding the do's and don'ts of weekend wedding planning

---

Earlier, I talked about an important fact concerning weddings of the 2000s: The boy next door seldom marries the girl next door. Gone are the days when childhood sweethearts grew up and married each other. We are a very scattered society. Travel is quick, efficient, and relatively inexpensive. In many aspects, our world has gotten smaller. You graduate from high school and move out into the real world—often far from your hometown. That world may include college, vocational school, the military, or the work force. Whatever a new environment brings, it's likely to offer you an opportunity to meet people from other parts of the country or even other parts of the world.

As you move out into the world, it's very possible that one of the people you meet will become your partner, and he or she also might live far from his or her family. Bringing that family across the country (or from halfway around the world) to meet with your family and help the two of you celebrate your union can be the springboard to a wonderful, fun-filled, romantic, and relaxing weekend wedding.

What Is a Weekend Wedding?

A *weekend wedding* is a wedding that offers your guests additional activities throughout the weekend beyond the normal wedding festivities. Instead of attending only the wedding and the reception, your wedding guests, often coming from all over the country, can choose to participate in several preplanned functions. The wedding and reception are the highlights of the activities, but you can plan other outings to help guests put aside their hectic schedules for a little while and provide them with a mini-vacation. It's a chance to meet new friends, a chance for your two families to do some bonding, and a chance for your friends and family to spend some quality time together—and with you.

Nuptial Notes

A **weekend wedding** is one that offers your guests additional activities throughout the weekend beyond the normal wedding festivities of ceremony and reception.

Weekend weddings have been around for hundreds of years. In ancient times, the Romans and Greeks celebrated weddings with very elaborate feasts and parties that lasted for several days. During the Middle Ages, the wedding festivities were often days—and sometimes weeks—long. These events were related to our modern fairs or carnivals and included storytellers, dancers, jugglers, various foods, musicians, and, of course, in King Arthur's time, jousting tournaments. Even in the American colonies, people brought family and friends from far and near to help celebrate in a wedding feast that lasted for several days. So, while the term weekend wedding might be relatively new, the idea certainly is not.

As I mentioned earlier, the weekend wedding is becoming increasingly popular because we are such a scattered society. Many couples have been on their own for quite a while before they marry, so they choose to make their wedding celebration a longer and more elaborate event, bringing together the people from all parts of their respective lives. Couples want their guests (the people most special to them) to get to know each other, to build memories, and to help make their wedding truly memorable.

Many times, the weekend wedding can bring a family back to an area where there is common ground. The University of Notre Dame in South Bend, Indiana, for example, houses a gorgeous cathedral where couples who are alumni may be married. Cyndi Basker of Celebrated Events in South Bend specializes in weekend weddings there and provided much of the research for this chapter. The couples she works with come from all over the country to be married in the cathedral at Notre Dame.

Other colleges and universities have couples return to be married in their facilities. St. Mary-of-the-Woods, a women's college in West Terre Haute, Indiana, also permits alumni to be married in its beautiful church. I've worked with several couples who have brought their guests to St. Mary's for their wedding day, and we've added activities in the area to fill out the weekend.

Coming back to a place that holds special memories is not the only reason for a weekend wedding. This kind of wedding also offers the couple the opportunity to include many people in many different activities and to make the wedding a truly memorable event.

Guest Activities

Your guest activities for a weekend wedding can be as unique as the two of you and the location you have chosen. You can arrange those activities around a theme or a time of the year. You should plan for a variety of activities—enough so that guests feel special, but not so many that they become physically exhausted. All guests are asked to participate in the activities, except for those requiring specific invitations (the rehearsal), and they may or may not choose to take part.

Here's a sample weekend format to give you some ideas and to get your creative juices flowing.

Thursday, September 5
(for guests arriving early)

6:00–10:00 A.M.	Continental breakfast in lobby
11:00 A.M.–4:00 P.M.	Shopping in the new mall (bus will transport to and from hotel)
7:00 P.M.	Notre Dame baseball practice at the new stadium
8:00 P.M.	Informal gathering at Coaches Bar
Late night	Hotel hospitality suite—may include snacks, drinks, and board games

Friday, September 6

6:00–10:00 A.M.	Continental breakfast in lobby
9:00 A.M.	Golf tournament (see Jim to sign up)
10:30–11:45 A.M.	Campus tour—main circle
6:00–7:00 P.M.	Rehearsal (wedding party)
7:00–7:30 P.M.	Musical ceremony at the Grotto
7:45–11:00 P.M.	Rehearsal dinner at The Commons
Late night	Hotel hospitality suite

continues

---

continued

Saturday, September 7

7:00–11:00 A.M.	Continental breakfast in lobby
8:30–9:45 A.M.	Campus tour—main circle
11:00 A.M.–2:00 P.M.	Notre Dame vs. Michigan football game party in hospitality suite
3:00–11:30 P.M.	Wedding and dinner reception
Late night	Hotel hospitality suite

Sunday, September 8

7:00–11:00 A.M.	Continental breakfast in lobby
8:45 A.M.	Mass in the Crown Room

The preceding example shows activities for the weekend wedding in which the hotel is the focal point for most guests. This is also an example of bringing the wedding guests to a point of interest other than the hometown location. In this case, the couple chose to bring everyone to the campus of Notre Dame.

This next example involves guests more with family, friends, and hometown activities.

Friday, October 8

10:00 A.M.	Van picks up guests at airport and delivers them to hotel and guest houses.
4:00 P.M.	Hospitality time for guests at Aunt Helen's home. Those guests arriving may pick up their welcome packages and get the agenda for the weekend there.
7:00–8:00 P.M.	Rehearsal at St. Stephen's Church (wedding party).
8:30–11:00 P.M.	Rehearsal dinner at the River House.

Saturday, October 9

10:00 A.M.	Brunch for all at Brown's Restaurant (Julia Miller, host).
1:00 P.M.	Tour of the art museum or historical society (see John for details).

5:00 P.M.	Wedding at St. Stephen's Church. Childcare is available at hotel (see John for details).
6:30 P.M.	Wedding reception, dinner, and dancing at St. Mary's.

Sunday, October 10

11:00 A.M.	Brunch at Uncle Fred and Aunt Margaret's home.
2:00 P.M.	Tennis and golf at the country club—games for the children included.
5:00 P.M.	Picnic at the park (Jane and Jim O'Shea, hosts).
9:00 P.M.	Fireworks display.

Monday, October 11

9:00 A.M.	Continental breakfast at Jane and Bob's home.
After 11:00 A.M.	Guests depart.

This sample showed more local family members involved. With this type of weekend wedding, either the bride or the groom or their parents probably lives in the area.

Depending on where and what time of year your weekend wedding will be held, here are some other ideas you could incorporate:

➤ Organize a golf outing. This is very popular with both sexes. Include a breakfast or lunch, and you have a great way to spend some quality time with folks.

➤ Set up a softball game—maybe a tournament.

➤ Take a trip to the local zoo.

➤ Tour a historical district.

➤ Visit museums, including children's museums.

➤ Take shopping trips to malls or unique or quaint areas.

➤ Spend a day at a spa; treat your wedding party to the works: a manicure, pedicure, and body massage.

➤ Have a picnic or barbecue in a park or backyard.

➤ Rent a bowling alley.

➤ Go see a play.

➤ Have a scavenger hunt through the city with prizes.

Practical Tips

Whatever place you choose to bring you wedding guests for your weekend wedding, be sure to do your homework. Because you're including more activities, you'll need to do more research and get more help than if you were planning just one day.

You can get help from various sources, including family and friends. If you're having a weekend wedding in a distant city, however, you might want to consider hiring a bridal consultant from that locale to work with you on the planning. This can save you time, money, and heartache.

Teddy's Tips

Be sure to check with the local chamber of commerce for other events scheduled for the weekend. If you can stay away from busy times in your chosen city, you'll be better off.

Cyndi Basker, of Celebrated Events, offers some suggestions for early planning: "When choosing your date for the weekend wedding, it is very important to check with the local chamber of commerce about other events that may be taking place on the weekend you have chosen."

Are there major trade shows in town? Is there a big sporting event? What about a festival or a convention? "It will be impossible to book hotel rooms, and navigation around the city will be difficult for your guests if there are other major functions going on," says Cyndi. "Weddings on busy weekends will turn out to be a frustrating experience for your out-of-town guests who are not familiar with your city."

Booking a Hotel for a Weekend Wedding

After you have decided on a weekend and have checked out the date with the local chamber of commerce to make sure it doesn't conflict with another major event, your next step is to find a good hotel. Depending on your circumstances, this can be the gathering place for the majority of your guests.

When choosing the hotel, there are several items to consider. Is the hotel easily accessible to the church and the reception? If the hotel offers a ballroom, will it accommodate your reception? That makes things extremely easy for guests: They just walk up to their room following the reception. Not many states have drinking and walking laws.

Choose a hotel with as many amenities as possible. Does it have an indoor pool? A sauna or whirlpool? Tennis courts, work-out rooms? Some hotels in downtown areas offer shops with a distinctive flare. Does the hotel have shuttle service from the airport? This is a big point if you have many guests arriving by plane. Will the hotel provide a shuttle from the hotel to the local mall? Will the hotel help you offer a hospitality room for your guests? Many times, you may have to rent a room for this, but it's a nice gesture. Can you bring your own snacks to the hospitality room, or are you required to use the hotel's food service?

How wedding-friendly is the hotel? Cyndi explains that it's very important that the hotel you choose for your wedding weekend have a good attitude. How much is the staff willing to go above and beyond the call of duty? For example, say you have 75 rooms reserved at the hotel for your guests. When each guest or couple registers at the front desk, they are to receive a balloon bouquet with the weekend agenda tied to it. Will the hotel instruct its front staff to make sure to present the balloons to your guests? Cyndi stresses that the front staff needs to be helpful and friendly, and to make all your guests feel welcome. After all, the staff is probably the first contact your guests have with your weekend wedding.

Ask the hotel about reduced rates for large blocks of rooms. Many hotels will discount your room costs if you book a large number of rooms at once. Does the hotel have good banquet facilities? Is the food well rated? Your guests could be eating here quite a bit over the weekend, and you want their tummies to be happy.

Finally, what's the overall appearance of the hotel? Is it well kept? Does it have a good reputation in the area? Is the manager accessible, and does he answer your questions fully and in a timely manner? There's nothing worse than being put on hold for days while waiting for an answer to a seemingly simple question.

Teddy's Tips

After meeting with the hotel manager, if you detect a bad attitude or are treated poorly, see what other facilities you can find in your area. With a weekend wedding in which the hotel is a primary focal point, you need the hotel's full cooperation.

Travel Advice

With many of your guests arriving from various parts of the country and by all modes of transportation, getting good information to them early on will help alleviate all types of problems.

Make sure that you investigate discounts on travel for a number of guests coming from the same locale. Often, your bridal consultant or travel agent can negotiate discounted airfare. Be sure to ask.

Let guests know the basics of your weekend plans well in advance. You don't have to send them an entire agenda with times and places, but sending them the information that, yes, you are getting married on July 5, in Madison, Wisconsin, will give them the opportunity to plan around that time. (See Chapter 15, "Extra! Extra! Read All About It!" for newsletter and "save the date" ideas.) Maybe guests were thinking of taking a vacation later in the summer. By receiving early information, they might be able to include your wedding in their vacation plans.

Make sure you have shuttle transportation or vans and/or cars lined up to pick up your guests as they arrive. You should know their travel plans so that you can get all those details coordinated in advance.

Make sure all your guests have a map of the area clearly marked with the sites where activities will take place. Also, make sure the map clearly shows one-way streets or any construction that might be going on during that time.

Consider how guests will move from event to event. If the majority of your guests arrive by plane or train, they will not have access to cars. What kind of shuttle service can you work out with the hotel or a rental company? Here's where a bus is ideal. It can hold large numbers, and as the old commercial goes, "Take the bus, and leave the driving to us."

Consider walking as a mode of transportation. As long as your guests are not expected to walk vast distances in subzero temperatures while carrying your 14-tier wedding cake, they might find a nice walk to the mall or museum refreshing. Of course, if you have guests with disabilities, you need to make appropriate arrangements for them.

Hear Ye! Hear Ye!

When planning for the weekend wedding (whether you're having it in your home city with family and friends coming in from all over, or whether you've made arrangements for it in another location), there are some do's and don'ts to follow.

Always think of your guests' comfort and enjoyment during the weekend. Make sure you take care of their needs. They may be coming from great distances to help share in one of the most fun, exciting, and romantic times in your life. Here are some additional things to help make everyone's visit more pleasurable:

➤ Get the word out early about the wedding date and location so that guests can begin to think about how they can incorporate your wedding into their plans.

➤ Send a newsletter closer to the wedding date, describing parties, events, weather conditions, hotel information, hosts for parties, and attire for the events.

➤ Update the schedule, and let guests know of major changes.

➤ After the invitations go out, you may, if you need a count for a particular event, send out response cards (postcards will do) to get an idea of the number of guests you're expecting for certain events.

One of the more elaborate weddings I worked on was a weekend wedding with the majority of guests coming in from out of town. In the invitation, a response postcard was included that asked guests when they were arriving, which hotel they were staying at, their choice of entrée for the reception, and if they had any special needs, dietary or otherwise. To this day, I'm not sure why, but the response rate for those cards was 100 percent. Ask any consultant, bride, or mother of the bride today, and they will tell you that generally the response rate on receptions is terrible. As a society, we are often very lax either in our knowledge or in our expression of proper etiquette when it comes to responding to an invitation. Many of us don't know what *RSVP* means, or we choose to ignore it.

➤ Make guests feel welcome when they arrive. Place some kind of welcome package in their hotel rooms. This doesn't have to be fancy or expensive, but it needs to be from you and your partner (or your parents). Your guests have traveled far to help you celebrate this wonderful day. Make them feel that much more special by having some kind of greeting in their rooms.

➤ Leave copies of the wedding weekend agenda at the front desk of the hotel, in the hospitality room, and with both sets of parents. That way, if a guest misplaces an agenda, another one is readily available.

> **Nuptial Notes**
>
> **RSVP** is French for *répondez s'il vous plaît* and means, simply, "please respond." If you see it written on an invitation, it means that you are to call the host or return a response card to indicate whether you can attend the function.

➤ Provide a list of baby-sitters, or have sitter arrangements made for those guests who are bringing small children for the weekend. Some activities the adults will want to participate in but are not children-friendly. Your guests will certainly appreciate your thoughtfulness in finding reliable sitters for the children. Sometimes, hotels can provide names of qualified sitters. If you're in a college town, check with the college's education department for names of students who would be willing to sit.

➤ Think about your guests. Are they the athletic type? Are they sports fans? Do they drink? What kinds of activities would most of them enjoy? Plan your agenda around your guests' likes and dislikes.

➤ Have some of the activities geared toward children. Consider hiring a social director to come in and organize a children's party for the kids while the adults are entertained somewhere else.

➤ Try not to overplan. You want to offer activities to your guests so that they can take part, but they should not feel overwhelmed or as if they're at summer camp. Don't overload the weekend with so many activities that everyone is exhausted by the time the wedding rolls around. Maintain a balance in your agenda.

➤ Remember that the wedding and the reception are the high points of the weekend. Everything else is optional for most of your guests.

Weekend weddings are meant to encompass all the beauty, love, and grace that a one-day wedding holds, plus give your guests more of a feel for celebrating in a variety of ways. Do your homework, stay organized, and plan ahead. You can then relax and enjoy what should be a memorable weekend for everyone involved!

The Least You Need to Know

➤ If you're bringing guests in to a locale where you do not have family, get some professional help with the planning.

➤ When checking on your wedding date, be sure to check with the local chamber of commerce for other events scheduled on that date that might affect hotel room availability, traffic, and so on.

➤ Make sure the hotel where your guests will be staying is wedding-friendly and cooperative.

➤ Do not overplan. Maintain a balance in your weekend agenda. Consider your guests' interests and needs; give them time to rest and relax.

➤ Remember that the wedding and the reception are the highlights of the entire weekend. No other activity should overshadow these two events.

Chapter 22

Mickey and Minnie, Here We Come!—Destination Weddings

In This Chapter

➤ Learning what a destination wedding is

➤ Planning a destination wedding

➤ Covering some practical tips

➤ Discovering some popular sites

In Chapter 21, "Hey! What Are You Doing This Weekend?" I talked about weekend weddings. A destination wedding is very similar to a weekend wedding in format and principle, but the kind of location you choose for the wedding is the primary difference between the two. Like a weekend wedding, a destination wedding should offer fun and relaxation for everyone involved. These weddings also require some extra time and organization to pull off successfully.

What Is a Destination Wedding?

A *destination wedding* takes place somewhere where you might take a vacation. That's probably the biggest difference between a destination wedding and a weekend wedding. While a vacation in South Bend, Indiana, or Iowa City, Iowa, might not be at the top of your list, you definitely would consider a vacation to Disney World in Florida or to the Hawaiian Islands. Think of it this way: With a destination wedding, the majority of activities you can offer your guests are already in place.

For example, let's say you're a big country music fan. What better spot could you find than Nashville, Tennessee, and Opryland to enhance your destination wedding dreams? Nashville is a stately, southern city filled with beautiful plantations, the home of Andrew Jackson (a former U.S. president), and the center of the country music industry. Think of all the activities right at your fingertips! For a weekend wedding in South Bend, Indiana, on the other hand, you would have to plan, coordinate, or organize all the activities you offer your guests. Don't get me wrong—destination weddings still require quite a bit of organization and planning to ensure that all systems are go. With a little help from the staff at the site, however, or with other professional help (this is where a good bridal consultant can be a lifesaver), you can be in for a wonderful and memorable event.

A destination wedding can be as elaborate or as simple as you want, depending upon your budget. Many times, families take extended vacations at resort spots and include the wedding festivities. One bride and groom, who came from opposite sides of the country and met at college, planned their destination wedding so that it would be a vacation for both sets of families. They enjoyed a wonderful seven days of fun and excitement before the big event. After the wedding, the couple left for their honeymoon, and both families stayed on another two days for more fun and more time to get to know each other.

Keep in mind that with destination weddings, your guests are responsible for their own transportation costs and housing expenses. Very rarely would you house them in family homes at a destination wedding unless there were family members in the vicinity.

Nuptial Notes

A **destination wedding** sometimes is referred to as a travel wedding (because you travel to the location) or a honeymoon wedding (because the destination also serves as your honeymoon spot).

How to Plan a Destination Wedding

Now, there are several items to consider when thinking about a destination wedding. Following are the key considerations.

Do Your Research!

If you have an area in mind or have some interest you want to fulfill, start arranging for your destination wedding by doing research. Browse travel magazines to get ideas of where you might want to go. Check out Web sites to see photos and hear others' experiences and reviews. Read all you can about a particular spot before you head for the travel agent. You need to be well-informed on the area so that you can ask intelligent questions. (Remember lecture number 201, "How to Be an Intelligent Wedding Consumer"?)

You can contact tourist boards, the chamber of commerce, and travel agencies in the area for advice. Almost every large city in the country has a tourist board or a tourist information office that you can call to request brochures and resort information.

If you know someone who had a destination wedding, ask for suggestions and recommendations, but be careful you don't compare apples and oranges. Just because they spent time vacationing in the Virgin Islands doesn't mean that the resort they stayed at can pull off a wedding. You need specifics about what the resort you want to use can offer in the way of wedding services.

If you belong to the American Automobile Association (AAA), check with this group for locations and resorts. The organization offers a wealth of information, and it's all free with your membership. Many times, staffers can answer your questions over the phone.

Ol' Mother Nature, Again

Think about the weather conditions where you're hoping to hold your wedding. Maybe a wedding planned for a remote beach in hurricane season isn't such a good idea. A veil blowing gently in the breeze is one thing, but gale-force winds could be overkill. Get some expert advice about the weather at that location at the time of year you're considering.

A Place in Your Heart

When choosing a location, think about a spot that might have some meaning to you. One couple, who met at Hilton Head, South Carolina, and had vacationed there several times during their courtship, couldn't think of a more appropriate spot for their wedding. They contacted the hotel where they had stayed previously and knew exactly which balcony overlooking the beautiful beach they wanted for the backdrop of their wedding. Only their immediate family members were present, but the couple could not have been more pleased. After they returned to their hometown from their honeymoon, they hosted a huge reception, including dinner and dancing, and celebrated with friends and family members who couldn't attend the wedding. During the course of the evening, a video was set up in a separate room off the main ballroom. It played the wedding service continuously during the evening, and guests could wander in and out at their leisure to enjoy. How fun for guests to see the wedding on tape! It made them feel more involved with the reception because they could witness the actual wedding service.

Teddy's Tips

When selecting the hotel or resort for your destination wedding, always read the fine print in the contracts. Trust me, there's a reason it's so small.

Accommodations and Amenities

After you choose a location, you need to select the accommodations you'll use. If you have more specific choices to make, such as choosing a particular Hawaiian or

Caribbean island, then you'll want to do more research to find just the right resort for your wedding. Take into consideration the extras the resort offers, such as which amenities are free and which ones guests have to pay extra for (such as golf, tennis, swimming). You don't want your guests spending big bucks on airfare and hotel accommodations only to find that they have to pay every time they use the pool or ask for a clean towel. Find out those details ahead of time.

Teddy's Tips

Find out the rules and regulations of marrying at the site you've chosen. Rules change from state to state and from island to island. Don't make the reservations until you're sure you can be married there.

Is It Legal?

Just because you have every detail in place and have talked at length with the hotel and the airlines, don't make that first deposit until you're sure you can be married in your chosen spot. Some destinations require a long residency; others require up to a 30-day waiting period after you apply for the license before you can marry there. Take some time now to determine whether your dream location actually can become a reality.

Guest Activities

Unlike the agenda for a weekend wedding, your guest activities are readily available. Because of the locale you've chosen for your destination wedding, planning activities to keep you and your guests busy will not be a chore.

Again, go with the flow. If you're on an island and have great beaches and fishing at your disposal, make that a focal point. Why not have the rehearsal dinner on the beach? Add volleyball and a picnic supper, and your guests can relax, eat, drink, and have fun either enjoying the game or watching the sun set into the ocean.

Let the destination determine what activities you'll have guests involved with; the choices are endless. It's up to you and your groom and just takes a little imagination.

Practical Tips

To meet your dreams of having your wedding and reception on an island paradise or with a castle as a backdrop, you'll need to make sure you have all your bases covered.

Here are some suggestions to help you utilize your resources and still get to the church on time:

➤ Work with the local chamber of commerce or tourist board in the area you've chosen for your wedding.

➤ Hire a bridal consultant from that locale. Many times, the hotels can provide names of local consultants. As I mentioned in Chapter 2, "Wake Me When It's over—Hiring a Bridal Consultant," you also can obtain names of bridal consultants in a particular locale or who specialize in destination weddings by contacting the Association of Bridal Consultants in New Milford, Connecticut, at 860-355-0464. (Ask for Jerry or Eileen, and tell them that Teddy sent you.)

➤ When you talk with the bridal consultant, whether you choose to work with a private company or a staff member at the resort, make sure that you write down all your questions before you make the call. Make good use of both your time and the consultant's time. Include all the items you need to discuss: ceremony site, music, floral arrangements, photography, videography, food, liquor, and the fee for staff. You don't want any surprises 2,000 miles away from home. Get those details in writing now.

➤ Make sure you have the legal requirements for marrying in that locale in writing: waiting periods, residency requirements, and what paperwork you have to bring with you, such as identification, birth certificates, blood test reports, proof of citizenship, passports, and parental consent (in the case of minors). Be sure you know the age requirement for marrying in that particular locale. This fact varies from place to place, so be sure to check. Work out all these kinks ahead of time!

➤ If at all possible, make a trip to the site before the wedding just to be sure that everything is as you want it and that there are no hidden agendas with hotel staff. What you are told and how that statement is interpreted by all parties might not be the same thing. For example, you might be assured that the backdrop for your wedding site is a pure white-sand beach with crystal-clear blue water. The fact that the hotel forgot to mention the oil rigging outfit offshore could be a really big interpretation problem. Sometimes a face-to-face conversation can save you misunderstandings later.

➤ Be sure to send a newsletter to those guests who have indicated that they would like to share in your destination wedding. In the newsletter, include information on airlines, hotels, costs, choices of accommodations, what's available onsite, dress style for the stay, and anything pertaining specifically to that destination. You can enclose a brochure of the hotel or resort in the newsletter to entice those guests even more.

Wedding Woes

Don't forget to include in your overall budget the long-distance telephone calls that pop up frequently as you plan for this wedding. The telephone is probably the cheapest, fastest, and most convenient way to communicate with the resort staff carrying out your plans. If time is short, you also can look into faxing items back and forth or using e-mail.

➤ Make sure that your arrangements are confirmed and that you have everything in writing. Look over contracts very carefully. Read the fine print—no surprises, please.

➤ If you're bringing your wedding gown with you, it must be boxed carefully with sheets of tissue paper between the folds. Think carefully before you decide to check it through with the luggage: Losing your wedding gown two days before the wedding would be a big headache. You might want to put it in a garment bag and hang it on the plane. Linens and silk taffeta are not good fabric choices for travel; stick with cotton, satin, cotton voile, or a silk crepe for the least amount of upkeep. Check with the hotel or resort about pressing or steaming services.

➤ If you aren't bringing your gown, think about renting one onsite, or go with the culture of your locale. Instead of our Americanized wedding gown, go with what the locals wear. Have fun!

Popular Sites

You can consider any resort area that can accommodate a wedding for your destination wedding. Choose the wedding site as you would choose your honeymoon site. What activities are you interested in? What activities would you like for your guests? Is there a fantasy you want fulfilled, such as spending time exploring a castle, snorkeling off the coast of Bali, or deep-sea fishing in the waters of Bermuda? Whatever your fantasy is, see if you can find someplace that fulfills it.

This doesn't have to be a big-time resort, either. If there's a state park or nature area that you find particularly inviting and you can envision yourself surrounded by family and friends on top of a mountain, go for it. Make this your special time, and offer your guests the opportunity to participate with you as you celebrate your wedding.

Disney World

Disney World, in Florida, and Disneyland, in California, have seen a huge jump in weddings performed on their properties. Both facilities now have full-time staff and departments that handle all the arrangements for destination weddings on their premises. In keeping with Disney's general theme, "Fairy Tale Weddings" is the name of the department that handles arrangements for these weddings. Call 1-800-934-7639.

Having been a guest at a destination wedding at Disney World a few years ago, I can say that it did, indeed, have a fairy tale quality about it. The ceremony was held on the lawn in a private area of the hotel. A platform had been erected in the front, and white chairs were set up in rows on either side of an aisle. On the platform were two lovely, large floral arrangements. In the distance, across the lake, we could see the castle. As we entered the site, we were greeted with the music of a string quartet. The fall sun was bright, but not too hot, and the setting was beautiful.

The processional started, and from the side came the minister and the groom with his best man. Down the aisle came the maid of honor and the ring bearer. As we heard "The Wedding March" begin, Cinderella's coach arrived, complete with a footman and six white horses. What a sight to behold! Out stepped the lovely bride, and then she marched down the aisle on the arm of her father.

The ceremony was simple but very sincere. I asked afterward if their minister had come all the way to Florida to perform the service. They replied that, no, he was a local minister who frequently performed weddings at Disney World. We thought he had known the couple for years.

At the conclusion of the service, the couple boarded the coach and was whisked away for the reception. There was something very magical about it.

Hawaii

The islands of the fiftieth state, Hawaii, are perfect for destination weddings. Whether you want the backdrop of Diamond Head or a deserted beach on Maui, Hawaii probably has what you're looking for.

The perfect climate, nearly all year, is one reason this is such a good selection for a destination wedding. The low season is November through April, when there usually is more rain, but in reality, it often only sprinkles. During those months, you can get good prices on lodging. Watch for better airfare prices at that time, too.

> **Teddy's Tips**
>
> A fascinating book on the market now in its eighth edition, *Places* (Hannelore Hahn and Tatiana Stoumen, 1998), might help you find a unique destination for your wedding. The book's subtitle says it all: "A directory of public places for private events and private places for public functions." Check out this book, and let your imagination run wild.

Las Vegas

If you want something totally opposite from the laid-back, relaxed atmosphere of the islands, try Las Vegas. The nightlife never stops; you can see a wonderful show every night, and a wedding chapel greets you at almost every turn.

One nice thing about Las Vegas is that it's relatively inexpensive to stay there if you choose your hotels wisely; room rates and food are especially inexpensive. (That's because they want you to have more money to spend in the casinos.) If you want a destination wedding and you're on a tight budget, give the folks in Las Vegas a call. The City Tourist Office number is 702-892-7575.

Cruise Ships

A cruise ship can be an attractive spot for your destination wedding. Whether your tastes take you south to the Caribbean or north to Alaska, a cruise ship can be a real treat for you and your guests.

Bouquet Toss

The romantic notion of being married by the ship's captain is false. Unless he is a Notary Public or an ordained minister, the captain cannot perform the service. Most couples have the ceremony at dockside—off the ship—and then go aboard and have the reception, followed by days at sea for the honeymoon. (Don't worry—your guests don't go on the honeymoon with you.)

A destination wedding can be fun, romantic, and intimate for all involved. It can be a wonderful vacation idea for guests and a good opportunity for family and friends to get to know one another. Your options are endless and can be as exotic or out of the ordinary as your budget will allow. Whatever destination you choose, just be sure to do your homework, and enjoy!

The Least You Need to Know

➤ Destination weddings offer a vacation atmosphere and many of the activities you might want to schedule for your guests.

➤ Make sure that you check about legal requirements for the marriage license in the locale in which you plan to have your wedding.

➤ Wherever you decide to have your destination wedding, work with a bridal consultant either from that area (an independent consultant or one who works with the resort) or a bridal consultant who specializes in destination weddings. She can be invaluable in helping you achieve the type of wedding you desire.

➤ Try to visit the site before the wedding to make sure it's what you have in mind and to make sure you have accurately communicated your desires to the local staff.

➤ Allow enough time for your guests to plan for a destination wedding; send them informative newsletters to help them prepare.

Part 7

Surviving the Big Event

Well, this is it! The big day is quickly approaching, and you're ready. You've met with countless vendors, looked at dozens of bridal bouquets, leafed through numerous invitation catalogs, and picked out some wonderful favors for your guests to enjoy. This is where all your hard work and dedication is going to pay off. Everything should be in place now. You have a few last-minute details to take care of, and then you just have to get yourself to the church on time.

In this part I'll discuss the importance of the wedding rehearsal and tell you how to prepare for your big day by eating right and getting some sleep. Then I'll walk you through the ceremony, the photography session, and the reception so that you know what to expect. Read this part, and prepare for a day to remember.

Chapter 23

Much Ado About Everything: Prenuptial Preparation

> **In This Chapter**
>
> ➤ Practicing at the wedding rehearsal
>
> ➤ Getting yourself ready for the big day
>
> ➤ Reducing your stress level
>
> ➤ Remembering items to take to the church

I've discussed nearly all the details you need to know to help you prepare for your wedding. Now, you're zeroing in on the big day. Preparation is the name of the game; it has been all along. Now, even more than ever, I want you to prepare just a little bit more as you move right up to the big day!

The Dress Rehearsal

The wedding rehearsal is an important event in the wedding planning process. It's your insurance policy that the members of your wedding cast know their lines, places, cues, what to do, and what not to do come wedding day.

This is Preparation with a capital P. For example, ushering Grandma to the wrong pew does not make for a smooth start to the ceremony. With a little run-through to work out the bugs and fine-tune the mechanics, you should have all your bases covered.

The wedding rehearsal usually occurs the day or evening before the wedding is to take place. Sometimes, the rehearsal doesn't take place the eve of the wedding. Many times, the Jewish rehearsal takes place the morning of the wedding. Plan the rehearsal for whatever time your individual circumstances dictate. Sometimes, with many members of the wedding party arriving from out of town, you can't logistically work in the rehearsal until early on the wedding day.

Practice Makes Perfect

The whole purpose of the wedding rehearsal is to practice what will take place during the ceremony. As in a play rehearsal, the director (officiant or bridal consultant) conducts the rehearsal so that everyone in the cast of characters (wedding party) knows their parts, responsibilities, and duties.

It's best if the musicians are present for the rehearsal. One of the prime functions of the rehearsal is to practice both the processional (when the wedding party enters) and the recessional (when the wedding party exits). If the musicians are not present, it's more difficult for the wedding party to get a feel for rhythm and timing.

I've also found that a rehearsal without music does not provide the true spirit of the dignity you hope to achieve. A wedding should certainly be a dignified event, regardless of whether the ceremony is being held in a church or in your backyard. Wedding parties tend to be louder and more unruly when there's no music at the rehearsal.

Sometimes, however, when you use musicians other than the standard organist or pianist, such as a string quartet or choir, those musicians consider the rehearsal a second performance. In other words, they expect to be paid for attending the rehearsal. If you are hiring performers from an outside source, you also need to take into account that they might have another engagement the night of your rehearsal. In either case, it's a good idea for them to send a representative to determine their placement and to see how many attendants there are so that they can judge how long the processional will be.

Teddy's Tips

If you have a chapel-length veil or a cathedral-length train, you might want to rehearse with a substitute to get a feel for what it will be like on the wedding day. Once a bride puts on the gown and starts dragging around all that extra material, she comes to understand rather quickly how heavy and awkward those appendages can be. With a little preparation and imagination, you can avoid an awkward or embarrassing scene.

There's an old superstition that says a bride is not to participate in the wedding rehearsal. I'm not sure where that came from, but it makes no sense. She's the one who's going to be on stage at the wedding, and it makes all the sense in the world for her to walk through her paces at the rehearsal. An actress would never go on stage for a play without first rehearsing. A football or basketball player would not go into a game without practicing with the team beforehand. The same applies for a wedding. Now, you may or may not repeat your wedding vows to each other. You may just be given a cue line and then leave out the actual vows. Either way, both the bride and the groom should practice at the rehearsal.

I Did Say "Dress Rehearsal"

The rehearsal is a good time to try out any bridal accessories, such as an exceptionally long train or veil, that might require some extra attention or special accommodation during the ceremony. One bride I worked with chose to wear a full-length veil that extended four feet behind her on the floor. She did look radiant floating down the aisle on the arm of her father. Dad, naturally, was feeling rather nervous. When they reached the altar area, instead of stepping back away from the veil, he stepped right on it and pulled it completely off the bride's head. He reached down, rolled up the pile of tulle, and tossed it to his wife in the first pew. Words do not begin to describe the look on the mother's face.

I now use a practice long veil and long train on the bride during the rehearsal, if it's determined that will be a concern. Brides are amazed at how awkward and cumbersome those long veils can be during the wedding; by practicing, it gives them a much better feel for movement and placement.

Whom to Include

Those who should attend the wedding rehearsal include all members of the wedding party, including ushers, the flower girl, the ring bearer, readers, the soloist, musicians, and, of course, the officiant (except in a Jewish wedding). If you're including train bearers or pages, they should attend as well. You also will want your parents present, especially if they have a part in the service. Many times, the mothers will light the family candles at the beginning of the service. If they can practice at the rehearsal, they won't be as nervous during the ceremony.

It's All in Fun

Approach your wedding rehearsal with a relaxed attitude. After coordinating more than 260 weddings, I realize that often this is asking the impossible, but try very hard not to get so upset with the little things that you lose sight of what's taking place. After all, you're dealing with humans, and humans do make mistakes. If mistakes are made at the rehearsal, try to keep it all in perspective. After all, it's just the rehearsal. Barring any national emergency or natural disaster, you will be married by the time your wedding day comes to an end. Don't sweat the small stuff; you will enjoy the whole process if you can just relax.

Who's the Boss Here?

In Chapter 4, "Get Me a Church on Time!" I told you the tale of the clergyman who decided to get back at one bride's mother who had worked against him every step of the way. During the ceremony, in a very public manner, he had the last word and showed her who was in control. Well, the officiant should be in control or in charge of the wedding rehearsal. Some facilities have a wedding director on staff who oversees the rehearsal. If that is the case with your ceremony site, work with that person.

Also, if you've hired a bridal consultant, make sure she knows her role at the rehearsal. Unless she has been asked by the officiant to help out, she should assume a backseat role; she shouldn't run the show.

Over the years, I've found that the best rehearsals are the ones conducted by the person who will perform the wedding service. Whatever circumstances you face, go in with a positive attitude. Try to work out all the ceremony details long before the rehearsal. It does little good for you or the officiant to be deciding reading selections the eve of your wedding. If at all possible, get those items ironed out beforehand.

If the officiant does not take charge of your rehearsal, you could be in for some rough waters. The more in charge the officiant is at the rehearsal, the smoother the wedding ceremony goes.

One bride I worked with was a very take-charge kind of person, and she decided to make it her mission to single-handedly direct her rehearsal. Although she gave it her best, she was quite unorganized. She also insisted that everything be rehearsed to perfection. Halfway through the rehearsal, the officiant, frustrated with the bride's attitude and her constantly saying, "But I want it perfect," threw his hands toward the heavens and walked out. This does not generate a warm and fuzzy feeling. It can be frightening to see the man who is supposed to perform your marriage service in less than 24 hours walk out the front doors of the church. If he walked out at the rehearsal, will he show up for the wedding? Who knows?

When the officiant walked out, the bride burst into tears, threw down the wedding program, and stormed out. Her mother also burst into tears and ran after the bride. None of the wedding party knew whether there would be a wedding the next day. There was, but the tension between the bride and the officiant was thick enough to cut with the proverbial knife.

Remember to have respect for the person who is going to perform your service. Make him your friend, not your enemy. Above all, remember why you're at the rehearsal in the first place. You're here to practice for your marriage service, the day the two of you vow to spend the rest of your lives together. Don't lose track of what's really important.

A Little Pre-Party

A discussion of the wedding rehearsal brings to mind one other little item we should talk about: the bachelor or bachelorette party. Promise me one thing—and don't do this for me (hey, I'm not your mother), do it for yourselves. Do not hold this final fling the night before your wedding. It can be a great time to share with your friends, but the bottom line is that you need to be in good shape for the wedding day. If you've been out too late and partied too much, you might not be in any shape to do anything, much less something as important as getting married. All right, enough from Mother Teddy.

The Bachelor Party

Historically, the bachelor party began as a way the townsmen could help a prospective groom get all the philandering out of his system before he took a wife. Today, the bachelor party is an opportunity for the men in the wedding party to get together for a night on the town, a baseball game, or maybe a sailing trip. One groom who loved to gamble got his guys together for a trip to Las Vegas for a weekend. Although this was a more elaborate event than most bachelor parties, they did have a great time, and it gave them a chance to spend some quality time with each other.

If you're a camping nut, why not take your friends to the woods for a camping trip? Fishing and sitting around a campfire telling jokes can be a relaxing—and relatively inexpensive—way to get away from it all for a while.

Some grooms prefer something less dramatic, maybe a night in their favorite pub with just a few close friends or ringside seats at a prize fight. Whatever strikes your fancy, try to incorporate those ideas into your bachelor party.

The Bachelorette Party

While the men are living it up in a local bar, the women can be doing the same thing with a bachelorette party. One of the neatest bachelorette parties I've ever heard about occurred a few years ago. The maid of honor made up a scavenger hunt for the women in the wedding party. The group divided into several carloads, and each group was given a list of items to find and bring back to the host site within a certain time limit. Of course, there was no alcohol on the road, but a couple bottles of champagne did await the winners. The bride later shared with me how much she had enjoyed the evening. Many of the items for which they were searching were things her groom-to-be would like, such as a deck of cards or a book on old cars.

Teddy's Tips

Keep the "Check-Off List" in this book handy, and use it!

Whatever you decide about pre-wedding parties and your friends, just make sure you play it safe, keep it fun, make sure people know the ground rules. Be sure to hold the party several nights (or weeks, or months) before the wedding as well.

Getting Yourself Ready

Okay, time is marching on. You've made it through the rehearsal in one piece, and you have been the honored guests at a lovely rehearsal dinner. You say good night and head home for some much-needed rest.

I've tried to emphasize throughout this book how important it is for you to be organized. I don't keep repeating that phrase because I have a limited vocabulary. I say this because of all the ways you can help yourself, staying organized and knowing what to do is the key to a successful, stress-free wedding day.

You Are Getting Sleepy

When you come home (or back to the hotel—wherever you're staying the night before your wedding), take a nice, hot, relaxing bath. Now, I'm not a bathtub fan. I much prefer showers, but for this particular event, I think you will find a nice, warm bath very soothing. That's what we're after here. You need to be relaxed so that you can get some much-needed sleep. You've probably been going about 100 miles an hour for the last several months. Now it's time to slow down and savor the day to come.

While you're taking it easy in the tub, try sipping some warm milk (not chocolate) or some herbal tea. Milk can be very soothing to the body and soul, and research has proven that warm milk releases in the body some chemicals that bring on sleep. As you relax in the tub, focus your attention on a peaceful setting: the green hills of a favorite park, a campfire growing dim, or the brilliance of a sunset. Peace, tranquillity, and a sense of calm (use imagery to stimulate that sense)—that's what you're after. Put on some soft music to help set the mood, or listen to a relaxation tape. Maybe the sounds of water or wind gently blowing can soothe your soul. This is "be good to yourself" time. Indulge yourself. Try to block out every possible negative vision you can. You want to be at peace, inside and out.

When you finish with your bath, follow your normal nighttime routine. Get as much sleep as possible. The wedding day will be exhausting. You need a lot of sleep now so that you can feel and look great in the morning. A bride or groom with huge circles under their eyes from lack of sleep is not a pretty sight.

You Are What You Eat

Just as important as enough rest is the right kind of food in your body. As I've mentioned several times in previous chapters, you must keep yourself on track by eating right and getting enough rest. With all the appointments to keep, fittings to schedule, and vendors to call, nourishment is important. Try to avoid fast food.

Even if you're not a breakfast eater, try to be one on your wedding day. Even if it's just a bagel and some juice, get a little something in your tummy. Believe me, depending on the time of your service, there might not be time to eat later, or you might be too nervous. If you do enjoy breakfast, then include in your menu some carbohydrates (for energy), some fruit or juice (for vitamin C), and maybe a little protein (milk, cocoa, eggs, or cheese). If you aren't a heavy breakfast eater, don't change now. The important thing is to get your body revved up for the endurance test of a lifetime.

If your wedding is late in the day, it's a really good idea to bring some snacks to the ceremony site for the wedding party to nibble on. You don't have to provide a meal, just some small sandwiches (without mustard, ketchup, or mayo—don't take a chance on staining your wedding finery) and maybe some pretzels and soft drinks. That way, wedding party members who haven't had a chance to eat can get a bite and not be so famished before the reception begins. Also, if you're serving alcohol at the reception, the snacks help to ensure that your wedding party will not start drinking on empty stomachs.

Making a List—Checking It Twice

By now you should have a check list of what goes to the church with you, what goes to the reception, and what goes on the honeymoon. Just as I keep empathizing to keep yourself organized, keeping a list and adding items to it as you think of them will help keep your stress level down and get you to the church on time and with what you need.

What I suggest to my brides is to find a room in their home where they can keep everything that goes to the wedding (church, reception, or on the honeymoon). As you find something or buy that cute bathing suit you've been wanting, put it in THE room at home. That way, when the time comes to divide up all those items, at least you won't have to go all over the house to find things. Make a box or large bag for items that go to the church with you. Make another box for items that go to the reception. Keep your honeymoon luggage open, with a packing list on top, and as you put something in, you check it off the list. Lots of things will be happening the closer your wedding day nears, and the more you can do now to keep organized, the better off you will be. See "Dressing Offsite" and "Dressing Onsite" sections later in this chapter for more information.

Don't Forget the Decorations!

Remember that sometime early on the day of the wedding you have to think about how to make your reception site look the way you want it to look when the guests start streaming in. If you've made arrangements with the florist and bridal consultant to take care of the details, then you're all set. Relax and skip to the next section about getting yourself to the church. If you have to provide the decorations and do the decorating yourself, you'll need to get the help of some reliable relatives and friends.

It's better to have too much time to decorate than not enough. If you think it will take you only two hours to decorate 30 tables, allow three to four hours and play it safe. This is your wedding day, not a marathon. You want to be as relaxed as you can possibly be.

One bride who wanted more than anything to decorate her reception site took on more than she had bargained for. She had already made the centerpieces for the tables, but she couldn't even let her friends and relatives take on the task of setting up the room. No, she wanted to personally oversee every detail. So, she worked and worked and the minutes were ticking off her wedding day clock. At 4:30, and with a 6:30 wedding time, she left the reception site and headed for the ceremony site. She was running late, and the pictures were to start at 5:15.

She wanted to take a shower because she had gotten hot and sweaty working on the decorations. She hopped in the shower, turned on the water, and screamed. Hot, rusty water poured out of the faucet. After she calmed down enough to talk and to understand that she hadn't been burned by the water but instead was just covered in rusty water, she grabbed a towel, her robe, her car keys, and ran to her car. Where she disappeared to, no one will ever know, but she arrived back at the church, rust-free, about 20 minutes later. How she ever got her makeup on, her hair dried and styled, and her gown on and still made it down the aisle on time is anybody's guess.

Moral of the story: Don't push yourself so much on the wedding day that you're literally out of breath as you start down the aisle. Let others help; delegate some responsibilities. This is one day when you should not rush.

Teddy's Tips

Don't forget the marriage license. Most officiants ask that it be brought to the rehearsal.

What to Take to the Church

In the Midwest, at least, it seems that most brides choose to dress at the ceremony site. They don't dress at home and then ride to the church in their gowns. While this practice will vary depending on your part of the country and your own preferences, you still will need to take some items to the church.

Dressing Offsite

If you dress at home or at the hotel, have someone take these personal items to the church or other facility for you: lipstick, pressed powder for touch-ups, breath mints, and tissues. You also have to make sure that someone—a friend, relative, or your bridal consultant—gets these general wedding items to the ceremony site: guest book (if you're using one at the ceremony) and pen, your ceremony programs, any payments that still have to be made to vendors on the day of the wedding (usually the musicians or the limousine company), your unity candle (unless the florist is providing it), and any other decorations that you were to provide.

If at all possible, take some of these items to the rehearsal and leave them there, or give them to your bridal consultant. If you can get some of these items taken care of early on, you'll be able to concentrate on just getting yourself ready and to the church in good fashion.

Dressing Onsite

If you're dressing at the ceremony site, you'll have a little more baggage than the bride who dresses at home. For starters, you need your gown, slip, shoes, hose, veil or headpiece, special undergarments, plus your personal makeup and hair-care items. Your bridal consultant or gown shop may deliver your gown and veil to the dress site.

A particularly nice treat for brides on the wedding day is to have both their makeup or hair done at the ceremony site. Come early in your sweats, and treat yourself to a professional to make you beautiful. This a wonderful addition to the day, and photographers tell me the pictures are just that much better. If you plan to have that done, be sure to allow enough time for it.

Over and over again, I remind the brides I work with to allow plenty of time to dress for the wedding. This is one time in your life that you probably want to go all out in getting yourself ready, and you don't want to be rushed.

Something Old, Something New

Whether you choose to dress at home or at the wedding facility, be sure to include in the bag of tricks you're taking with you the items in the verse: "Something old, something new, something borrowed, something blue, and a lucky penny in your shoe."

"Something old" is used to show a sense of continuity. You can use a family heirloom or carry the family Bible or Prayer Book. I wore my grandmother's onyx-and-diamond ring on my wedding day and carried a hankie from my great-grandmother.

"Something new" equates to hope for an optimistic future. Most brides consider their gown to fit the bill.

"Something borrowed" refers to the old superstition that happiness wears off on others. So, if you borrow something from someone who is happy or from a happily married friend, you're to have a happy future.

For "something blue," brides include a blue item of some kind to bolster the favorite old line, "Those who dress in blue have lovers true." Blue has long been considered the color of fidelity, purity, and love. Brides in Israel wear blue ribbons to denote purity and fidelity. Blue also can be associated with the Virgin Mary. Many brides choose to wear a blue garter and "a penny in your shoe." In England, it's a sixpence; in Canada, a quarter; and in the United States, a penny. These all help ensure a married life with fortune.

Other customs around the world suggest what a bride should carry on her wedding day. Brides in Greece, for example, place a lump of sugar in one of their wedding gloves to give them the sweetness of life. Brides in Belgium embroider their name in a bridal handkerchief that is framed after the ceremony and passed on to other brides in the family.

The Emergency Kit

Ah, the emergency kit. If you've hired a bridal consultant to coordinate the weekend activities, you can skip this section and move on to the next chapter; she should take care of having these items available for you.

If you're braving this adventure on your own, well, take heed. Some items you will need at the ceremony site, just for insurance. Of course, you will not need all these things, but it's a good idea to have them, just in case. My emergency kit grows after each wedding. I take items that fill two very large canvas bags, plus an organizer and a tool kit. It's better to be safe than sorry. When you need a big safety pin to hold up the groom's trousers, you don't want to spend time trying to figure out where (in proximity to the church) you can find such an item.

Start with the basics: sewing kit, scissors, safety pins (various sizes), tissues, masking tape, and a stapler. (You might be surprised at the repairs you can make with masking tape and a stapler.) To that, add a hand towel, a wash cloth, soft drinks/juice/water, saltine crackers, static-cling spray, breath mints or mouthwash, and sanitary supplies (you never know). There are hundreds of other items you can add, and at every wedding I discover another item that would come in handy.

Being prepared, both physically and emotionally, and staying organized are ways to keep you on track for your wedding day. It's time-consuming, but it pays off when you glide down that aisle relatively stress-free and looking wonderful.

Go get 'em!

The Least You Need to Know

➤ The rehearsal is a very important part of the wedding activities. Just as an actress wouldn't go onstage without rehearsing her lines, don't show up for your wedding day unprepared.

➤ It's great if musicians can be at the rehearsal; it helps set the tone and adds dignity to the proceedings.

➤ The person officiating at the wedding should be the person in charge of the rehearsal. Work with your officiant to make the rehearsal go as smoothly as possible.

➤ One of the best ways to help get you ready for your big day is to get enough sleep the night before and eat a good breakfast the morning of the wedding.

➤ Allow plenty of time to dress for your wedding; you do not want to be rushed. Pamper yourself.

➤ Be sure to put together a kit of emergency items to take along to the ceremony site for last-minute crises.

EEEK!!

click!

Honeymoon Suite

Chapter 24

Say Cheese!

In This Chapter
➤ Deciding when to take pictures
➤ Using settings other than the ceremony or reception site
➤ Working with a videographer

As I mentioned in Chapter 14, "Pretty as a Picture—Photographers and Videographers," photography is a vital part of your wedding day activities. When everything is said and done, when the last dance has been danced, and the final crumb of wedding cake has been eaten, you will want some way to hang on to all the wonderful memories you've just created. Photography and videography can help accomplish this.

You want to make good use of your time spent with the photographer or videographer. You need to have the details ironed out before these professionals ever arrive at the church (time, what pictures you want, if there are special shots you want captured, etc.). Aside from that, let the photographer guide you through the special moments of the day that should be captured on film. After all, he's the one with the eye for photographic moments. Allow him some freedom to use his creativity.

When to Take Those Pictures

One of the biggest dilemmas couples face today is how to work in time for the wedding pictures. When I was married, it was considered bad luck and improper for the bride and groom to see each other before the walk down the aisle. I remember being at the church for our wedding. I was in the sanctuary checking the flower arrangements when someone yelled, "The groom is here!" I made a mad dash back to the dressing room, nearly falling over a wastebasket, and for what? To hide from the man I was about to marry? Doesn't seem to make a lot of sense now, does it?

As far as we know, the tradition of keeping the bride and groom apart before the wedding probably developed in the days of arranged marriages. That way, the groom would not see the bride and back out of the wedding if he didn't like what he saw. The question you and your groom have to answer is, "Do we want to see each other before the ceremony?" This is a personal choice, but before you make up your mind, let's talk about available alternatives. Basically, you can choose from three time periods for your wedding photography.

All Before the Wedding

This is probably my first choice of when photos should be taken. Most photographers will tell you that they not only get better pictures when they do everything beforehand, but it also relieves some of the pre-wedding tension. If you do everything before the service, you're more relaxed than if you take the pictures after the service, when you're wondering what's happening at the reception and if everything is okay.

If all the pictures are taken beforehand, you're free to leave the ceremony site along with your guests. Couples tell me they enjoy the wedding and reception so much more because they aren't worried about pictures. Grooms tell me that there's still something very mystical, magical, and romantic about the moment when the organ goes into "Bridal Chorus" and the bride starts her walk down the aisle—and even if they have seen their bride before the ceremony, it's still a very moving moment.

Teddy's Tips

Allow enough time to accomplish whatever photographic style you've chosen. It's always better to allot too much time for this than too little.

One thing I do for my clients who want to take all the pictures beforehand is to find some private time for the couple to see each other in their wedding finery for the first time. The bride gets dressed in her gown and veil while the groom is putting on his tuxedo. I find a private room somewhere at the ceremony site, take the bride to the room, and then bring in the groom. Then I close the door and give them some private time. Some couples use this time to give each other their gifts or cards. I even had one groom who sang to his bride.

I've learned over the years that this private time might be the only quality time the couple will have the entire day until they get in the car to exit the reception. Some couples find this hard to believe, but experience wins out here. Once that ceremony starts, you're on a roll; things don't calm down much until late into the reception. You might want to gaze longingly at your groom as you walk down the aisle, but there's so much else going on that this usually isn't possible. Also, depending on the site, once you start down the aisle and the congregation stands (as they usually do), the groom's view of the bride—and the bride's view of him—is obstructed by the guests (unless, of course, you're both eight feet tall).

If you choose to have all your wedding pictures taken before the service, allow enough time to accomplish this task. Your photographer should give you a timeline for the picture schedule. For example, if you're taking all the pictures beforehand, the photographer might start taking pictures with you and then add your groom. Your parents might be next in line. The photographer will build up the photography session so that she finishes with the entire wedding party. Thus, you don't have lots of people standing around with nothing to do but wait to have their pictures taken.

Try to build in some extra time for just relaxing after the pictures are completed. Posing for pictures is work—don't let anyone tell you differently. If you can build some extra time into the day for just sitting back and maybe even slipping off your wedding attire and resting for a while, it can make all the difference in the world later.

After the Ceremony

You might have to take pictures following the ceremony if you choose not to see each other until after the wedding, or you might be scheduled into a church where there just isn't time to take pictures beforehand. If you're having a Catholic wedding at 6:30 in a church in which Mass is scheduled for 5:00, for example, the only way you can have pictures taken before the ceremony is to go to the church very early in the afternoon and take them at that time.

In most cases, the photographer should be willing to come in and do some candid shots, perhaps in the dressing room or at your home while you're adjusting your veil, or maybe take a picture of you and your mom. The bulk of your photos will be taken after the ceremony, however.

You need full cooperation from your wedding party. Let me repeat that: You need your wedding party, your parents, and anyone you want included in the photos to be cooperative with the photographer. Make sure everyone understands that pictures will be taken immediately following the ceremony and receiving line (if you're having one). One bride did not make that clear, and three of the ushers headed directly for the reception. They had to be called back to the church so that the pictures could be finished.

Teddy's Tips

Trying to finish pictures without the entire wedding party is difficult. Make sure your wedding party knows when and where the pictures will be taken and who's expected to be photographed. Never assume that they know what your plans are.

For pictures after the ceremony, the photographer probably will reverse the strategy and begin with the large group shots, working down to the shots of just the bride and groom. Sometimes, he may photograph the parents first so that they can leave and greet guests at the reception. Pictures taken following the wedding will take some time, but they don't need to take hours.

Before and After

Probably one of the most common ways to work in all the photos you want taken is to take some before and some after the ceremony. If you're determined not to see your partner before the wedding, this is probably the method you will choose for getting all the shots you want.

Teddy's Tips

If you're truly not comfortable, for whatever reason, with seeing each other before the ceremony, do not let anyone—the photographer, your mother, your future mother-in-law, or the bridal consultant—talk you into going against your wishes. This is something that is definitely up to you.

When you have some photographs taken before and others taken afterward, the photographer usually starts with the bride and then adds her parents, maybe the bridesmaids, and then perhaps the grooms-men. Then he'll do the same sort of routine with the groom. In other words, the photographer takes as many pictures as possible without you seeing each other before the ceremony.

Following the ceremony and your receiving line (if you're using one), you can do the larger pictures: the couple with the entire wedding party, the couple with the parents, and so on. It shouldn't take too long if you work with the photographer. She's not a magi-cian, so get your wedding party there on time, let them know what to expect, and smile.

Location, Location, Location

There are other locations besides the ceremony and reception sites to take photos. There may be a site, such as a park or a garden, that is special to you. Maybe there's a mansion whose owners would allow you to come in and have some photos taken. Look around for the unusual. Make those photos unique.

At the Ceremony Site

If your wedding is taking place in a church with an altar area, don't assume that all your pictures have to be taken at the altar. Your photographer is your best judge of what will photograph nicely and what won't. I've learned over the years to trust the professionals' judgment. They have an eye for seeing things that someone without a photography background is likely to overlook. So, while you may insist that you have a picture taken with the pipe organ in the background, if the photographer says it won't work, it's probably because through his camera, it looks as if you have horns coming out of your head. This doesn't mean there aren't other settings within the church or ceremony site that you can use for backdrops.

One church I've worked with has a beautiful cherry staircase leading to the upstairs sanctuary. For weddings, it's usually decorated to coordinate with the flowers in the sanctuary. Many couples have had their pictures taken on that staircase.

Maybe your church has a small chapel that is picturesque. Check ahead of time to see whether the church allows you in other areas. If you get the go-ahead, look around and explore. Look at the outside of your facility. Some of the most majestic wedding photos I've seen are of wedding parties or the couple alone outside with the church as the background.

If the photographer is not familiar with the setting, ask him to meet you there before the wedding day so he can see what he will be working with. He may find a backdrop that will photograph well that you hadn't thought about.

Finding Other Hidden Treasures

Of course, you will want pictures taken at the ceremony site and at the reception, but you might want to consider using some other sites to add some different backdrops to your pictures. There are hundreds of choices out there; use a little imagination.

One bride who dressed at home and whose parents boasted a beautiful garden and yard had some of her formal pictures taken there. It was a lovely May day, not too sunny (outside pictures are best when taken on overcast days so that the subjects of the pictures aren't all squinting), and the photographer was able to get some great pictures.

Maybe you have a garden or a park in your area that you've admired for years, or maybe there's someplace special to you and your groom and you want a photo to remember it by. One couple married in a lovely outdoor ceremony near a lake where they had spent many of their dates fishing. When they had finished the formal pictures, the

Wedding Woes

If you plan to go to different sites for photos, try not to include so many that it creates more stress for you.

Teddy's Tips

Any kind of garden setting or a university campus where you met (providing that the wedding is close by) can add some special background and sentimental meaning to your pictures.

groom turned to the photographer and said, "I want a picture of us by the lake." So, we hopped in a golf cart (that was our mode of transportation) and drove to this se-cluded lake. The fall foliage was at its peak, and the lake was crystal clear. There were even some Canadian geese floating by. The photographer posed the couple in front of the lake and the colorful trees; a goose even cooperated and swam by right on cue. That picture will mean more to that couple than most of the others because the set-ting had special meaning for them.

Don't Forget Anybody!

Most photographers have lists of favorite photo shots a couple might request. Be sure to look over the list and check those photos you want captured as your day unfolds. This will also help keep the photographer on top of the wedding photo scene. He needs to be in charge at this time. Too many requests from family or you at the last minute can eat up time—very precious time—on your wedding day. Should you have a large and extended family or if you have special people you want included in those pictures, then your photographer needs a list of those people. Unless he is familiar with your family, he will need help getting those members rounded up. This can be a real chore, especially if the numbers are large. You might ask a family member to help the photographer locate those family members whose photo you want. He should also have a schedule of events or agenda of the reception so he can capture those "Kodak moments" for you.

Your wedding pictures are meant to last a lifetime. When everything is over, they are what you have left to remember this special time. Work with the photographer to help capture the very essence of your day.

Teddy's Tips

If your videotape won't be edit-ed, you probably will have shots of the photographer on the tape. Because it has not been edited, what you see is what you get.

Adding Videography

In Chapter 14, I talked about adding videography to help capture your wedding memories. Videotaping your wedding and reception is a great way to make sure you don't miss any of the day's events. A good videographer can capture on a single frame what a still photographer cannot.

When you decide to add video to your wedding day, make sure that the videographer and photographer are willing to work with each other. Sometimes this is a difficult task. Both are concerned with their own work (and should be), but they need to cooperate with each other to help give you the best possible coverage of your wedding. If they are professionals, there should be no problem. They are there to do two entirely different things: one to take photographs, one to get on film the events as they unfold. What you don't want to see when you get your pictures back is a shot of the videographer holding his camera. Actually, you don't want to see the videographer or the photographer on film at all.

Most video companies will send a representative, if not the camera crew, to the ceremony site during the rehearsal to check out placement and entrances so that they can set up the equipment to get the best vantage point possible. They also will want to talk with the officiant to find out what's acceptable and what's not. Although you want them to have a good vantage point, you might not want them to be too visible to the guests (or block their view). After all, this is a wedding ceremony, not a TV production. You should be able to have a good tape of your ceremony with two cameras. Always be sure to go over the day's agenda (or your bridal consultant can do this) so that the special things you want taped are done and not overlooked.

One video company a bride hired came to tape the ceremony at the church with not one, not two, but five cameras. I kept waiting for Dan Rather to appear at any moment. There were wires and tape all over the floor. When they went to plug their microphone into the church system, the minister suggested that it was not a good idea. The church had some problems with the system, and he didn't want anything to go wrong during the ceremony. The videographer assured the minister that everything would be fine. Famous last words. In the middle of the ceremony, a hard rock station blasted throughout the church sanctuary. Needless to say, the couple was very embarrassed and upset that this happened during their ceremony. The bottom line here is to try not to turn your ceremony or reception into someone's electronics extravaganza.

The Least You Need to Know

➤ Pictures can be taken at different stages and different time periods during the wedding day. Make a decision early about when to have the photos taken.

➤ Work with the photographer to make sure you have plenty of time to complete all your pictures. Let members of your wedding party know when photographs will be taken, and ask them to be on time and to work with the photographer.

➤ Look around the ceremony facility and see if you can find some unique backdrops to use for your wedding photographs.

➤ Consider using sites other than your ceremony facility, such as a park, a garden, or someplace special to one or both of you. Just make sure it doesn't turn your already busy day into a hectic outing.

Chapter 25

Let the Party Begin!

In This Chapter

➤ Planning your reception agenda: when to do what

➤ Handling gifts at the reception

➤ Implementing security

➤ Making your grand exit

You're done with the formalities at the church, and you're feeling somewhat more relaxed. The religious and legal portions of the day are over. Now, prepare to be the guests of honor at one of the greatest parties you've ever attended. Whether you're having a small, intimate celebration with only family and a few close friends, or the party of the century with dinner and dancing until dawn, you and your partner want to enjoy it. Let others do the worrying for now. You want to concentrate on your new spouse and your friends and family who have come from all over to share in this day. And the best way to do that is to have certain things decided ahead of time, and to make all who need to know aware of the schedule.

Activities to Include

What happens when you arrive at the reception? Should there be some kind of order to the events? Can you just mingle and do things as the spirit moves you? The answers are both yes and no.

Remember that this is your reception. The agenda needs to be of your choosing, not because Cousin Sarah says that a reception is supposed to include this and that.

Discuss your options and what you want to see happen at the reception. For example, do you want your guests to be welcomed with a glass of champagne? When is the best man going to make his toast? Do you want to throw a bouquet and garter? Do you want a rigid dance order that specifies who dances with whom and when? Setting an agenda helps determine how the activities will flow.

Teddy's Tips

Here is another great opportunity to make a relative or close friend feel very special. Instead of relying on an MC, a DJ, or a band leader, why not have someone you know (and who knows the guests and can pronounce their names!) handle the introductions. Obviously, it should be someone who can stand up in front of a crowd and speak without tripping over his tongue!

Call it whatever you like, but even at an informal, family-only reception, there should be some kind of an agenda. You need an idea of what events are to take place and an approximate time of when each should happen. For your agenda to be carried out, you need someone to help move the events along. This is another place where a bridal consultant with experience can be invaluable.

A Big Hand for Mr. and Mrs. ...

Many couples want to be introduced as they arrive at the reception. This can be accomplished by working with your band or DJ. Ask them to do the honors if you aren't using a master of ceremonies (MC) for the evening. Most are more than happy to assist. Consider whether you want your entire wedding party to be announced or just you, the couple. Also, be sure that each individual or couple knows where to move after the introduction. Decide whether you want them to walk to the head table or directly to the buffet line. The type of food you're serving for the reception will dictate some of these decisions.

Bouquet Toss

The term **toasting** dates back to the sixteenth century. Those attending a function placed a spice-laden crouton in the bottom of a wine glass. This was either for flavor or nourishment—who knows? Anyway, the last person to drink from the glass and find the toast not only claimed it, but was also given good wishes.

Usually, ushers/groomsmen are introduced first with the bridesmaids they walked with at the ceremony. Then the children attendants are introduced (if they're old enough to participate in this; otherwise, they can be acknowledged at the table where they're seated with their families). The best man and maid of honor are introduced next, followed by the new couple (that's you).

You've been introduced, and you're famished; get something to eat. Your guests can wait for a little while, and you should be able to enjoy this meal. Put everything else on the back burner. If you're having a formal seated dinner, this will not be a problem. Guests also will be seated and waiting to be served.

Raise Your Glasses

When you're finished eating, you might want to schedule in a toast or two. Traditionally, the best man offers the first toast of the evening. He stands, gets the guests' attention, and makes a toast to the two of you. The toast should be simple and sincere, and he might choose to share a funny (and tasteful) story. The groom then should thank him and offer a toast to the new bride. After that, it's an open floor (anyone can offer a toast or it can stop there).

When a toast is proposed, all should rise—except the person or persons who are being toasted. In the examples given in the preceding paragraph, both the bride and groom would remain seated for the best man's toast. For the groom's toast, only the bride would be seated.

The Cake Cutting

Following the toast, and depending on what you've decided to do, you can go right into cutting the cake. This is another place you will want formal photographs, so make sure that your photographer knows the order of events.

Your photographer will work with you on where you should stand at the cake table. Follow his guidelines and suggestions so that he can get the best possible photograph. According to tradition, the groom places his hand over the bride's, and together you cut the first slice. The angle from which the photographer wants to shoot and the way your cake has been constructed usually determine where you make the cut for the first slice. Sometimes, the photographer might ask you to pretend to make the first cut from a higher layer so that the angle is better for the photograph. After he has snapped the picture, you then can normally cut the first slice from the back of the bottom layer of the cake.

Have a plate and napkin ready at the table to place the cake on and to wipe sticky fingers. Then take turns feeding each other a small piece of cake. Notice the word *small*. I find it very interesting when a couple gets into a food fight while they are feeding each other the cake. Must be all that wedding tension finally coming out.

Bouquet Toss

As with many of the wedding traditions we still observe today, the cake cutting dates back to ancient times. In ancient Rome, the couple would share a hard biscuit, taking only a bite from it. The wedding officiant would then take the remaining biscuit and crumble it over the heads of the couple. This was thought to bring bounty to the couple, good luck, and many children. Guests at these ancient weddings would rush to the site where the cake had crumbled and try to obtain any leftover crumbs for their own good luck. Over the centuries, this cake crumbling has evolved into modern wedding guests having a piece of cake at the reception or taking a piece home with them.

Sometimes, after the cutting ceremony, the cake is taken into the kitchen to be sliced and served. At one second wedding, however, the bride and groom cut the entire cake while their children served the guests. It was a nice way to involve the children and recognize that so much of a family's life centers around food and serving others.

Cutting a wedding cake is an art—don't let anyone tell you otherwise. If the catering staff is willing to cut the cake for you, by all means, let them. If you don't have any expert assistance available, however, this task becomes the responsibility of your cake server, who might never have attempted this task before; the following diagram may provide some assistance. Be sure to share this information with your server so that she can be prepared for the big day.

Always remove the layer you want to cut. Never cut a layer while it's on top of another layer. About two inches from the outside of the cake, make a circular cut all the way around the cake. Then from the outside into the cut, slice pieces off. Repeat this process, moving in two inches at a time, all the way to the center of the cake.

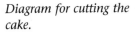

Diagram for cutting the cake.

Front

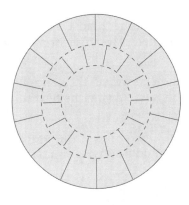

Looking Down

Get Your Dancing Cards Ready

If your reception includes dancing, the dancing can begin following the cake ceremony. Your groom is the first person you dance with at the reception, and some couples choose a favorite song for that first dance. The bride and groom can dance the entire first dance, or the bride's father can cut in and finish that first dance with his daughter. Some brides request the first dance with their groom and the entire second dance with their father. A popular song for the dance with dad is "Daddy's Little Girl." (Check with your local music store for sheet music if the band or DJ doesn't have it.)

Once you have the first dance or two out of the way, it's time to let loose and get the party moving. This is where the homework you did before you chose your DJ or band should pay off. If your dance floor is filled with dancers most of the night, you get an A for all your advance work.

Wedding Woes

Don't make the dancing segment of the wedding so complicated that the cast needs cue cards to tell who's dancing with whom and to what song. I normally recommend two or three special dances.

It's a Toss Up

Later in the reception, if you choose, you can throw the bouquet and garter. Here again, you will need help to make the announcement. Ask for all single women to join the bride on the dance floor. Work with your photographer, too. Let him determine the best placement. It's customary for the bride to turn her back to the single women and, after a countdown, toss the bouquet. Tradition has it that the woman who catches the bouquet will be the next to marry.

Now it's the groom's turn. Instead of using a chair to sit on while the groom removes your garter, why not ask the best man to kneel on one knee so you can sit on his leg? It makes for a great picture and is certainly warmer than a cold chair. Sometimes, the band or DJ provides a drum roll here and then plays "The Stripper" for the actual garter removal.

When the groom has the garter in hand, he moves off the dance floor and, with his back to his single male friends, tosses the garter. Again, the next to marry is the man who catches the garter.

Remember, you don't have to incorporate any of these customs into your reception. After all, this is your wedding, and you should plan your agenda around the things you want to include.

There might be more things you want incorporated into your wedding reception. Perhaps there are some religious customs or prayers you'd like recited (such as the prayers over the wine and bread at a Jewish wedding). Some sororities and fraternities have rituals they perform during the evening. Maybe there's someone you want to honor with a special dance. One father purchased a magnum of champagne at the time of his daughter's birth, with the intention of opening it on her wedding day. He did this, and it was quite a nostalgic moment for the family as he talked about the little girl who had grown into a lovely young woman.

Wedding Woes

Do not have the gift table set up in an outer lobby. There are too many sticky fingers out there, and you want to make it as difficult as possible for a would-be thief to exit with your wedding gifts.

Handling Gifts at the Reception

According to proper wedding etiquette, all wedding gifts should be sent to the bride's home or her parent's home before the wedding. In our busy, hectic society, however, guests sometimes fail to abide by this rule. Often, you have numerous wedding gifts to deal with at the reception. When you talk with the reception site manager, ask to have a table specially set up in the main room for wedding gifts.

Safety First

I hate to have to say this, but your gift table needs to be in a place that is hard to access, such as a distant corner away from any exits. It's much harder to walk clear across the dance floor with gifts than to grab one and go out an exit. Make the table hard to get to and away from, and you'll take home the gifts intended for you.

Assign someone to greet guests and take any gifts they may bring to the reception. This person doesn't need to stand guard over the table all the time—he just needs to be there at the beginning of the reception to help guests. If you anticipate receiving cards containing monetary gifts, have either a basket or a box placed on the table to collect those. If you use a basket, make sure you empty it frequently during the evening. Cards can walk away even more easily than wrapped presents. The best solution here is to have a sealed box that can be opened only by breaking the seal.

It's Not Christmas Morning

You should not open gifts at your wedding reception. The only time when that might be appropriate is at a small, family-only reception where you can do the honors without creating too much hassle. Always have someone record who gave you what so that you can send thank-you notes. Do assign someone to load up your gifts and secure them for you, especially if you're leaving for your honeymoon.

Security

You might think security is a strange subject to discuss in a wedding planning book, but nothing is further from the truth. Weddings can bring out the good, the bad, and the ugly in your guests. Throw in a little too much to drink, and you can have some fireworks that you didn't expect or want.

Most of the larger facilities used for receptions have security guards on the premises who patrol the area just in case they're needed. They're not there to embarrass you or intimidate your guests, but when you need them, you'll be glad they're around. In one case, a rowdy group of groomsmen who had consumed way too much alcohol decided that dancing on top of the tables at the reception would cap off their evening very nicely. The catering manager asked them to get down and tried not to make a scene. It was the end of what had been a very long day. The parents were upset. The couple had already left for their honeymoon. The catering manager tried one last time; when he couldn't get them to move, he called security. Not a pleasant sight, but a needed one. The men were escorted off the property and driven to the hotel where they were staying.

If you're serving alcohol at your reception and your reception facility doesn't provide security, you might want to look into hiring a security guard for the evening.

Designating the Designated Driver

Any discussion of alcohol brings up the topic of watching out for those who have indulged too much. When I first started in this business, I would see people drinking to excess at almost every wedding reception; that usually is no longer the case. It doesn't matter the age of the guests or the age of the couple—fortunately, I haven't been seeing the overindulgence I once saw.

What I do see is a more attentive society with guests taking it upon themselves (and rightly so) to make sure others are sober enough to drive when leaving a reception. I have had couples take car keys from their guests and turn them over only when the driver was someone who had not been drinking. I have had parents book cab companies to come gather guests after a reception and deliver them safely to their homes or hotel. On several occasions, couples have rented buses or trolley cars to transport guests from the reception back to the hotel. There are all kinds of ways for you to make sure that guests from your wedding reception do not leave the reception and drive under the influence of alcohol.

Teddy's Tips

Most reception facilities now require you (the renter) to provide proof of liability insurance that names the facility within the policy. Each facility requires a different amount depending on the event and circumstances, but most do require the extra insurance. You can obtain this coverage as a rider on your homeowner's policy for a 24-hour period, and the cost is minimal. I've personally had to do this for two parties I've hosted, and both times the cost was about $50. Be sure to check with your insurance agent for details, as laws vary from state to state.

The best way to protect yourself from any chance of liability is to make sure that you're working with a licensed liquor agency in your state and that bartenders check the IDs of guests who appear to be underage. It's everyone's responsibility to make sure that each guest who leaves is capable of driving a car. You don't need your wedding day memory to be a terrible auto accident involving one of your wedding guests. Take some time now, and develop a plan for seeing that you have a safe and happy reception.

Childcare

"Childcare?" you ask. "What does this have to do with my wedding?" Well, for openers, if I live to be 100, I will never understand why parents cart their toddlers and babies to weddings and receptions, especially evening weddings. Parents don't enjoy the time spent at the wedding or reception when the baby is along. There's nothing enjoyable about trying to keep a crying baby still during the wedding vows or trying to con Junior into not playing leapfrog on the dance floor with the other two dozen children.

If your guests insist on bringing their children, try to provide some activities that kids will enjoy. Children like to be kept busy; children are basically very busy little people. And I love kids; truly, I do. (Ask my kids. Well, you can ask them now that I've finished writing this edition.) Plan activities for the kids. You can apply the following ideas to both your ceremony and your reception.

➤ If the church or reception facility has a separate room, ask to use that room as the entertainment lounge. Give it a fancy title so the kids think they're getting a great deal.

➤ Maybe rent some cartoons and bring in a VCR and a TV for "movie night." Provide some kid snacks and nonsugared drinks (apple or orange juice).

➤ Have coloring books, crayons, easy-to-read books for the older children, puzzles, trucks or cars, and maybe some blocks.

➤ Check with a local university (early childhood department) or a high school home economics class (family development) to see if you can hire students to come in and work with the children. Notice I said "work with," not "watch"—there is a vast difference between the two.

For one wedding reception, the couple decided that because several children would potentially be at the reception, they would plan something specifically for them. At the beginning of the dancing segment, one of the groomsmen brought out a heart-shaped piñata, and we had all the kids line up and take turns trying to break the piñata. When it finally broke apart, the kids scrambled for the candy and trinkets inside. They were occupied for several hours playing with the trinkets and sampling candy (try to keep the sugar count down). The adult guests enjoyed watching the kids have their own special fun.

Teddy's Tips

It helps to know in advance the ages of any children who might be attending the wedding and reception so that you can plan appropriate supervision and activities. Consider including an additional enclosure card with the invitations you send to those with small children. This card can have blanks for the names and ages of the children, and guests can return them in the same envelope as the reception response card.

House-Sitters

During the final consultation with my clients, I suggest that if they don't have a good security system on their property, they consider hiring a house-sitter to stay at their home during the ceremony and reception. At the very least, you need to make sure the neighbors know what's happening on the wedding weekend, and ask them to watch out for anything or anyone unusual in the area.

Burglars know when weddings are happening—they watch for them. These potential party poopers scan the newspapers for wedding and engagement announcements and marriage license announcements. They know that there will be a lot of movement and a lot of gifts arriving at the home, and that they can count on the family being gone for hours the day of the wedding. Don't give them the opportunity to steal you blind. With a little preparation now, you won't be sorry later.

It's also a good idea to add a rider for your wedding gifts to your insurance policy. This is a short-term policy that you can usually add through your homeowner's or renter's insurance policy. It doesn't cost much, and it can save you thousands of dollars if you happen to be unlucky enough to be robbed. This is different from the liability rider I talked about earlier.

Teddy's Tips

Petals, either fresh or dried, are a wonderful alternative to bird-seed. They don't get caught in your clothes and hair, and they smell wonderful. They are natural as well, so you don't have to worry about the environment. Check with your florist.

Bouquet Toss

It was once thought that the couple should leave the reception at some point so that all the guests could stand around and throw rice at them. Rice is now out (it's too easy for someone to slip and fall on it, and it's bad for the birds), that's for sure, but rice has been replaced by birdseed or, better yet, rose petals or bubbles. The showering simply means good luck and, according to legend, also promotes fertility.

Making Your Grand Exit

The time has come, my dears, to make your getaway.

You and your groom need to decide when you want to leave your wedding reception. Most of the couples I work with want to stay for the whole reception. After all, it's a party for you, given in your honor. Most of these couples don't want to miss anything: the fun, the music, the dancing, and talking with friends they've not seen for months. So, if that's what you'd like to do, go for it.

But let's say you do want to leave earlier than most of your guests. Maybe you have a plane to catch or you just want to find some time for yourselves. If you're changing clothes at the reception, then you need to do that before you leave. It will be easier not to travel in a long gown, complete with train. Besides, you can leave your gown with your mom or a good friend to be taken to the cleaners. (Yes, it will need to be cleaned and preserved after your wedding.)

After you've both changed clothes and gathered the items you need to take with you (hopefully your luggage for the honeymoon will already be in the car), it's time to say goodbye to your folks. Now, most times, moms and dads at this stage of the game are glad things have gone well. They're happy, they're sad, they're tired, and they love you. Give your parents a hug; thank them for this wonderful day and for all their support. Do the same with your new parents-in-law. Then, make your exit. If you have petals or birdseed you want guests to toss as your make your mad dash to the waiting car, have one of your bridesmaids gather guests by the exit and pass out the birdseed or petals.

The photographer will want to capture this moment on film. Give her time to get set up and then run—do not walk—to the car and wave goodbye. Now, you're off. You're alone for the first time since earlier that day, or maybe even the previous day. It's now your time to enjoy each other, relax, and have a great honeymoon!

Teddy's Tips

It's best to check with a reputable dry cleaner before your wedding to see about having your gown not only cleaned but also preserved. This is a process in which, after the gown is cleaned, it's packed in an airtight box and sealed. This process will protect your gown for many years from the aging process or bugs.

Wedding Woes

One bride lost a $100 deposit when a guest, not knowing the rules, passed out birdseed to the guests to toss. The church claimed the deposit as a clean-up fee. So, check with facility beforehand!

The Least You Need to Know

➤ It's important to plan a reception agenda so that the reception has a continual flow and so that the photographer can be ready for each activity.

➤ Have the reception manager place a table for gifts in the main room of the reception, and ask a friend to direct guests bearing presents to this table.

➤ Check with the reception manager about having security available during the festivities. It's good to have some expert assistance if guests become rowdy or out of control.

➤ Check into hiring a house-sitter for the periods during the wedding weekend when you will be gone for an extended time. Also check into purchasing a short-term rider to your homeowner's or renter's insurance policy to protect the value of your wedding gifts in case you're burglarized.

Part 8

Tales from the Altar

How do brides and grooms ever survive this thing called a wedding? How do they manage to enjoy the day? What would they change if they could? The couples in Chapter 28 have some stories to tell; they might have some advice that can help you. Read on for some solid suggestions on how you can survive the big event!

Part 8 also reveals some vendors' and bridal consultants' insights and tips to help get you through the whole process more easily. They, too, have survived many a wedding.

But first, we'll take a look at some popular wedding trends around the country. You'll find out what is currently hot in photography packages, wedding cakes, reception menus, centerpieces, and wedding transportation. You can also get great ideas for your own wedding by seeing what other couples are trying.

Chapter 26

Tips from the Pros—What's Hot, What's Not

In This Chapter

➤ Getting free advice from experienced bridal consultants

➤ Learning what trends are current around the country

➤ Checking out what trends have died on the vine

One of the benefits of belonging to an international trade association is the opportunity to meet people from all over the world who share a common desire: to provide the best possible services and products for wedding clients. Over the years, I've had the pleasure of hearing other professionals speak and the opportunity to share ideas about our profession. I've learned so much from them, and I want to share some of this valuable information with you.

This chapter includes tips and advice from professionals to you, the prospective bride and groom. These wonderful consultants also have included trends they are witnessing in their particular areas of the country. Enjoy this free advice as you read on.

Bridal Consultants

Good bridal consultants have only one thing in mind: helping you enjoy your wedding. Here are some suggestions, new ideas, and advice from some of the best.

Colin Cowie

Colin Cowie, of Colin Cowie Lifestyle, has been designing and producing weddings for 15 years. His business is a full-service event, design, and production company with offices both in New York and Los Angles. The author of four books, Colin's two latest are *Colin Cowie for the Bride: A Guide to Style and Gracious Living,* and *Colin Cowie for the Groom: A Blueprint for a Gentleman's Lifestyle.*

These wonderful books hit on subjects that other authors either leave out or don't know how to write about. Not only is Colin a brilliant producer of some of the most famous weddings in the world, but he is also a humble, kind gentleman and has a wonderful sense of humor. He is a member of the Association of Bridal Consultants, appears on *Oprah,* and is the National Spokesperson and designer for Lenox China.

Here's some advice from Colin:

> There are really no rules in this industry now. (Remember how I talked about the wedding police in Chapter 2, "Wake Me When It's over—Hiring a Bridal Consultant"?) However, style should always prevail in everything we do, not with how we look, but rather how we behave. If you are worried about something you are doing with your wedding at any stage, stop and ask yourself, "Am I offending anyone by doing this?" If the answer is no, then embrace your ideas. Make your wedding unique to you, the couple. (See, I told you!)

> Do not lose sight of what this wedding is all about. If something goes wrong, roll with the punches. The bottom line is that you are marrying someone for the rest of your life, and you shouldn't be concerned with all the details. Embrace your ideas to the fullest, and get your groom involved.

Shelby Tuck-Horton

Shelby Tuck-Horton owns Exquisite Expressions and Events, Inc., in Mitchellville, Maryland, and has been in business 15 years. She is an Accredited Bridal Consultant through the Association of Bridal Consultants. Shelby offers this advice:

> Personalize your wedding to reflect your taste and personal style. Even when planning a traditional wedding, you can incorporate your own unique taste and style, which will make your wedding like no other. Although most people, including family and members of your wedding party, may be happy about your wedding, remember that your wedding is not their priority. Everyone will not always be able to do what you need to have done at the time you designate. Communicate with your wedding party and keep them abreast of plans, schedules, timelines, and deadlines. Two to four newsletters during the planning period is an excellent way to communicate information to the wedding party without inundating them with too much information.

Joyce C. Smith

Joyce C. Smith is president of Weddings Unlimited, Inc., in Cincinnati, Ohio. She is a member of the Association of Bridal Consultants and has an extensive business there. Here's what she has to say:

> *Since many of the guests from both sides come to the wedding from other cities, states, and countries, they need a means to communicate about the happenings for the weekend. A good newsletter, either one they can pick up at the hotel desk or one enclosed with the welcome basket, is essential. Be sure to include a good map, detailed to the sites your guests will be attending. It should also include a note from the bride and groom to their guests.*

Elisa MacKenzie

Elisa MacKenzie is also from the Cincinnati area. She is a professional bridal consultant through the Association of Bridal Consultants and has been in business since 1996. She also belongs to and is active in the International Special Events Society. I met Elisa when she was first starting out, and I saw then her passion for this business. Elisa continues to maintain that passion while watching her business grow. This is her advice:

> *When looking for the professional wedding consultant that is right for you, look for the consultant that is not just a member of a professional organization, but an "active" member of that organization. Is that person involved with her peers? Does she have references within that organization? Is she continuing her education through that organization?*

> *The idea of the perfect wedding is just that, an idea. I tell my brides the goal isn't to be perfect, but to give that impression. Make everything look like, "We did it on purpose." My best example of this was when a florist forgot the aisle candles at the church. By the time the candles could be delivered, guests were already seated. I prepared the candles with their holders in the foyer of the church, lined up the ushers two by two and, just before the ceremony began, told them to pretend they were in front of Buckingham Palace. They walked majestically down the aisle with the candles and placed them in the holders, and everyone thought we had done that on purpose.*

Betty Jackson

Betty Jackson owns Friend of the Bride, in Indianapolis, Indiana. She is an Accredited Bridal Consultant through ABC and has been in business six years. Here is her advice:

> *For out-of-town guests, instead of placing information on restaurants and local attractions in the guests' rooms or welcome baskets, make up two or three books of local*

entertainment and restaurants. Place the books in the hospitality suite or other gathering place, perhaps the parents' suite or local home. This will encourage guests to mix and mingle, start some conversations, and even encourage guests to join each other for trips around town. My brides really seem to like it, as do the guests. Guys can mix with other men and do men things; women can do girl things, uninterrupted.

Merry Beth Turpin

Merry Beth Turpin, from Kirkland, Washington, owns Aisle of View. She has been in business since 1989 and has seen everything from the theme wedding to the very traditional.

As the rest of consultants are experiencing, too, Merry Beth has guests coming in from all over the globe. Here are a couple of her tips:

Work very closely with several hotels on blocks of rooms for your guests. Most hotels will give you a block of rooms without cost, up to a certain date. If you do a block of rooms, then it is easy for the hotel to give you a list of guests making reservations under your block. The hotel can also provide arrival and checkout dates, along with how many guests are booked per room.

Another idea is to prepare goodie bags for your guests. Depending on what you have to spend, these can be as simple or as elaborate as you want them to be. Just having something for them when they check in will make them feel special. In Washington state, it's easy to figure out some local items that will easily go into a goodie bag—red delicious apples, Seattle's best coffees, an umbrella, local wine and beer, and so on. It doesn't take much to make the goodie bag special, and it certainly makes the guests feel welcomed.

Karen DeKay

Karen DeKay, owner of KD Productions, Inc., in Daphane, Alabama, is a Master Bridal Consultant through the ABC. She started her business in 1992 and has branched out into television with a talk show, *Wedding Talk with Karen DeKay*. She has been consulted by *Elegant Bride* magazine on several projects as well. Here are some tips Karen offers:

Before purchasing your gown or selecting any other wedding merchants, book your ceremony site and reception location. This will allow you to determine the time of day or evening your wedding will take place. This also sets the tone for the wedding: very formal, formal, semiformal, or garden.

If young children are in the wedding party, you might place small chairs for those children who would rather sit than stand. Have the chairs decorated with chair covers and flowers. Some children behave better if they are seated.

Sue Winner

Sue Winner, of Sue Winner & Associates, Ltd., is located in Atlanta, Georgia. She is a Master Bridal Consultant, has 15 years of experience, and is the author of *The Complete Idiot's Guide to Budgeting for Your Wedding*. Sue has a lot of valuable information to offer, and this advice is really needed in our society.

Thank-you notes can be quite a chore, but your guests want to know that you received their gift, so you will have to get them written in a timely manner. I recommend that the bride separate the card from the gift and write on the back of the card what the gift was. Stack these cards standing up in a small box, with the card from the most recently opened gift in the back of the box. This will make sure the gift you received first is acknowledged first.

As you write the thank-you note for the first card, you can record the gift and that the thank-you note was written in your Wedding Memory album or on the guest list index card. Address the note, stuff it, seal it, and then mail it. Then throw the gift card away. Because this box is easy to keep on your desk, you will not have to worry about missing someone's gifts.

You can expect gifts to begin arriving shortly after your wedding invitations are mailed. Thoughtful guests will send them ahead and not bring them to the wedding. If you make yourself write thank-you notes daily for the gifts you received that day, you will not fall behind—and when you return from you honeymoon, all you will have in front of you will be the few gifts that arrived at the wedding or while you were gone.

Toni DeLisi

Toni DeLisi, of Waldwick, New Jersey, owns Memorable Events, Inc., and has been planning weddings and events for 12 years. She specializes in mansion and tented weddings and is an Accredited Bridal Consultant with ABC. She is also the New Jersey State Coordinator for the Association of Bridal Consultants. She writes:

For couples with a limited budget and a large wedding party, consider having the florist create bouquets that can double as a table centerpiece once formal pictures are completed. Always order an extra boutonniere when placing your floral order. As a special honor to your parents, have the band or DJ play their wedding song during the reception.

Arrange for shuttle transportation from ceremony to reception for those out-of-town guests. Instead of using table numbers for seating assignments, try using something that has meaning to the couple and that your guests can relate to. For example, instead of numbers, use lines from love poems on the table assignment card, and have the poem printed and standing (like a table number) on the table.

Priscilla Vasicek

Priscilla Vasicek, from Ypsilanti, Michigan, has been in the wedding industry since 1990 and is a Master Bridal Consultant through ABC. Her business, Forever Yours Weddings by Priscilla, is booming. She offers this timely advice:

> *Put a number on the back of a respond card corresponding with the number by the guest's name on the guest list. Sometimes guests forget to put their name on the response card when returning it, or their handwriting is illegible. You can refer to your numbered guest list to resolve the problem.*

> *Be sure the bride has at least two people who know how to bustle her gown. Ask the bridal salon to draw a diagram (especially if you aren't using a consultant). This can be a time-consuming event during a time when you want to be out meeting people instead of standing perfectly still while a crowd gathers behind you as you get hooked up. Do not bustle the gown until you reach the reception site; it will only come loose in the transit.*

> *Do not schedule your hair and makeup appointments too close to the time you need to start photos. This can be a huge cause of delays with weddings.*

Jean Picard

Jean Picard, of Ventura, California, owns and operates Jean Picard Wedding Consulting. In business since 1993, she is an Accredited Bridal Consultant and the California State Coordinator for the Association of Bridal Consultants. Her advice is this:

> *Let your first decision be to hire an independent professional wedding consultant so you can benefit from his or her expertise from the very beginning. Then proceed in a logical manner—there is a commonsense order in which to do things. For example, choose your wedding location before you choose your dress. A dress that can live up to a grand ballroom very likely will not work in a simpler setting, and the informal dress that would be perfect in a country garden will not stand up to a magnificent cathedral.*

> *If you are having a significant number of children at your wedding, consider providing childcare and/or entertainment. In one setting, we had caregivers who told stories and showed videos. At a formal evening wedding, a magician entertained the children in an adjoining room. One fun-loving couple occupied the children at their outdoor wedding with a moonbounce. This is a good solution for those couples who can't quite agree on whether to invite children. The one who feels perhaps that the presence of children will detract from the desired formality might not object to having a separate party for young guests; the one who would feel bad about excluding anyone's children can not only include them, but also can do so in a very special way. It's a perfect compromise.*

Christine Young

Christine Young is a Master Bridal Consultant; the owner of The Wedding Directory, a wedding consulting firm; and the editor-in-chief of *A Guide to Massachusetts Reception Sites and Services*. She is located in Rockland, Massachusetts, and been in business since 1988. Her advice follows:

> *Don't over-plan and don't become obsessed with details. A sequence of events is more important than the timing. Everyone wants their wedding day to be perfect, but worrying about the tiniest of details could ruin your day. A wedding should be about moments that are meaningful and fulfilling. Don't try to reproduce a page from a bridal magazine, and do remember to keep your sense of humor!*

> *Give the facility the names and numbers of all your vendors—just in case.*

> *And, never specify that something is "rush" if it is not, because you might find that the word "rush" could considerably increase the price.*

Norma Edelman

Norma Edelman operates The Wedding Casa, in San Diego, California, and has been doing so since 1981. She has done hundreds, if not thousands, of weddings by now and knows her business inside and out. She is a gem! Here is what she has to say:

> *Do not use white runners (aisle cloths). They look awful in the photos. The bride's beautiful gown gets lost on that white cloth. If you're outside (as are most of Norma's weddings), try using a red runner. (How royal.)*

> *Many weddings we do involve two faiths: Catholic and Jewish, or Hindu and Methodist. This is a test for life, and the bride and groom need to choose a ceremony that gives a bow to each tradition and yet a bridge between the two. For example, Jewish and Protestant might choose Unitarian. Each person is free to formulate their own theology and yet can sit side by side in the same congregation without being conflicted.*

> *Weddings and receptions need a beginning but also a great ending. Always plan a time and way to end the event. A great car, prescheduled, arrives and guests gather around it. All are given petals. As the crowd cheers, the bride and groom run the gauntlet into a car with tin cans on the back, champagne inside, and flowers on the dashboard. And their day ends in a blaze of glory.*

Frank Andonoplas

Frank Andonoplas, from Chicago, Illinois, is another Master Bridal Consultant and the Illinois State Coordinator for the Association of Bridal Consultants. I have watched Frank's business grow as he has developed and found his style with couples.

He's an excellent consultant and owns Bridal Consulting/Event Planning by Frank. He offers this tip:

> *Try using an alternative to the standard guest book. Guests can engrave a silver serving tray or sign a matting that will be framed around a wedding picture. Have guests sign their names on loose pages from a book. At the same time, have a photographer take a photo of the couple signing the guest book and then add the photo to the page at a later date. The book is then bound and given to the couple.*

Martha Cook

Martha Cook, from San Diego, California, owns Weddings By Design. She is an Accredited Bridal Consultant and averages 30 to 40 weddings per year. She offers this advice regarding divorced parents:

> *My advice to the couple is that they are no longer and have never been responsible for the actions of their parents. You are responsible for your own attitude and actions. Be kind and gentle, and talk through any issues that you can which involve the wedding. Letters may be the best way to communicate because what you say is in writing for better understanding and can avoid unhappy emotions.*
>
> *Ask them how much togetherness they feel comfortable with. Do let parents and step-parents know where they will sit, stand, and when. Surprises at the rehearsal or on the wedding day result in disaster. If you try to mediate problems but are unsuccessful, move on. You will now have the opportunity to learn from their mistakes and build your own marriage.*
>
> *Your wedding consultant can be invaluable to you when you have difficult family problems. The consultant can explain protocol to the parents and even be the "bad guy" in tough circumstances, taking the emotions from the bride and groom.*

Lois Pearce

Lois Pearce owns Beautiful Occasions in Hamden, Connecticut. She has been helping brides plan wonderful weddings since 1986. She is a Master Bridal Consultant and the Director of Ethnic Diversity of the Association of Bridal Consultants. Read on:

> *When planning your wedding, remember your heritage and your lifestyle. Very often the couple can make the wedding day unique and special for them and their families by incorporating religious or cultural aspects in very subtle ways. Not only are couples multicultural, but interfaith as well. Consider printing a program, which helps explain some of the rituals that may occur so that the guests may all be familiar with what is taking place.*

If you are considering cultural foods for your dinner, print a menu perhaps in the language of the culture, underscored in English—again so that all the guests will be familiar. You want your guests to have a great time. Also have an understanding with your clergy, consultant, and banquet manager so that there will be no misunderstanding. These are the key people who will carry out making the wedding day one to remember. For your favors or the groom's cake, consider some aspect of your lifestyle. Do you golf, ski, skate, travel, or collect items? Use these as ideas to express yourself. Most of all, have fun.

Kay Krober

Kay Krober, from Indianapolis, Indiana, owns Kay Krober Bridal Consultant. She has earned a nice following in the Indianapolis area and has consulted on several very large-scale weddings. One of her weddings was even picked up by *Elegant Bride* magazine. Here are some ideas from Kay:

Often it is difficult to move the guests from the cocktail area to the ballroom for dinner. We have been using a musician to signal the move. At one wedding where the cocktail hour was on the lawn of the country club, we had a bagpiper circulate, then lead the bride and groom, with the guests following, into the club. At another wedding, we had a jazz quartet playing during the cocktail hour around the pool of the bride's home. As we transitioned to the tent for dinner and dancing, the sax player led the bridal party down the petal-strewn path, lined with twinkle lights in the pine trees.

Gayle Labenow

Gayle Labenow, from Palm Beach Gardens, Florida, has been in the wedding industry both in New York City and now in Florida. She is a Master Bridal Consultant and the Director of Corporate Development for the Association of Bridal Consultants. One area of her expertise is tent weddings, and this is her advice:

For a tented wedding or reception, the first question to ask is what is the best time of year. This should be fairly obvious in your area. Know your weather patterns, including heat and cold. This doesn't mean that you can't have a tented wedding in Michigan on New Year's Eve, but it does mean that most likely you'll have to heat the tent to keep guests comfortable. Tents also can be air-conditioned. Both of these items require dollars.

A tent wedding, when properly set up, is never cheaper than having a wedding at a facility. However, there are advantages:

➤ *It begins and ends when you want it to, not when the management wants it to.*

➤ *It's always more intimate.*

➤ *It is definitely one of a kind.*

> ➤ *You can choose any vendor you want because you are not locked in to the management's selected list of suppliers.*

Finally, before proceeding with plans, always bring in an electrician to find out what the amps are from the power source outside the house into the house. Do you need the local power company to provide any temporary or permanent power into the house?

These are some early things to investigate before you decide to go ahead with the plans for a tented wedding.

Mary Jane Miles

Mary Jane Miles owns The Perfect Wedding in Evansville, Indiana. And, indeed, her weddings are almost flawless. She has been treating brides to her creative talents since 1989 and is an active member of the Association of Bridal Consultants. She shares some of these tips:

> *Lately we are having the mothers carry lighted candles in silver candlesticks down the aisle and then place them next to the unity candle on the altar. Another tip for the bride and groom is to be sure to toast their parents at the reception. It's a nice way of publicly saying thank you for all the support during the planning process.*

What's Hot—What's Not

Some of the trends mentioned in this section might give you some ideas that you can incorporate into your plans, or they can let you know if something you want to include is currently "in." As you know by now, this is your wedding, so go with your ideas and make it truly unique to you.

But read on to discover some of the trends in other parts of the country. The trends are listed by region and have been provided by some of the best consultants from around the country.

East-Coast Trends

Christine Young, from Rockland, Massachusetts, says that tiaras are definitely in. Instead of the bouquet toss, brides are making a special presentation to a dear friend or relative. Wedding couples are making donations of extra food to shelters and floral pieces to hospitals and nursing homes. A group shot of *all* the wedding guests, even if the wedding count is more than 200, is something we're seeing more of these days as well.

Items that are not hot include: changing into your going-away outfit, throwing the bouquet or garter, and using guest books and receiving lines.

Lois Pearce, from Hamden, Connecticut, says the East-Coast trends she's seeing include lots of detail. Invitations are layered with custom papers and ribbons, including organza and vellum paper. Flowers seem to be everywhere. Bouquets might be tailored, but the flowers are colorful and are allowed to open, permitting the beauty of the flowers to show. Bands are back, along with the Big Band sound. The charm pull is back as well. This is an Argentinean custom in which the wedding cake is baked with several silver charms inside, with ribbons attached on the outside of the cake. At a given time, either the bridesmaids or friends gather around the cake table, and each woman pulls a ribbon and a charm from the cake. The custom says that the girl who pulls the small ring from the cake will be the next to be wed.

Popular favors include a picture frame that doubles as a place card. Calling cards and chocolate bars, all personalized with the couples names and wedding date, are also favored (no pun intended).

From Maryland, Shelby Tuck-Horton notes these trends:

➤ The use of professional bridal consultants is still very popular, especially for the career-oriented bride and groom.

➤ Brides are choosing bridesmaids dresses that can be worn after the wedding.

➤ Wedding weekends are still popular.

➤ Thematic weddings are popular and can include ethnic customs and traditions. These weddings also help to create weddings reflecting the style and taste of the couple.

➤ Weekday weddings are increasing in popularity.

➤ Dancing is an important element at the reception, and the swing band is back.

➤ Couples are taking dancing lessons for their first dance.

➤ Disposable cameras aren't as popular.

Colin Cowie, of New York and Los Angles, sees a trend toward smaller weddings, making them more intimate. Also, brides are older, more sophisticated, and less like the "princess bride." Grooms are becoming more involved, too, and Colin stresses that having the groom involved in the whole planning process is a plus to the wedding itself. Colin also sees more destination weddings involving more cultural and interracial diversity that sets new trends and rituals.

West-Coast Trends

Norma Edelman, of San Diego, notes that theme weddings are big. She has done several productions, including a "titanic" wedding on an 1880 ferryboat. She says that couples also want to use parts of their lives in the wedding and reception. One bride collected quilts, so Norma draped a quilt over the guest book table so that guests could admire it. Reveal your personality and background on your wedding day.

Jean Picard, of Ventura, California, tells us this:

➤ More couples are recognizing the value of hiring an independent wedding consultant.

➤ Simple elegance is in; froufrou is out.

➤ The full receiving line is out. Usually just the bride and the groom receive guests.

➤ Most couples prefer to have the ceremony and reception at the same location.

➤ Outdoor weddings are very popular (remember this is a California gal talking).

➤ Big Band music is still popular with all age groups.

➤ Served dinners are more popular than buffets.

➤ Half the brides omit the bouquet toss, and most skip the garter toss.

➤ Couples are more comfortable with having uneven bridal parties, as well as bridesmen and groomswomen.

➤ Chair covers and specialty linens are in.

Martha Cook, from San Diego, California, suggests these trends she sees:

➤ Black is out for bridesmaids.

➤ Platinum, sage, champagne, and icy pastels are in.

➤ Wedding gowns have clean, tailored lines. Gone are the beads and mile-long trains.

➤ Rich, traditional classical music is in for ceremonies.

➤ Special lighting is in.

➤ Having mirrors on the tables is out.

➤ Using low centerpieces with flower petals on the table is in.

➤ Cake tables beautifully decorated and lighted are in.

➤ Journalistic style of photography, including video, is in.

Fran Myers, from Albuquerque, New Mexico, tells this: Couples ask for more black-and-white photography, as well as black albums with black pages. She is also finding that couples want alternative locations for their ceremonies because many of them are of different religious backgrounds; rather than requiring either to go to the other side, they want to stay on neutral ground.

Midwestern Trends

Mary Jane Miles, of Evansville, Indiana, says she sees the following trends:

➤ Sophisticated gowns for both the bride and the maids

➤ Hiring a personal trainer six months before the wedding for the perfect body—might not be a bad idea for stress relief, too

➤ Food stations with ethnic foods

➤ Beer and wine only after the cocktail hour

➤ Swing music

➤ Bagpipes used for a variety of musical interludes

Some trends she sees as on the way out are these:

➤ Black bridesmaids gowns

➤ Garter and bouquet toss

➤ Disposable cameras on the tables

Frank Andonoplas, of Chicago, Illinois, gives these trends in the Midwest:

➤ Clients want to leave the traditional banquet hall/hotel and do something different, such as a reception in the Chicago Museum of Art or a historic mansion.

➤ Grazing stations are becoming popular. We use no formal seating, but use interesting themes such as Asian wok stations, carving stations, seafood buffets, mushroom stations, soup stations, and pasta stations. This allows guests to move freely around and enjoy the venue.

➤ Guest count at an average wedding is about 180.

➤ Coffee stations after dinner are big.

➤ Couples are paying a lot of attention to tabletops so that the guests are wowed when they go to dinner. This includes elaborate centerpieces (more low than high), charger plates, menu cards, napkin treatments, and framed table numbers.

➤ September and October are the most popular months to marry.

➤ Groom cakes are on the rise, and this is the perfect place to use some personalization.

➤ Favors are still in.

➤ Lots of candlelight is used.

Priscilla Vasicek, in Ypsilanti, Michigan, notes the following trends:

➤ Aisle runners are not as popular.

➤ String musicians or a harpist are popular for ceremony music or the cocktail hour.

➤ Black-and-white photography is becoming more popular.

➤ Weddings are much more elaborate.

➤ More Friday and Sunday weddings are occurring. This year she had her first Monday wedding.

➤ Trolley cars or motor coaches are being used instead of limos so that everyone can be together.

➤ Bubbles are used when the couple leaves the church or for their first dance.

➤ Menus in beautiful ornate frames are placed on each guest table.

➤ Most popular favors have been the personalized candy bars or truffles in beautiful boxes imprinted with the couple's names and wedding date.

➤ Place cards are the trend for seating guests.

Kay Krober, from Indianapolis, Indiana, offers these trends:

A wonderful trend we have seen in wedding flowers is the use of hand-carried flowers for the mothers. Often, pin-on flowers are not complementary to the lovely dresses they select for the wedding. We have some wonderful Tussie Mussies that come with a little stand. The mother carries the flowers at the ceremony, and then I place the holder at her place at the reception. She then can leave the flowers in the stand to hold the arrangement. It is also a pretty way to mark her place. If the arrangement is made of roses or some other flower that dries well, she can leave it in the holder to dry, and it will make a nice keepsake from the wedding.

Cynthia Basker, of Mishawka, Indiana, notices these trends popping up:

Brides and grooms are more frequently opting out of the traditional receiving line and are greeting their guests table by table during the second half of the dinner hour. The head table is always served first, so they will finish eating first. Rather than spend that extra time watching others finish eating, they are making their way to each table to offer greetings. If they choose to do a receiving line, they are making it the short version with just the couple and both sets of parents.

Platinum, pewter, and tones of silver have become a new neutral. Perhaps it has something to do with the millennium, but it is certainly a popular choice in color for dresses.

The use of vivid color is back. Most of the 1990s was spent in subdued tones of creams and taupes, and blush pinks that are quietly elegant. Now I see the bright vivid colors, such as fuschia, magenta, and deep rose. Along those lines also in floral, I am seeing only one type of flower used for everything—including personal flowers, and ceremony and reception décor. It's really breathtaking. Baby's breath is back, too.

Guest lists are getting smaller, but budgets are remaining the same. The intimacy level of the event is increased dramatically, and there is more room in the budget for the extras that would have been cost-prohibitive with a large guest list.

Finally, I see lots of couples registering online, which helps everyone, near and far.

Southern Trends

Salli Goldstein, of Dallas, Texas, offers these trends in the South:

➤ Bigger, more elaborate weddings

➤ Big Band sounds

➤ Cappuccino bars

➤ Fruit, cheese, and crackers served at the end of the reception

➤ A resurgence of popularity for the groom's cake, mostly in chocolate or cheese-cake

➤ Black tie

Elisa MacKenzie, from Kentucky, sees these trends in her area:

Menu cards are very popular with my brides. It's a great touch and doesn't have to be expensive. The cards can be ordered from your stationer to match the invitation. Many brides choose to make the menu cards themselves. This can be a good project for the groom or the bride's brother, too. Tuck these cards into the napkin at the reception; adding a little touch of lavender or another similar floral piece can add a little something extra without being costly.

Elisa sees mock or fake exits being used to help speed the photography sessions along. The couple exits the church as though they were going on to the reception. Guests shower them with bubbles or petals, and then the limo drives around the block, giving the guests enough time to head for the reception. When the couple returns, they can get right to finishing the pictures while knowing that their guests are enjoying themselves at the reception.

Guest books are taking on new ideas. One of the favorites is the signature portrait. Guests sign their names on a large matting, and the picture is later framed.

Sue Winner, of Atlanta, Georgia, offers this new trend:

> *To forgo paying for extra cleanup after tossing petals or feathers or confetti, I have found streamers that can be tossed at the couple but that are easily picked up for cleanup. They are the size of a tennis ball, and the streamers are attached to the top of the ball.*
>
> *When guests open the cardboard tab and fling the streamers across the bride and groom, the streamers come out, but nothing else. All anyone has to do is to pick up the cardboard containers with streamers attached, and voilà, you have instant cleanup.*

The Least You Need to Know

➤ Trends are moving more toward unique or personalized weddings to you, the couple.

➤ Trends in photography are moving toward the photojournalistic style, with some posed photos thrown in.

➤ Vivid colors, especially in flowers, are more popular.

➤ Theme weddings are growing in popularity.

Chapter 27

Free Advice from Some Experienced Vendors

In This Chapter

➤ Using advice offered by bridal apparel retailers, florists, photographers, travel agents, videographers, caterers, and musicians

➤ Remembering those additional questions to ask your photographer and videographer before you sign on the dotted line

➤ Preserving your bouquet

➤ How to care for your dress before and after the wedding

I don't know where else you can go these days and not have to pay for the advice that follows in this chapter. Several generous vendors have graciously provided some great ideas, tips, and suggestions to help make your wedding planning and your wedding day as trouble-free as possible. Most of these folks have been in their respective businesses for years, and the advice they have to offer is invaluable. In addition, they all love what they do and truly want your wedding to be a special day.

Gowns—Bridal Retail and Designer

As I discussed earlier in this book, the wedding gown and bridesmaids' dresses can be expensive purchases. Read on to find out what advice the Director of Retail Services of the Association of Bridal Consultants and a bridal salon owner have to offer about purchasing your gown. Read also about how to care for the gown before and after the big day.

Mary Kelley, Director of Retail Services, ABC

Mary Kelley, the Association of Bridal Consultants' (ABC) Director of Retail Services, formerly owned a bridal retail salon in the Midwest and offers the following suggestions:

It's important that the bride (and her attendants) be aware prior to shopping for their gowns that the sizing is not the same as ready-to-wear. Bridal sizes run smaller. That means if someone usually wears a size 10, she probably will wear a 12 or 14 in bridal apparel. These garments are made to fit so closely to the body (unlike most ready-to-wear styles) that one size doesn't fit all. If on a manufacturer's size chart a bride has a size 10 bust, size 12 waist, and size 8 hips, the store probably will recommend that she order a size 12 (the largest measurement). A reputable store owner can sleep very well at night knowing that she gave the best possible recommendation if she recommends a size 12 and tells the bride up front that it will fit correctly in the waist, but the bust and hips will have to be altered.

The bride should get involved in choosing the right size so that she feels comfortable with the choice. Brides and bridesmaids should also understand that these gowns are intended to be altered or custom-fitted to each person; they are not custom-made by the manufacturer to a woman's measurements. Inside seams are purposely left raw so that custom-fitting can be done easily. If the bride and bridesmaids are aware of these facts before they go shopping for gowns, they will be much happier with the final outcome.

It's a very good idea for the bride to go in and try on her gown and check it over as soon as it comes into the store. The store has only a certain number of days to return any gown with which there are problems. If the bride doesn't come in until two months after she is notified that her gown has arrived and there's a problem with the gown, she may well be out of luck as far as returning it to the manufacturer for repairs or replacement.

Bridesmaids' gowns take about 8 to 10 weeks for delivery. There is less chance of a bridesmaids' order shipping extremely early because they are less likely to have six or eight different sizes and colors in stock. Bridesmaids also should come in to try on their gowns as soon as they're notified the dresses are in. Five of the six gowns may be perfect, while one may need replacement, but it might not be noticeable

Nuptial Notes

Bustling your gown refers to pulling up your train at the back of the gown so that you can move around more freely at the reception. This is usually accomplished by sewing tiny hooks and eyes or buttons onto the back of the gown at appropriate places. But some gowns look better when bustled from underneath with ribbons that are color-coded so that your bridesmaids can tie them correctly.

until the dress is tried on. Also, if one gown must be returned to the manufacturer, the entire order may have to be sent back to ensure that all gowns are from the same dye lot. It's amazing how "off" one gown can be if it comes from a different dye lot.

Almost all manufacturers charge extra fees for certain changes: larger sizes (over size 18), rush cuts, rush shipping, some phone orders, and some colors. These charges usually are passed along to the consumer as extra charges. They are not charges the shops just invent to make extra money; these are actual charges billed to the shop that they must then pass along to customers.

Ellen Prange, The Bridal Suite

Ellen Prange, from Ashton Bridal and Formal in Huntington, Indiana, says this:

> The biggest help a bride can be to a bridal shop is to not wait so long before ordering her gowns. Bridal wear runs small. Don't be offended if the shop takes measurements and orders a size larger than you wear in ready-to-wear apparel. We must order from each manufacturer's measurement charts, which are all different. Also, don't expect every shop to carry all the dresses you see in the bridal magazines. Sometimes if we don't carry it, we can order it, but not always.

Finally, she urges brides, "Always ask what alterations will cost. Our shop does not charge for alterations, but we are in the minority. Most shops do charge."

Wedding Gown Specialists Association

Former museum curator Sally Lorensen Conant, Ph.D., of Orange Restoration Labs, in Orange, Connecticut, restores vintage gowns to the true color and also cleans and preserves gowns. She is a member of the Wedding Gown Specialists Association. The Association offers the following tips for basic gown care before and after the ceremony.

Before the Wedding:

➤ Be sure your gown is hanging by loops inside the gown that are connected to sturdy side seams, never by fragile shoulder seams that can stretch or sag. If there are no loops, make some with ribbon and attach them with safety pins.

➤ Your gown will hold its shape best if it is stuffed with acid-free tissue. Bust forms, too, can be used to keep the bodice from wrinkling. Layering the folds of the train with tissue and stuffing the bottom of the garment bag with tissue to keep it from pressing against the dress also helps.

➤ If you are flying to your wedding site, carrying the gown in a transparent garment bag attracts very attentive care; flight attendants will store it for you in a forward cabin space.

➤ To remove light wrinkling when you reach your destination, hang your gown in a steam-filled bathroom. Heavier wrinkles are best removed with a hand-held or portable steamer. Some hotels and churches have steamers on hand that you can use. Most cleaners will press your gown for you.

➤ Avoid storing your gown in a plastic bag for any length of time, especially if the bag has a metal zipper, because plastic can emit fumes that yellow the gown. Instead, protect the gown from air and light by wrapping it in an old sheet or a length of unbleached muslin that has been freshly laundered.

➤ For long-term storage before the wedding, use a box to safeguard the gown. Line the box with an old sheet or laundered, unbleached muslin, and use lots of acid-free tissue to buffer the folds as you pack the gown.

During the Wedding:

➤ It's a good idea to know the fabric of your gown. Ask the bridal shop or look inside for the care label. If you spill something on a gown made of polyester or nylons, it's much easier to dab away the stain with water or even a baby wipe for greasy stains such as lipstick. Silk is water-sensitive, and any stain remover will often leave a ring.

➤ You also can try camouflaging spots with something white and relatively harmless, such as baking soda or baby powder.

After the Wedding:

➤ If you plan to keep your dress in the family, look for a cleaner who specializes in wedding gowns and cleans them onsite.

➤ Ask what precautions the specialist takes to protect delicate trims and decorations, how the cleaner guards against latent stains, and what guarantee is given.

➤ Ask to inspect the gown personally (yes, you can do that) before it is put into the container, which should be a pH-neutral or acid-free box lined with fabric or acid-free tissue.

➤ Ask how and where the guarantee may be redeemed, today or 25 years from today.

➤ Avoid storing your gown in the attic or basement, where there are extreme changes in temperature or humidity.

Florists

Flowers add so much to both the ceremony and the reception site: beauty, fragrance, and an aura of romance. It takes a great deal of planning and work by a professional florist with an eye for design to put the full magic of flowers to work. Read on to discover what some experienced florists advise.

Joyce Mills Edelen, Joyce, A Floral Specialist

Joyce Mills Edelen owns Joyce, A Floral Specialist, in White Plains, Maryland. She is an award-winning floral designer and has been in the floral industry for 29 years. Joyce offers this advice to the wedding couple:

> *Interview the florist. You want someone who will listen to your dreams. This includes a reflection of your wishes, your physical size, the wedding style, the season, the time of day, color, and, most of all, your budget.*
>
> *Obtain a photo or sketch of the gown and bridesmaids' dresses. Bring a fabric swatch with you to the interview for color ideas. This information will be very important to the florist so that he or she can offer you the best suggestions on bouquet styles.*
>
> *Select your florist 6 to 12 months in advance so that he or she can reserve the date, time, and location on the calendar. Fine-tune the order in the months ahead, and always review your order one to two months prior to the wedding.*
>
> *The bride and the financially responsible party should go to the first floral consultation (too many people will hinder your decision-making). The consultation should convince and assure the bride that she has made the correct decision and that the floral order is in good hands.*
>
> *The traditional split on expenses is like this: The bride's family is responsible for the largest portion of the order. The groom's portion is usually the rehearsal flowers, the bridal bouquet, the men's boutonnieres (the bride gives the groom his), and the mothers' and grandmothers' corsages.*

Dale Miller, Miller Floral Company

Dale Miller, of Miller Floral Company, in Terre Haute, Indiana, is one of the most creative floral designers I've ever had the pleasure of working with. It must run in the family, because he is the fourth generation of Millers to run the business. With his degree in art, he can create almost anything on paper and turn it into the floral arrangement of your dreams. His floral creations are truly magic. He also offers some great ideas for new and different centerpieces. He has this advice for brides and grooms:

> *Go over some initial ideas with the floral designer to get a feel for his or her creativity. Have the designer show you various pictures and sketches of designs; tell the designer*

what you like and dislike about the pictures so that you can get on the same wave-length for what you want. It's important not to shop for price at this point; there are many florists out there who will always beat the other florist's price.

Shop for quality and the floral shop's ability to create the floral designs of your choice. There are many ways to sense whether the shop will meet your needs and desires: the freshness and style of the designs in the sales cooler, the pictures of past weddings and parties the shop has done, the cleanliness of the sales floor, the courtesy of the staff, and just plain and simple word of mouth.

Be honest with the floral designer in your discussions; tell him or her your concerns about your budget, colors, style, and the feeling you want to convey at your wedding. It's very important that the florist understands these points.

After establishing trust in the floral designer's creativity and ability to listen to your ideas and concerns, reserve your wedding date with him or her. This is important so that the florist does not overbook your day. Some florists require a deposit for this privilege, so be prepared to pay up to 25 percent of the estimate. After you have paid the deposit, you have the right to ask for a copy of your estimate.

There are many ways to save money on your wedding. The classic advice is to use flowers that are in season. This is good advice, but "in season" does not always mean inexpensive. Your florist can advise you of what is in season and in your budget. If you decide on a style of bouquet (nosegay, cascade, crescent, free-form, hand-tie, or arm bouquet) and choose your colors, the floral designer can best tell you what flowers will fit your style, color, and budget.

If you have a favorite flower in mind that's unavailable, ask to incorporate silk flowers into your bouquet. More flowers are becoming available for longer seasons now, partly because of the many countries that are growing flowers for commercial use. A good florist should have a number of different resources to locate the flowers of your choice. Keep in mind, though, that finding flowers that are a little out of season, or using certain flowers at floral holiday times (such as roses near Valentine's Day), may mean you have to pay a premium price. Have the florist give you three different price points for the bouquets for you to choose from (small, medium, and large).

At the reception, keep your main decorations at your head table and the cake table. You can save money here by using some of the flowers from your ceremony at the reception. For example, a low altar arrangement makes a great head table piece. Keep in mind the time it might take to transport these flowers from the ceremony to the reception—you must give the florist or whoever is moving the arrangements time to accomplish this task. You also can have your bridesmaids' bouquets sit on the front edge of the head table for decoration.

Your throw-away bouquet can double as a cake topper. Or, have your florist use loose flowers to decorate your cake rather than intricate arrangements. For centerpieces on the guest tables, gather different interesting vases and containers from yard sales and flea markets, and have your florist fill them with loose bouquets of flowers—no one says that every design has to be the same. Another centerpiece idea can consist of a simple single flower floating in a bowl surrounded by a few votive candles. See if your florist will rent you the bowls and votive cups so that your money goes into the flowers and not the purchase of containers.

Another idea for a centerpiece that will double as gifts for your guests is a centerpiece using varying heights of bud vases arranged on the table to appear as a single unit. The vases can easily be taken apart so that each woman at the table can take home a memento from your wedding.

The key is talking with your florist and telling him or her up front of your budget and style concerns. The florist should be able to design a wedding that meets all your needs.

David Kurio, David Kurio Floral Design

David Kurio owns David Kurio Floral Design in Austin, Texas. He has been in business for 10 years and, from our conversation, obviously loves his business. David offers this to the bride:

> *When a bride calls and books us, we ask her to sit down with some wedding publications and look through those to get a feel for flowers. We ask the bride to find pictures of flower bouquets and displays she both likes and dislikes, and to put those into separate folders. When she comes in for the appointment with those folders, we can look through them and have a better idea of what she has in mind. It saves all of us time. By using this method, we can see something in a publication and pull the same idea from our portfolio. Then we can incorporate the colors and design style with her wedding flowers. We always ask her to bring a sample of the fabric of both the wedding gown and the bridesmaids' dresses and a photograph of the dresses if at all possible.*
>
> *I recommend that brides use a bridal consultant. The consultant can be a real lifesaver, both in terms of saving money and headaches.*

Karen Hopkins, Making Arrangements

Karen Hopkins, of Making Arrangements, a floral company in Sammamish, Washington, has been in business for more than 15 years. She is a member of the Association of Bridal Consultants and has some very practical advice on trends she sees coming as we move into a new century.

➤ Because couples have been liberated during the past couple decades by being encouraged to plan their wedding around their individuality rather than tradition, flowers have been an obvious medium through which to accomplish that expression. One thing I have seen as a result of that expression is the use of a great

335

deal more color in the visual aspect of the celebration. Color is becoming more important to a bride as she plans her wedding because it is a perfect way for her to express who she is and to separate her wedding from others.

➤ Roses have always been a popular wedding flower, and the vast majority of brides today seem to be unwilling to sacrifice roses to save on the budget. The wonderful thing about that is that they shouldn't have to. Roses have become more available in almost every color for today's bride. The versatility of the rose is hard to surpass and works for any flower requirement, from boutonnieres and corsages to bridal and bridesmaids' bouquets, to the largest church arrangement. They just work. So many other beautiful flowers are available to us today as well, and they should be used, but don't feel that you can't afford to have roses.

➤ Props are playing a larger part in today's weddings. It is no longer enough to place an arrangement on the altar at the church. We now have to go on searches for the perfect pedestal or antique table on which to place the arrangement. Table centerpieces are more visually appealing if they are lifted off the table with the use of a footed container. Many couples are incorporating family heirlooms into their flower planning. A great-grandfather's golfing trophy serving as a container for head table flowers, a grandmother's antique vase used to hold flowers on the cake table, and a mother's collection of crystal bowls used for centerpiece flowers all add personal meaning to a couple's special day.

Florists are renting more pieces to the couples to save from having to purchase props that they will probably never use again. This enables them to put more of their budget toward the flowers, therefore giving them more bang for their buck.

As with everything else, wedding flower styles change. Your florist should be up-to-date on the latest styles and should have the ability to combine your personal taste and personality with the newest trends as he or she helps you plan your day. Flowers add that finishing touch to your wedding and help set the tone for your entire event by providing beauty, elegance, and romance.

Sali Widner—Bouquet Preservation

Sali Widner owns Florescence in Silver Springs, Maryland.

> *Over the years I have had brides say to me that they want to preserve their bouquet. That's a lovely sentiment, but this is just like anything else you are planning for your wedding; it needs to be planned out long before the wedding day.*
>
> *The best way to dry flowers now is the freeze-dried method. There are other methods, but the freeze drying seems to keep the flowers as close to their size, shape, and texture to fresh and are more durable. This method also offers the highest success rate.*

For best results, flowers should be delivered to the preservationist as soon as possible after the wedding.

Remember that fresh flowers are fragile and should be handled with care to minimize bruising and wilting. Here are some suggestions:

➤ *Assign someone to be responsible for the flowers.*

➤ *Bouquets on their natural stems will keep better if placed in a vase with water at the reception.*

➤ *If using the bouquet as part of the décor, try to place it out of crushing distance.*

➤ *Make sure your florist knows that you are having your flowers preserved. If a certain flower is not a good choice for preservation, substitutions can be made.*

➤ *If possible, put the flowers safely away if no longer needed.*

➤ *Keep your flowers in cool but not frigid conditions. Do not freeze them.*

➤ *If refrigerated, place the flowers in a large plastic bag and tie it closed—this will protect against moisture loss. Many hotel refrigerators are too cold; put flowers in a box first. If using a cooler, use a towel or newspaper to protect the flowers against direct contact with ice packs.*

Teddy's Tips

Most of the preservation companies in this country will provide for you the mailing container with complete instructions. After the wedding is over, the flowers can be prepared and then delivered to a mail service for overnight delivery to the preservationist.

Depending on the variety of flower and the preservation method used, the colors of preserved flowers might vary from their fresh state: Some pinks may dry mauve, reds may become burgundy, and whites will mellow to ivory or parchment. In general, greens do not dry well.

Framing protects the preserved flowers so that they will last many years, and your care is extremely important in extending their original color. Display your keepsake in low light and low humidity conditions. Maintain moderate temperatures, avoiding extremes of heat or cold.

For the latest information on freeze-drying flowers and local preservationists to contact, check out the International Freeze Dry Floral Association (www.ifdfa.com).

Again, it's best if you investigate your options well before the wedding. You will find a great variation among floral preservationists with regard to method of preservation, quality, keepsake choices, and prices. Ideally, see their work in person; ask about their methods, and specifically about preserving your choice of flowers. Base your decision on the quality of the flower preservation, artistic presentation, the craftsmanship of materials, and, of course, price. When comparison-shopping, consider the whole package, not just one element. A small display well done is better than a large piece poorly executed.

Claire Webber, Claire Webber Florals and Events by Design

Claire Webber, from the San Francisco Bay area, owns Claire Webber Florals and Events by Design. Claire is a florist and an event designer. She can take an ordinary hilltop and turn it into Camelot, or she can take a large hall and turn it into the most elegant setting for a celebrity wedding. She not only works with flowers to help create these scenes, but she also incorporates fabric treatments, greens, plants, props, linens, chair covers, and special sound and lighting. She has been in business since 1988 and serves a national clientele. For some advice to a couple, Claire says this:

> *Hire a designer who will help you create the big picture that suits you best and is within your budget. Working with a designer who has an ongoing relationship with the various vendors you will need will help you shuffle your budget and get your best value for your dollars.*

> *It's important for you to use a bridal consultant during the planning stages. If that is not in your budget, at least hire a wedding coordinator for the day. So many details are not part of a design package, such as giving direction to the ushers and making sure the bridesmaids are all dressed on time.*

Photographers

Smiling pretty for the photographer can be helped greatly by understanding what the photographer is trying to accomplish and knowing a little about wedding photography. In this section, several experienced and knowledgeable wedding photographers offer their suggestions. There are different types of wedding photography out in the wedding world now, and you, as the wedding consumer, need to understand which type is best for you and your particular situation.

G. Gregory Geiger, CPP, Gregeiger Company Unlimited, Inc.

Gregory Geiger, CPP (Certified Professional Photographer), of Gregeiger Company Unlimited, Inc., in Orange, Connecticut, has photographed weddings all over the country. I've seen his work several times and have always been quite impressed. Some of his magical pictures appear in this book. Gregory offers some questions that you should ask the prospective photographer in the initial stages of planning:

➤ Do you have any particular philosophies about your approach to photographing wedding events?

➤ Do you have any set goals as you approach each wedding?

➤ How long do you expect to be with us on the day of the wedding? Beginning at what time? Until when?

➤ How can we best help you perform your duties while photographing our wedding?

➤ What kind of educational background and/or experience have you had in developing your photographic technique? When was it last updated?

➤ How will you present the preview pictures for our final album selection? What kind of time frame are you looking at for preparing the preview pictures for selection? Are you providing us with proofs or slides? May we keep them? For how long? Are they for sale?

➤ How can people who live out of town order, pay for, and expect delivery of reprints and/or albums?

➤ How much money would you expect us to spend before you think we would be completely happy with our wedding coverage?

Gregory also suggests calling an industry organization or association to provide you with names of reputable wedding photographers in your area:

Although the organization may offer a list of members, this should not be taken as a recommendation. If your photographer does belong to such a group, however, call the association to learn its policy concerning backup vendors if yours is not cooperative or suddenly goes out of business. Once you've chosen a photographer, ask if he or she is familiar with the site of your wedding. If not, you should visit it together. If you're dealing with a studio that employs a staff, as opposed to an individual, ask for the home telephone number of the photographer you have requested. Don't hesitate to call if you have any questions or want to verify the time and date.

Geno, Classic Contemporary Photography by Geno

Geno, of Classic Contemporary Photography by Geno, in Indianapolis, Indiana, is a very creative photographer who has been in the business of photographing weddings for the past 11 years. He started out in Chicago and moved to Indianapolis. He truly loves what he does, and it shows in his albums. Remember in Chapter 14, "Pretty as a Picture—Photographers and Videographers," how I talked about photojournalistic photography? Geno is just that and more. He tries to blend the uniqueness of the photojournalistic approach with the spontaneity of the event to create the story of the wedding with all the emotion that goes with it. Some of his creative work is featured in this book. Look for the emotion his pictures bring to mind. As they say, "A picture is worth a thousand words." Here's what Geno has to offer as advice for the prospective couple:

You might have noticed the revival of black-and-white imagery in the past few years and now there are more and more photographers offering the photojournalistic coverage to complement the formal, traditional portraits. Newlyweds are excited about the possibility that they, too, can now have pictures like the ones they see in the magazines. However, couples are finding it increasingly more difficult in attempting to understand the variety of ways in which photographers structure the pricing of their services. Do to the wide array of today's packaging, I suggest to couples to meet with at least three photographers to determine the best value.

Some photographers charge by the hour or day and then the prints and enlargements are additional. Therefore, ask about any additional fees (travel, overtime, and assistants) that the photographer hasn't discussed during your initial meeting.

Teddy's Tips

Both of our sons have been ring bearers in several weddings. I always asked the photographer to take pictures of our boys being boys. The photographer was always most cooperative, so I have two small albums of my sons as ring bearers, behaving as most small boys do. Those albums can never be replaced. They are truly priceless! The memory fades some, but it makes my heart warm to look at those special pictures and remember a time long ago.

The photographer's work/portfolio should speak for itself and at the consultation, a couple should immediately know whether or not that particular photographer's work suits their style and preference. One thing I think couples should take into account is the level of comfort and rapport they have with the photographer. Couples will intuitively know if that photographer's personality will fit in well with the wedding party and families. Most of us have heard at least one story about the not-so-friendly photographer and how that affected or spoiled the mood for the day.

Ask recently married friends or co-workers for referrals and ask what they liked about the photographer and also suggestions of what they would have done differently with their photography, if anything. Simply put, don't let price be the sole factor in who you select to document your celebration.

Have the wedding you've always imagined by following your dreams, listening to your heart, and trusting your instincts.

Jim and Lois Wyant, Wyant Photography

Jim and Lois Wyant, from Wyant Photography, in Indianapolis, Indiana, are another pair of great, award-winning photographers. Watching them shoot a wedding is truly a pleasure. You can view some examples of their wedding photography in this book also. The Wyants offer this advice for brides- and grooms-to-be:

The United States does not require a license, examination, apprenticeship, or degree to practice photography. So how can you judge those calling themselves professional photographers? Here are some guidelines to help you determine true professionalism:

➤ **Credentials.** Professional Photographers of America (PPA), founded in 1880, is the world's oldest and largest association for professional photographers. The organization provides educational services and sets standards of professional performance for its more than 14,000 members and 250 international affiliated organizations. The PPA degree program is the foremost appraisal of the professional photographer. The Master of Photography, an earned degree, is presented only to those photographers whose superior competence and technique have been recognized in exhibit competition. The photographic Craftsman Degree (Cr.Photog.) is awarded for teaching, lecturing, and service to professional photography associations. (Note of caution: Many photographers claim to be Masters, Artists, and so on, but be sure to check for diplomas and proper credentials.)

➤ **Ethics.** Always consider a photographer's honesty, attitude, and character. For example, make sure that images viewed in brochures, albums, and so on are indeed the work of the photographer you are considering.

➤ **Organizations.** Membership to most professional organizations requires little more than paying dues. Look for someone with active involvement and participation in competition, which indicates an interest in learning, sharing, and creative growth.

➤ **Competition.** Take note of any awards received by the photographer. This is an excellent measure of talent, technical knowledge, and artistic ability. Be sure recent honors are documented and are awarded through professional organizational competitions, such as those of Professional Photographers of America, the Professional Photographer's Organization (PPO), and/or the regional or state affiliates of these organizations.

➤ **Consistent quality.** Look around the consultation room at the images displayed along with the images in albums. Do they all display the kind of quality you're looking for, or do some of the images fall short? Ask yourself, "What level of quality can I expect to receive?" Pay close attention to the photographer's expertise in the areas of lighting, posing, and composition.

➤ **Education.** Ask where the photographer has studied to gain his skills and whether he is continuing his education.

➤ **Emotional impact.** Technical skills are important, but the ability to reach beyond the rules of photography is the mark of a true professional. Look for images displaying expression, enthusiasm, and feelings.

Michael Colter

Michael Colter is a second-generation wedding photographer who started out shooting for a small-town newspaper, photographing teams at the Indianapolis 500. His business, Colter Photography, is located in Rushville, Indiana. He is a delight to work with and absolutely loves what he can do with a camera. He is one of those few photographers who can really get into the wedding. He's all back-stage, but he seems to be everywhere—and his finished product shows it. Couples today are asking for more black-and-white photos than they did 10 years ago. Michael is an expert at black-and-white photography, and his work is also printed in this book.

What makes black-and-white photography different is not simply that they are standard wedding images printed on black-and-white paper. There is a difference in line, composition, perspective, shadow, and the ultra-wide angle. When I pick up my camera loaded with black-and-white film, I look at the wedding day in an entirely different perspective.

Photojournalism means "to tell a story with pictures," and that is exactly what I strive for. I arrive before the bride is dressed and am frequently the last one to leave. This allows me to be available for those moments when people are unaware of me and are able to be themselves. I try to be unobtrusive, to tell the behind-the-scenes story of the wedding. I can capture honesty and emotion. I shoot first and ask questions later, taking hundreds of images without taking the time to consider whether they will be purchased, working on instinct alone. These captured moments will be among the most tender, hilarious, and heartfelt memories of the wedding day—the icing on the cake.

One of the beautiful things about still photography is its ability to freeze a small slice of time and preserve it forever. Even if the bride and groom did not view a particular moment of their wedding day, it can become part of their memory forever because their sensitive photographer has captured it for them. It's a great life!

Stephanie Hogue

Stephanie Hogue, of Stephanie Hogue Photography, does business on the West Coast—Oxnard, California, to be exact. She has been in the wedding business for eight years now and loves what she does. Her passion is "capturing moments in our lives that might otherwise be gone forever." You will find great examples of her work in this book, too. Here's some advice from Stephanie:

When you've chosen the photographer, include her in the planning of the timeline for the day. This will help her in knowing where the action will happen next so that no precious moment will be missed. Talk about where and when all the posed photographs will be taken. This is very important, especially for a photojournalistic-style photographer, because you want the posed photos to go as quickly and efficiently as possible so that it doesn't detract from the day. There are always many options as to when and where posed photos should be taken, and these will be dictated by the locations you have chosen, the time you'd like to spend, and the convenience of the family members taking part in the photos.

Your photographer should have lots of suggestions as to how can make the day go as smoothly as possible from a photographic standpoint, but don't let anyone push you into doing something you really don't want to do. A good photographer should be flexible, too, and will let you know what the benefits are to suggestions, but the final decisions are up to the couple.

Above all, I believe that once you've chosen a photographer you're happy with, the most important thing to do to ensure that you will love your photos is to enjoy your day. Love every minute of it, and your photos will radiate your joy. Don't get caught up in the details that you've worked so hard in planning. If things go wrong, try to have a sense of humor because nothing in life is perfect. Not only will this attitude help your photos be beautiful, but it will also ensure that the day is a success and everyone will have a joyful memory.

Travel Agents

Whether it's "Aloha" or the Mickey Mouse theme song for your honeymoon, the expert help of great travel agencies is a must for perfect planning.

Steve Schrohe and Virginia Pfrommer, IT Travel, Inc.

Steve Schrohe, president of IT Travel, in Terre Haute, Indiana, and Virginia Pfrommer, one of his experienced leisure travel consultants, offer this advice to couples seeking that perfect honeymoon. IT Travel has been in business since 1980, so they have seen trends come and go.

When you meet with the travel consultant for the first time, you should see a red flag if the travel agent has a preconceived idea of what he or she thinks your honeymoon should be. Just because you are looking for honeymoon sites does not mean you want to go to Hawaii. They need to be able to listen to your wants and desires.

Also, look for an agency that is fully computerized. They should have Web sites that you can access and do your own booking. With IT Travel, if you use their Web site to book your trip, they will waive all the fees associated with arranging the travel. You also can pull up other information from a good agency's site, such as weather, currency exchange rate, and other details.

For trends, Virginia says that the all-inclusive resorts, which started in Jamaica and have spread all over the world (Sandals is probably one of the most famous), are still high on couples' lists, but the cruise has gone through the roof in popularity. She also stresses experiencing a honeymoon away from the norm. Most couples take a week's vacation.

Virginia suggests that you should start talking to the travel agent as soon as you set your date. You are what the travel industry calls "not date-flexible," meaning you don't have lots of options on when to leave and return. Allow yourself plenty of time so that the agent has the time needed to research all the possibilities well in advance of your wedding date. Another advantage in seeking advice early is that the further out you book trips, the bigger the discount on prices. The typical honeymoon today—either a cruise or an all-inclusive resort—is about $3,500.

Steve Ledewitz, Worldtek Travel

Worldtek Travel is one of the top 30 travel agencies in the country in size and volume of sales. Because of the company's size, staffers work closely with the airlines to get better service and lower rates for their clients. This is the official travel agency for all the routine NCAA's travel and tournaments and is known for the ability to rapidly change large group's schedules. Worldtek is a corporate member of the Association of Bridal Consultants.

Steve says there are three things a couple should watch for in a good travel agency.

1. Response time. How long does it take an agent to get back with you? Does this person have your questions answered when they do return your call?

2. Is the agent listening to you? Does he take the time to incorporate your ideas, dreams, and budget into the plan?

3. Is the agent selling you a product that is right for you? In other words, does he have a preconceived idea of what the honeymoon should be?

If the agency falls short on one or more of these points, then you might want to look elsewhere for some guidance.

Worldtek sees one of the most popular honeymoon sites now as Disneyland or Disney World. Also, cruises and the all-inclusive resorts are popular and definitely help with budget because everything is included. You know what your honeymoon will cost before you leave for the plane. Steve also notes that adding the honeymoon package to the gift registry is becoming more popular.

Videographers

Wedding videography is a wonderful way to help capture the memories of your day as they unfold. In Chapter 14, I talked about what to look for when you choose a videographer. In this section, you get some valuable advice from three professional wedding videographers. One professional trade organization dedicated to videographers is the Association of Professional Videographers (APV). If you have questions, contact Steve Short, at 919-231-9245.

Jim and Cindy Wright, Video Magic Productions

Jim and Cindy Wright, owners of Video Magic Productions, in Clinton, Indiana, have been doing wedding videography for 18 years. They are true artists in every sense of the word, and every one of their videos is unique to that couple. Here are their suggestions:

> *The single biggest problem facing most wedding videographers today is the misconception that we can capture credible footage in just about every conceivable lighting situation: from the father and bride entering the church through an open door with a blazing sun at their backs, to the murky shadows of a 150-year-old mausoleum lit by the twinkling of too few candles.*
>
> *Light is nature's oldest special effect: a genie capable of painting life's robust and myriad images at 30 frames per second across the canvas that is videotape—but only if the brush is grasped correctly.*
>
> *Often what the couple envisions for this, the most romantic day of their life, and what the videographer delivers a few weeks later are poles apart. Visiting several videographers early in the planning stages of your big day can allow a finished product that finds the best of both worlds—yours and the videographer's.*
>
> *Unlike the still photographer, who documents the wedding through a series of staged shots, the videographer is charged with capturing the emotions of the day: unrehearsed, unexpected, and in constant motion.*
>
> *Armed with a little preplanning and basic knowledge, the couple and the consultant can find a nice balance between what is expected and what is delivered.*

Patrick and Jodi Harris, Sight and Sound Video Productions and DJ Entertainment

Patrick and Jodi Harris, of Sight and Sound Video Productions and DJ Entertainment, in Las Vegas, Nevada, are really into this industry. Not only do they offer video work, but they also offer DJ services and host a weekly radio show for brides and grooms. I've been interviewed several times on their show, and couples can call in and ask questions. They are a real asset to the wedding industry. Their advice on hiring a videographer follows:

> *The biggest mistake a bride and groom can make is having a friend or family member videotape their wedding. Many a friendship has ended and a family feud has started because of a bad wedding video. Your friend's efforts can't compare to a professional's. Professionals have better equipment, more knowledge, and more experience to create masterpieces.*

> *Don't shop for a wedding videographer over the telephone. Video is something that has to be seen. How can you compare the quality of work between one company and another over the telephone? No two video companies shoot the exact same way. You need to find the company whose style best matches what you are looking for.*

> *Ask your videographer if he or she belongs to any videography associations. Ask if he or she attends industry conferences, expos, conventions, or seminars. These are the videographers who stay up-to-date on current trends and technologies that can only enhance your video.*

> *Make an appointment with your wedding videographer before the wedding to pre-plan what will happen and when. Discuss shots that are important to you. Tell the videographer who the special people are that you would like to have on the video (for example, your grandparents).*

Caterers

I've talked at great length throughout this book about food for your reception. Food is an important aspect of any wedding reception. In this section, catering managers provide you with some more food for thought.

Donna Rader, Jim Herman, and Kent Beckman; Marriott Corporation, Education Services

Donna Rader, Jim Herman, and Kent Beckman are the catering managers for Marriott Corporation at one of my favorite local reception sites: St. Mary-of-the-Woods College, located outside the city limits of Terre Haute, Indiana. The St. Mary's facility itself is quite elegant, and working with Marriott makes my life and the couple's life worry-free. These three professionals offer the following suggestions:

> *Have an idea of what your budget is, and plan the location, meal type, and size accordingly. It's hard to make a large, elegant place appropriate for a small punch and cake reception. But it's just as difficult to get the full benefit of a full meal reception if it's overcrowded and the facility is in poor condition.*

When choosing a menu, do not be satisfied with a set menu if it is not what you want. Any good caterer will work with you on setting a menu and its presentation to match your expectations. Keep in mind that this is your event, and it should be the way you want it to be.

When you begin planning your reception, look at the starting and ending times. When the reception begins at 4 P.M. and ends at 8 P.M., your guests most likely will make a meal out of your menu whether you have hors d'oeuvres or a full meal. The costs will be fairly similar. A full menu after 9 P.M. most likely won't be eaten as a meal, especially if it's a buffet; hors d'oeuvres may be the better way to go at that time. The caterer should charge less after 9 P.M. than during a meal period.

If you choose to serve alcohol, your best bet is to hire a bar caterer who has sufficient liability insurance. One liability ordeal can wipe you out financially if something happens and you don't have proper coverage. It's also good to provide alternative beverages all evening. Examples would be coffee, iced tea, and soda. Shutting down the bar 30 minutes before the entertainment stops is always a good plan to follow.

Jerry Green, The New Savoy

Jerry Green, president of The New Savoy, in Bronx, New York, has been in the business of catering weddings, parties, and nightclubs for 30-plus years. With that much experience, his advice is important. Here are some of his thoughts:

Be very honest with the banquet manager regarding your budget. A good banquet manager is capable of saving you money if you are truthful with him.

Always have a definite wedding date or alternate date in mind. Many banquet managers will not take you seriously unless you have a specific date. Be as outspoken and forthright as you can. If you say very little to the banquet manager, he might not feel you are a serious customer. Never tell an experienced banquet manager what you think he wants to hear. He has too much experience and will see right through you. Always be pleasant and polite; you will receive twice what you give.

Susan Sluyter, Indiana State University Food Services

Another Marriott branch is on the campus of Indiana State University, Terre Haute, Indiana. Susan Sluyter, the catering manager, has a vast amount of experience and offers the following suggestions:

The best advice that I can give a bridal couple is to trust your caterer! This begins by doing research. Ask for references and pictures from past events. Be sure you feel comfortable with the salesperson. Ask to meet the supervisor who will be present the day of your wedding. Once your decision is made, communicate your expectations and then put your wedding in the caterer's hands. Allow your caterer to perform magic.

Teddy's Tips

To ensure that prime rib is done properly, you have only a 15-minute leeway in which to serve it. Fifteen minutes isn't a lot of time, but it can sure ruin your dinner if your timeline is off much.

Be sure to provide the caterer with a wedding day timeline. Be realistic when establishing that timeline. This is where the advice and expertise of a good bridal consultant can really pay off. Many prime rib dinners have been served long past their prime.

Tell your caterer exactly what your budget is, and do this up front. This tells them exactly what they have to work with. Champagne taste on a beer income is acceptable if all parties know ahead of time. A good caterer can share many inexpensive tricks.

Instruct the caterer to cut the cake (after you first cut it, of course) in the kitchen. Cake debris is often gruesome to the eye, but it sure tastes good.

Jacquelynne T. O'Rourke, Edelweiss Caterers

Jacquelynne T. O'Rourke has owned Edelweiss Caterers in Danbury, Connecticut, for many years and is an offsite caterer. Offsite caterers do not work in one facility; they work in diverse locations. (Chapter 11, "Eat, Drink, and Be Married," will remind you of this.)

I met Jacquie at a conference six years ago where she was one of the speakers on catering. I think you will find value in her advice to couples:

Whether the couple selects a gorgeous mansion, an incomparable garden reception, a modern art gallery, or a historic museum, the caterer should be qualified to assist in all phases of planning the wedding reception.

Ask about the little extras, such as an immaculate service staff with white-glove presentation, petite strawberries in the guests' champagne glasses, butler-style hors d'oeuvres, carving stations with chefs in white jackets, and flaming Crèpes Suzettes prepared at each guest table.

Your caterer should have the ability to help you select and order all your required rental items. Depending on your physical setting, those should include linens, china, silverware, crystal, tables and chairs, tents, and so on. Ask questions concerning damage waivers, time of delivery, and pickup of everything.

Request several references, and call each previous bride, especially if that reception took place in the same facility that you are considering. Schedule a complimentary tasting of some of the entrées that you are contemplating.

Finally, this day should be free from worries and stress, and the proper caterer will make you feel like a guest at your own wedding!

Music

Over the years, I've heard music blend with the ceremony and reception, and I've heard such outrageous songs that the hair on the back of my neck stood straight up. In this section, several professional musicians offer some things to consider when you are deciding on music for your ceremony and reception.

Bill Cain, Keyboard Musician

Bill Cain, of Terre Haute, Indiana, is a talented professional musician. When I know that Bill is our organist or pianist for the ceremony, I know we are in good hands. Bill offers the following practical advice for couples:

> When determining your vocal selections, ask yourself if the song that sounded so perfect at the local hotel lounge on Saturday night is really the song you want your grandmother to hear at your church wedding.

> Also, when you are using a musical selection that is available only on tape or CD, ask yourself if it's really fair to the musician to ask him to transcribe that music onto sheet music so that it can be played at your wedding.

Kenny i Orchestras

Kenny is president of Kenny i Orchestras in Somers Point, New Jersey. His bands perform all over the East Coast and get rave reviews wherever they go. They are truly magical music makers. Kenny offers the following advice for selecting musicians for your reception:

> Volume is a key item when selecting the "make or break" factor of the reception—the music. Not only does the band have to be conscious of volume, but it also has to be sensitive to all those involved in the wedding: the consultant, the photographer, the caterer, the videographer, and, of course, the guests.

> Auditioning the band is crucial. Recommendations are extremely important and can come from people who have enjoyed the entertainers at previous events. A referral from a reception site or caterer also can be respected.

> Note the band's poise, professionalism, volume, selections, overall appearance, and timing. Remember that the band's personality is a mirror image of the elegance and excitement level of the party.

> Ask the band leader several key questions: Is the band's contract clear regarding getting exactly who you've hired, especially guaranteeing that the leader or MC will be present? How early does the band report to the site? Does it have liability insurance? Can it provide music for the cocktail hour if it's in a room separate from the dinner dance? The music helps make the dream wedding a reality. Select it with care!

349

Patrick and Jodi Harris, Sight and Sound Video Productions and DJ Entertainment

As I mentioned in the video section of this chapter, Patrick and Jodi Harris, of Sight and Sound Video Productions and DJ Entertainment, in Las Vegas, Nevada, not only offer video work, but they also offer DJ services and host a weekly radio show for brides and grooms. They have been in business for 15 years. I've been interviewed several times on their show, "Weddings Done Right," where couples get good information and can call in and ask questions. Here's their advice for hiring a DJ:

> *Know who your DJ/MC will be. Meet your DJ before your event to go over all your information. Some large companies send out whoever is available without telling the bride and groom the name of the DJ; you meet the DJ for the first time at your wedding reception. You have specific requests, needs, and ideas. By meeting your DJ before your wedding, however, you can assure that your entertainment is customized to meet your needs. Your DJ will be with you many hours, and you want to make sure you all get along.*

> *Professional DJs do more than just spin discs. You need to find one who will help coordinate events and make announcements of all reception formalities, such as the first dance, father/daughter dance, bouquet toss, garter toss, cake cutting, and so on, tastefully. A good DJ will also work with all your other services, such as your photographer, videographer, bridal consultant, and catering manager, letting them know when things are going to happen to give them enough time to prepare.*

> *Find out what time your DJ/MC will arrive. Are you being charged for setup time? Most DJs arrive at least one hour prior to the start of the wedding and don't charge to set up.*

> *Look at a video demo of the DJ's work. This doesn't necessarily mean that your party will be like the one on the video, because not every party is the same. However, this will give you an idea of how the DJ is dressed and how he or she makes announcements and sets up activities.*

Sharon Thompson, Sunny Moon DJ Entertainment

Sharon Thompson is the owner of Sunny Moon DJ Entertainment and has been in the business for 19 years. She is the best DJ I've seen in action. Her company is located in Noblesville, Indiana, and has a great reputation. When you're looking for either DJs or bands, Sharon offers this advice:

> *Music formatting and dance floor psychology are very important. The atmosphere you wish to create is enhanced by the music selection. If you have an afternoon, garden-type reception, you might want to choose classical and New Age selections for the cocktail and dinner hours. Afternoon receptions usually have less dance floor activity due to*

the time of day; however, a professional DJ or band will still enhance your event by playing tasteful music. Evening receptions are more party-oriented when you reach the dance segment.

Professional companies will offer you a song booklet that will assist you in selecting particular favorites. Music will enhance all aspects of the reception, including the opening acknowledgments, bridal party announcements, cocktail and dinner hours, cake-cutting ceremony, first dance, parents' dance, bridal party dance, father/daughter dance, and garter/bouquet toss. It's very important that you not only note these items on your planner for your entertainer, but that you also meet with your entertainment a month prior to the event. Professionals are there for you *and will be there for* you *every step of the way.*

Do not let an entertainer control your wishes. If you choose not to do special dances, such as the Chicken Dance, Macarena, Dollar Dance, Electric Slide, and so on, just indicate that you do not wish these to be played. It's your *day. Professional entertainers will politely explain to the guest who is requesting a particular song that you have requested it not to be played.*

Read your contract carefully! Make sure your entertainer has backup in case of any unforeseen misfortunes. Check to see if he or she has a cancellation policy. The majority of the entertainment agencies have a nonrefundable deposit.

Your length-of-play package refers to the amount of time you feel is needed for the reception. Professional companies will work with you in planning the correct start and end times. The start time should always coincide with when you expect your first guest to enter the reception site. Commit to the hours you know you will need, and ask for the overtime fee.

Remember that you are paying for play time. It's the responsibility of the entertainer to arrive one hour prior to the start time to set up and be ready by the indicated start time on the contract.

The following is a suggestive questionnaire you can use when booking entertainment:

➤ Are you available on (date)?

➤ What's your name, and how many musicians do you have? Where can we see you in action prior to making a decision?

➤ Will you play special requests?

➤ Do you have a song list?

➤ How will you dress?

➤ How many hours will you play?

➤ If booking a band, ask how much time is considered play time. Does a set consist of 40 minutes of play time with 20-minute breaks, and does the band play music during breaks? If you are booking a combination package—that is, a band/DJ—your professional DJ will fill the gaps during the breaks.

➤ What does the lighting package consist of, and is there an extra cost for it? Professional DJs and bands both have lighting effects available.

➤ How much time do you need to set up? How much space do you need for the setup? What kind of electrical service do you need? DJs require two banquet tables. It's the responsibility of your catering facility to assist you with making sure your entertainers have ample tables, space, and electrical sources. Do you need to have your entertainers set up early? Is there an early setup fee?

➤ What's the cancellation policy?

➤ How much does overtime cost?

➤ Will you act as MC? Do you have a wedding planner?

➤ Are you a licensed agency? (ASCAP and BMI are the two most common.)

The Least You Need to Know

➤ Make sure you order your wedding apparel as far in advance as you can. Ask about alteration costs. Make sure that you go back to the shop to try on the dress as soon as you are notified that it has arrived. Check about having your gown preserved.

➤ Select your florist and book your wedding date with the florist as far in advance as possible. Actual floral decisions don't have to be made until about three months before the wedding, after you have finalized your wedding colors, style, and budget.

➤ Choose your photographer carefully. You will be spending a lot of time with this person, and you want to feel comfortable with him and the work he offers. Think carefully about what kind of photos are important to you for capturing your wedding day on film.

➤ Find a competent travel agent to help you plan your honeymoon. Tell the agent your budget, and let him or her help you stay within it. Consider inclusive deals, such as all-inclusive resort getaways or cruises.

➤ Be careful in your music selections. Make sure that the songs you want to use don't have to be transcribed to sheet music from a tape or CD. If you are using a band or other musical group, try to see the musicians perform before you hire them.

Chapter 28

True Confessions— Couples Tell How They Survived

In This Chapter

➤ Listening to brides and grooms share their wedding stories

➤ Seeing what worked for them

➤ Learning about what they would change

A long time ago, I learned to listen and take advice from those who had experienced a similar situation I was about to experience. After all, they got through it and lived to tell about it, so why couldn't I?

In this chapter, eight couples share their wedding days with you. You should find this chapter especially fun to read. These gracious couples are sharing with you ideas they used and things they would either keep the same or change. They will tell you what they learned in the process of planning their weddings and how to avoid some of the pitfalls they experienced.

These eight couples were asked to be part of this book because of the ways in which they handled their wedding planning process and the type of wedding they had. We have everything from the mom helping to plan, to the couple doing it all themselves. And we have some very unique ideas—individuality—to share.

A wedding is the blending of two families into a new family. Your individuality should shine through. Read on, dear couples, and learn how these eight couples lived to tell their tales.

Kelly Kristin Potts and Scott William Locke

Date: May 31, 1997

Hometown: East Lansing, Michigan

Guests: 125

Colors: Navy and ivory

Attendants: Maid of honor, best man, two ushers

Reception: Buffet dinner with DJ for dancing

This couple comes from Michigan. They brought everyone for the wedding to the campus of Indiana University where they met. They were married in a delightful chapel in a private ceremony for 40 guests and then had a delayed reception later that night for 125 guests. We actually had some time for them to relax, take off their wedding attire, and order a pizza!

In keeping with the simplicity and budget of this couple, we used all white roses to go with the navy-and-ivory theme. Because the chapel was so small, we decided to put our budget into the flowers and food for the reception. Kelly chose hurricane globes, and the florist placed two ivory roses tied with some gold ribbon on each. Her mother had made flower favors for everyone and wrapped them in gold foil, which helped add color. The couple also used menu scrolls tied with gold ribbon at each place for an additional bit of uniqueness.

Kelly and Scott have traveled extensively. During our first meeting, I asked them what they liked to do; when they told me how much they love to travel (they fell in love in Paris), I knew we had to incorporate traveling into the wedding.

We had assigned seating. But, instead of table numbers, guests were seated at tables with the name of a city Kelly and Scott had visited. For example, the place card for Mr. and Mrs. Jones read, "You are seated at the Naples table." Guests had fun trying to find their city table, and Kelly and Scott made a list of all the cities and why they were so important to them. This was placed in a lovely frame by the place cards. This was another unique idea using what is special to that couple.

The buffet also reflected the international theme by offering foods from all over the world.

Here are some tips from Kelly:

> Think seriously about all the traditions associated with weddings and receptions. If you are not comfortable with a tradition, don't feel that you have to observe it. Teddy told us many times, "It's your wedding, do what you want."

> Make the wedding yours—just for the two of you. You are the only ones getting married. Make the decisions together, and make your day a reflection of yourselves. We are a unique, nontraditional couple who loves to travel and have fun. We feel that both our wedding and reception reflected that about us. It was hard work, but we wouldn't

have done it any other way. We really enjoyed the reception, and it was so satisfying to receive so many compliments on our original ideas.

Use a reputable wedding coordinator, whatever your budget. The time and money he or she can save you, in addition to providing a calming presence on the wedding day, more than pays for the fee.

We met privately about 20 minutes before the ceremony, just Scott and me. This really helped calm my nerves so that I could focus on the ceremony and not have to worry about crying.

I wouldn't do anything differently. The stress was intense at times, but it also made our day a huge success.

And here are some tips from Scott:

Kelly and I planned the whole rehearsal dinner, wedding ceremony, and reception ourselves. We knew this celebration was about us and our relationship. We realized that the best way to personalize our celebration was for both of us to plan and make all decisions regarding that weekend. (The planning process is very stressful, but you learn a great deal about each other and how the dynamics of your relationship work.) This way makes everything about the wedding, from the food to the music, a manifestation of you both. This is not to say that help and advice are not needed, because they are, but the final decisions need to be both of yours. I feel our wedding was a huge success because we made it us! And, by all means, hire a coordinator.

Don't sweat the small stuff. Keep focused on the meaning of the wedding and not the troublesome details.

Gretchen Elaine Whalen and James Jeffrey Moore

Date: August 2, 1997

Hometown: Indianapolis, Indiana

Guests: 225

Color: Forest green

Attendants: Five bridesmaids, five groomsmen, two ushers, flower girl, ring bearer

Reception: Formal seated dinner with DJ for dancing and entertainment

This wedding was a very special wedding for me. Gretchen had worked with me for about five years as an assistant, and when it came time to coordinate this wedding, there was a big lump in my throat. I always try to stay calm and collected for my brides, but I had to fight the tears when she got ready to go down the aisle.

Gretchen's favorite color is forest green, and that's what the bridesmaids wore. She added lots of color with her flowers using shades of reds, pinks, and lots of greenery. It was really a lovely combination.

One of the highlights and certainly fond memories of this wedding was the DJ they hired. He was from South Carolina and wasn't just a DJ; he was an entertainer and was a wonderful addition to this wedding reception.

When I walked into the ballroom for the reception, I took one look at the wedding cake and knew we were in trouble. The DJ came over to introduce himself and said. "I don't want to tell you your business, but that cake has been sliding since I arrived two hours ago." That was all I needed. I told the DJ to announce for guests to be seated and that the bride and groom were going to cut their cake. I went to Gretchen and told her that we needed to cut cake. She replied, "But it's not time to cut the wedding cake." Whereupon I said, "Do you trust me?"

"Yes," came this meek reply.

"Gretchen, your wedding cake all over this ballroom floor will not be a pretty site. Let's cut cake." And so, we did, and no one knew we hadn't planned it that way.

I asked each couple to write about anything unusual that happened during the wedding, and Gretchen told me she forgot to kiss Jim at the end of the ceremony. The minister had to pull her back to get the famous kiss in.

Gretchen also offers this advice:

> *Plan well and use a wedding coordinator so that you can enjoy this day. It goes by so quickly. Have a video of your wedding made as well. The ceremony and reception go by so fast, and it's all such a blur that having the video to watch later reminds you of what you missed or what everything looked like.*

> *I think I had a head start on my planning by working with Teddy. I had so many ideas and knew what I wanted and what I didn't want from helping Teddy with weddings. My biggest advice would be to get a good wedding coordinator. And take all the pictures before the ceremony.*

> *If I had it to do over again, I would practice the kiss at the rehearsal and make sure I didn't have a leaning cake.*

> *Everything else went very well. I would also take pictures from magazines in to the caterer to show them what I wanted the food presentation to look like.*

> *After the wedding, if it doesn't come with your photography package, pay the photographer to put together your album. We started out picking out the pictures and trying to decide what size they should be and where they should go, and it was a big headache. Just let the professionals do it.*

Becky Lynn Williams and Greg Bryce Swenson

Date: August 1, 1998

Hometown: Denver, Colorado

Guests: 125

Colors: Celedon green with bright assorted Gerbera daisies

Attendants: Four bridesmaids, four groomsmen, three ushers

Reception: Very informal reception at the local country club using lots of food stations and a DJ for music

From the minute I met Becky and Greg, they kept saying, "We want it simple, and we want to have fun at the reception." And so we did. Part of the secret to this wedding's success was that Becky relaxed and focused on what was of prime importance. She didn't let the little things get to her, and she was able to turn things over to me and relax.

Her centerpieces were absolutely darling—tiny vases in various heights with mixed bunches of Gerbera daisies (no two were alike). We bought the daisies in bulk and arranged them ourselves. We took the same idea with the church flowers. This was a charming country church. Becky told me what I could spend on church flowers, and my assistant and I went to the nursery the morning of the wedding and bought plants of all kinds—ferns, flowering, large, small—and then just arranged them. It was just right for that particular church, and it was just the look Becky had in mind.

Here are Becky's words of wisdom:

> *It may sound like a cliché, but it is your wedding. The wedding should look and feel like the two of you; otherwise, you won't feel comfortable. Once the wedding is underway, have fun. We have a theory: As goes the bride and groom, so goes the wedding. If you have fun, so will everyone else. The crowd will take your lead. And remember, no one—including you—will remember what the centerpieces looked like, but they* will *remember the fun!*

Shanna Marie Toney and Jon Anthony Bradbury

Date: August 8, 1998

Hometown: St. Louis, Missouri

Guests: 200

Colors: Periwinkle blue and light yellow

Attendants: Three bridesmaids, three groomsmen, junior bridesmaid, junior groomsmen, flower girl, ring bearer

Reception: Buffet with DJ for dancing

Shanna was a most creative bride. She made her attendants gifts of jewelry (necklace, earrings, and bracelets), along with the boxes to put the jewelry in. What a gift! And because it took time and energy to do this, she says it really meant something to her, too. A gift from the heart!

Her attendants were dressed in simple, floor-length periwinkle gowns that a family friend had made. They carried a single yellow silk rose with ivy and blue ribbon. Shanna used tulle, greenery, and yellow ribbon in the church, again keeping the design simple, yet very pretty.

She chose not to use a wedding program to save on costs and used the seal-and-send invitations, which also saved on costs.

This is Shanna's advice to you:

> Take your pictures all beforehand. We did that, and before we started, we had some private time, just the two of us, to see how we looked all dressed up. Jon even got down on one knee and proposed all over again. By taking all the photos beforehand, we got to join our guests a lot faster. We dismissed the congregation by pews and then went directly to the limo amid a shower of bubbles. It was wonderful, and we got some great pictures of that.

> If you are planning from out of town, as I was, give yourself plenty of time. Put a day between the wedding and leaving for your honeymoon. We got to bed late and had to get up at 5 A.M. to drive to the airport.

> Always double-check your airline tickets and reservations ahead of time. We got to the airport and found out that our travel agent had booked us to the wrong city! We had to fly standby all day to get to our destination. (We survived our first catastrophe beautifully.)

> Make sure your DJ understands exactly what you want played. He did not play our first dance and played odd selections throughout the night. But we went with the flow and still had fun.

> Hiring a wedding consultant was great for me. Being from out-of-town, we knew there was someone local who was in charge and knew what she was doing.

> It is the best feeling in the world to see all your family and friends enjoying themselves at your party. I know people will remember our wedding for years to come. I'll never forget my grandmas doing the Chicken Dance.

Just remember, it is *your* day. If it doesn't go exactly as planned, so what? Don't let it bother you and get you upset. This day goes by so quickly, so try to commit as much as you can to memory. You can laugh about all the small stuff later.

Virginia Longyear and Phillip Wayne Whitaker Jr.

Date: May 29, 1999

Hometown: Mechanicsville, Virginia

Guests: 125

Colors: Deep plum and desert clay

Attendants: Three bridesmaids, three groomsmen, two ushers, flower girl, ring bearer

Reception: Hors d'oeuvres with DJ for dancing

Virginia lived in Virginia, where she wanted to be married. Her mom hired me to get her started in the right direction and then offer advice/counsel where needed. As Virginia will admit, she is picky. But, by holding onto her ideas and not giving in to someone else's idea of what her wedding should be like, she finally found a solution that worked for her.

Here's some advice from Virginia:

> *The bride needs to get away from everyone the night before the wedding (including your mom). I chose to stay downtown at the Omni with my maid of honor. It was so convenient! The rehearsal dinner was right across the street, and the reception was at the Omni, so I was in the middle of all the action, in case I was needed. The day of the wedding, the other bridesmaids met us at the hotel, where we had our hair done. That was so nice. The last thing you need to do is run errands on your wedding day.*

> *At the rehearsal (and be sure to check ahead of time), bring everything you can (gown, shoes, veil) so that all you have to get to the church on the wedding day is you.*

> *Do not use a friend or family member to do your pictures or your video just because they will cut you a deal or even do it for free. Think about your pictures and video carefully. That is all you have left when the wedding day ends. Do not cut corners on these two aspects of the wedding. We just cut our budget in other areas.*

> *I wasn't sure what flowers I wanted; I just knew that I wanted something different. One florist got so frustrated with me that she began telling me what I wanted and started picking out flowers. Needless to say, I got another florist. If you are extremely picky like me and you are set on a certain color but cannot come up with the flower to suit that color, go get silks or even dried flowers of that hard-to-match color and mix them in with your fresh flowers. That's what I did, and it worked beautifully.*

> *Every girl dreams of an elaborate wedding, but don't go overboard. Sometimes less is more.*

And now from the mother of the bride, GiGi Longyear:

> *If you bought this book, you have the best tool on the market today for planning a wedding. Virginia's wedding was in Virginia, while I live in Indiana. A long-distance wedding was not as hard to plan as one might think. You need to start retaining*

vendors at least a year to a year and a half in advance if time will allow. Because I worked and could not spend a lot of time in Richmond, I had to depend on good vendors that we could rely on. This may cost you more, especially if the wedding is held in an area where costs are higher, but it's worth it.

Believe it or not, I made only one four-day trip to Richmond to scout around for vendors, especially a site for the reception. You can do a lot by phone with 800-numbers, computers, fax, and plastic (credit cards).

Keep in mind who is getting married. Even though you will have dollars invested in this wedding, the wedding is only about the bride and groom.

Plan a budget, and discuss the budget with the bride and groom so they know not to expect more than you can afford. It will save a lot of stress and misunderstanding later.

Teddy helped with ordering and wording the invitations and answering questions. She also typed up a minute-by-minute itinerary for the MC (my sister-in-law) who took charge of the wedding party at the church. This was a great help. That way I could stay with my daughter while she dressed and did not have to worry about who was where.

One of the greatest moments for a MOB (mother of the bride) is to see her daughter walking down the aisle on her father's arm. To future MOBs, keep your eye on the groom also as his bride walks down the aisle to meet him. Phillip had tears of joy running down his cheeks. Needless to say, so did her father and I.

Gina Marie Tom and Preston Earl White

Date: July 18, 1999

Hometown: Terre Haute, Indiana

Guests: 375

Colors: Seafoam, gold, and white

Attendants: Seven groomsmen, six bridesmaids, junior bridesmaid, three ushers, two crown princesses, flower girl, ring bearer

Reception: Seated formal dinner with two choices of entrée and a band for dancing

Gina and Preston had a Greek Orthodox ceremony, which is very rich in tradition. It was also a very largely attended wedding and reception. Even with the heat index well into the high digits, everything went quite smoothly.

Two items that made their wedding unique were the individual wedding cakes on each table as centerpieces and the strawberry daiquiri slush machine. They also had a fountain of amaretto sours. It was something I'd not done before, but it worked, the guests loved it, and it made the reception fun (not to mention cooling people off on a hot July day).

Here are Gina's thoughts on her wedding:

I can honestly say that I feel we had a fairy-tale wedding. A lot of details I stressed about came off without a hitch. This is where my first suggestion comes into play: Hire Teddy Lenderman! Teddy and her staff made it possible for us to actually enjoy our wedding day. I knew I didn't want to have to make any decisions or solve any problems on the actual day, so having a professional wedding coordinator took that pressure off me and my family.

I'm very glad we took all our pictures before the wedding. This seemed to break the ice before the big moment. Also, before all the activities began, everyone is fresher and looks their best. Make sure the photographer has a list of desired photos before the wedding day. We had finger sandwiches and fruit for the wedding party to nibble on during pictures. We didn't want any gurgling stomachs in the church. Preston and I met privately for about 15 minutes before pictures began. This was a special time just for the two of us. We exchanged wedding gifts at this time.

One of the best investments I feel we made was our wedding video. The day goes by so fast, and the only thing you really have left to hold on to are the memories of this most special day. Our videographer was professional and creative and captured all the important moments as well as turning the video into our wedding story. Special graphics and interviews with family and friends have made the video one of our most treasured possessions.

We had a band that played a variety of music. It's difficult to please everyone, but our band did a really good job of keeping the dancing going. It's important to give them your favorite requests but also to give them the freedom to use their expertise to fill in what will really get the crowd up and dancing.

Try to enjoy your wedding day as much as possible. I spent one year planning the details of this wedding, and when the actual day comes, it goes very fast. Savor each moment and try not to stress over the details. Chances are that if something does go wrong, you are the only one who will know it.

(Gina gets a gold star for this last section—she is right on target.)

The process of planning a wedding is a very emotional time, especially for me. I am the only daughter and lived at home until I got married. Getting married for me meant a lot of life changes, and the stress level was very intense at times. My mom and I were at each other's throats at times during the planning stages, but this actually made our relationship grow. There were times I felt that I was the only one who cared about this wedding because my mom would put off the planning. Actually, planning the wedding was one step closer to the actual marriage, and she had a hard time seeing her little girl grow up. Your parents only want the best for you, so try to be patient. This is an emotional time for them, too.

Jennifer Ann Hofmann and Bryan Scott Redding

Date: August 21, 1999

Hometown: Indianapolis, Indiana

Guests: 200

Colors: Periwinkle blue with pastels for accent

Attendants: Three bridesmaids, three groomsmen, three ushers

Reception: Formal seated dinner with DJ for dancing

Bryan and Jennifer hired me early on to help with this wedding, and from the moment I met them, I knew they were a special couple. They both had major parts in the planning, and their planning paid off. Music was important to them, so they chose to use a string trio plus the majestic organ in this church. One of our challenges with this wedding was the actual size of the church and the guest list. The church holds 800, and we had only 200 attend. (That's fine with me—working with 200 is much easier than moving 800 bodies around.) The sanctuary was divided into three sections. The florist roped off the side sections using ribbon, tulle, and lovely arrangements, and we seated guests then in the center section. This focused the eye on the center of the sanctuary.

Here are Jennifer's tips for the bride:

> We wanted our wedding to be very elegant and romantic, with lots of candlelight, flowers, and beautiful music. Most of all, we wanted our wedding to be a true reflection of us. I can remember Teddy telling us more than once, "It's your wedding; you can do whatever you want." We planned almost every aspect of our wedding together, which was a great process for us. We learned a lot about decision-making, conflict resolution, and working toward a common goal. Decide what aspects of the day are the most important to each of you, and be willing to be flexible and compromise in other areas. We feel our relationship became stronger during the planning stages, and we ended up with the perfect wedding day we both envisioned.

> There is such a thing as too many choices in the wedding business, especially if you are having your wedding in a large city. Plan a budget and stick to it—otherwise, you can get carried away very easily. A wedding coordinator can help by recommending vendors that are right for you, which will give you a head start on the planning. Many of our vendors had worked together in the past, and that made everything run more smoothly.

> Try not to worry too much about all the details. If you do your homework and stay very organized, everything should fall into place. Hire a reputable wedding coordinator, and trust her to pull everything together. Teddy was a real blessing to us during the wedding weekend. The time flies by very quickly, and it was so nice to be able to relax and enjoy spending time with our family and friends, knowing that Teddy was there to handle any unexpected problems that might arise.

We re-entered the sanctuary following the recessional and released our guests from the pews. This worked more effectively than a receiving line and still gave us the opportunity to greet each of our guests and thank them for coming. We would also recommend having the majority of your photographs taken prior to the ceremony. After the ceremony, we couldn't wait to get to the reception to celebrate, and we didn't want to keep our guests waiting. We were alone when we saw each other for the first time before the ceremony, and that was a special, private time for us to exchange gifts and get all our tears out of the way.

The most important piece of advice I could give couples is to always stay focused on the true meaning of the day and the life you will have together after the wedding. The wedding day is only the first day of a whole lifetime together. Bryan gave me several cards throughout our engagement telling me how much he was looking forward to spending his life with me. Whenever the stress became intense, I would look at those cards and think that it would be worth it—and it was!

Rebecca Lynn Lueken and Todd Edwards Stewart

Date: October 2, 1999

Hometown: Chicago, Illinois

Guests: 175

Colors: Black and white, with a touch of rose

Attendants: 27 (more later)

Reception: Tented cocktail hour, formal seated dinner with DJ for dancing

When I first met Rebecca, I knew I was in for a treat, and I wasn't disappointed. Rebecca had so many wonderful ideas that made their wedding special—it's hard to know where to start. Let's start with the wedding party size. Now, 27 is a *big* wedding party, but with Rebecca's idea, it worked beautifully. Rebecca and Todd decided to include their immediate family in the wedding party—their siblings and spouses, and their nieces and nephews. They referred to it as a "gathering of both families." Rebecca's sister (matron of honor) and her three brothers with their families, plus Todd's two brothers with their two families, all processed down the aisle. At the correct pew, the family would be seated while the sibling walked on up into the altar area. It was really quite touching to see the whole family literally participating in this celebration.

Actually, I knew we were going to have a good time after I received her save-the-date card. The couple got engaged in January, and as Valentine's Day rolled around, they decided to send all the family and friends Valentine's card with their information enclosed. You will find this card in Chapter 15, "Extra! Extra! Read All About It!"

Instead of tossing petals or blowing bubbles, they released two turtledoves, which was very lovely and so romantic. At the reception, we had our cocktails in a tent behind the ballroom, and with the fall colors in the trees, it was very pretty. Then we entered the ballroom for a formal seated dinner. Rebecca and Todd decided to do their first dance at the beginning of the dinner, which worked out very nicely. Finally, they had such a unique engagement story that they had copies of the story framed and on each of the guest's table. As I said, they used some wonderful creativity in planning their special day.

Here's Rebecca's advice:

> *Start your planning early so that you can accomplish details throughout your engagement. That way it doesn't seem so overwhelming. Have fun, and enjoy the planning process because it goes by so fast. To you brides: If you have a good relationship with both your parents, take both parents with you to shop for your gown. It is a special time to share with both parents, and I can't explain what a special shopping trip that was. Plus, Dad loved telling the story to family and friends. Use humor during the entire process. When something doesn't go smoothly, keep laughing.*
>
> *Delegate planning items to your families and bridal party. Be sure to describe how you envision "finished" to look, and ask for the final right of refusal. That way, with only minor adjustments, you can check those items off the list.*
>
> *Hire a bridal consultant and vendors that you trust. That takes the anxiety and worry over details away. For example, our florist had great money-saving ideas, such as using my toss bouquet as our cake topper. Have the wedding videotaped. So many moments and expressions could be missed without it. After all, the bride doesn't get to see the wedding party walk down the aisle, and the groom doesn't get to see the final preparations, such as you putting on your veil. Finally, on your wedding day, remember that very few people will know all the details, so if something doesn't go exactly as planned, don't panic. No one will notice.*
>
> *We feel very blessed because we agreed on almost everything. Therefore, we planned a beautiful ceremony and a great party, including details important, unique, and special to us, and we had a wonderful day. We both agree we would do it all over again—with each other, of course.*

A Final Word

Over the past 15 years, I've learned so much about people, about commitment, and about what is *really* important to a wedding and the celebration that follows. I've worked with some absolutely delightful couples in my experiences. The trust and respect they have given to me makes me very humble. No amount of money could ever give me the satisfaction I've received from knowing these fine young men and women and being honored by them to help with one of the most important days in their lives.

The weddings you just read about are all different and unique to the particular couple—and they should be. This is *your* wedding—make it part of the two of you. It still amazes me how very different we all are and how we can take that uniqueness and use it to our benefit.

Enjoy this planning time. Spend it wisely, and spend it enjoying the time with each other. And, I do sincerely hope that no matter where you are, all your dreams come true and you live happily ever after. With blessings and my very best wishes!

The Least You Need to Know

➤ Use your imagination and uniqueness to make this *your* wedding.

➤ Delay leaving for your honeymoon for a day to give yourselves some down time.

➤ If at all possible, take *all* the photos before the ceremony.

➤ Have fun!

Glossary

birdseed, petal, or bubble attendants   These are the folks who will distribute birdseed, petals, or bubbles to guests at the appropriate time (your exit) so that you can be showered with them.

bodice form   A piece of cardboard shaped like a woman's upper body that the bridal shop places in the bodice of the gown to keep it wrinkle-free and looking fresh. This protects the gown during travel time from the shop to the home or ceremony site.

bridal consultant   Title used to describe both consultants and coordinators, unless specifically stated otherwise.

bustling   Hooks and eyes or buttons are sewn onto the back of the gown at appropriate places to bustle the gown. When the buttons are looped, the train is pulled up, or bustled, so that the bride can move more freely during the reception.

cash bar   If you offer a cash bar at your reception, your guests will pay for their drinks. You may offer wine and soft drinks; if guests want something else in the way of liquor, they can buy it from the bartender.

cathedral-length veil   A veil four yards long (12 feet).

chapel-length veil   A veil three yards long (nine feet).

elbow-length veil   A veil that brushes the elbows.

engraved invitations   Invitations in which the paper is stamped with a mold, leaving an indentation in the paper.

favor   A little gift you give your guests as a thank-you for attending your wedding.

finger-tip veil   A veil that just brushes the shoulders and frames the face.

gift attendant   At the reception, this is the person in charge of taking gifts from the guests and placing them in the appropriate spot (either on a gift table or in a locked room).

gift bearer   During a Catholic service, the gift bearer brings the bread and wine to the priest.

guest book attendant   This person, male or female, greets guests as they enter the ceremony site or reception site (depending on where the guest book is placed) and asks guests to sign the guest book.

honorary flower girl   An honorary flower girl is usually someone who is too young to be the official flower girl, yet is honored by being given this title.

in-house caterer   Refers to a caterer who provides the food for functions within a particular facility.

limited bar   A bar in which you limit what is served to the guests. Often a limited bar will feature both wine and beer, plus soft drinks or maybe punch.

open bar   A bar containing hard liquor for mixed drinks, plus beer and wine and maybe even after-dinner drinks. Nonalcoholic beverages should be provided as well.

outside caterer   An outside caterer is an independent caterer you hire on your own, from outside the facility.

personal attendant   This is a close friend of the bride who is there to help, run errands, and be supportive.

program attendant   This person usually stands by the guest book and distributes the wedding programs; this person also acts as a greeter.

readers   During the service, you may have several readings. This is a responsible job for the right person.

reception assistants   These folks, usually ladies, are asked to help with the reception foods, mostly cutting and serving the wedding cake.

wedding professional   Describes anyone in the wedding business, but doesn't specifically mean that the person is a wedding consultant or coordinator.

"within the ribbon" cards   Cards enclosed with the invitation that give guests special seating "within the ribbon" or in a reserved spot. Within the ribbon cards are usually used for very large and very formal weddings where many guests are expected and seating special family members is a must.

Further Reading

Books

Aertker, Paul, and Katherine Aertker. *Write After the Wedding*. Paint Press, LLC, 1994.

Batts, Sidney F. *The Protestant Wedding Sourcebook*. Westminster/John Knox Press, 1993.

Dlugosch, Sharon. *Wedding Plans: 50 Unique Themes for the Wedding of Your Dreams*. Brighton Publications, Inc., 1989.

Editors of *Bride's* Magazine with Antonia van der Meer. Bride's *New Ways to Wed*. Perigee, 1990.

Eklof, Barbara. *With These Words … I Thee Wed*. Adams Media Corporation, 1989.

Exley, Helen. *The Bride*. Exley Gift Books, 1998.

Feinberg, Steven L., ed. *Crane's Blue Book of Stationery*. Doubleday, 1989.

Glusker, David, and Peter Misner. *Words for Your Wedding*. Harper & Row, 1983.

Goldman, Larry. *Dressing the Bride*. Crown Publishers, 1993.

Klausner, Abraham J. *Weddings: A Complete Guide to All Religious and Interfaith Marriage Services*. Alpha Publishing Co., 1986.

Lipsett, Linda O. *To Love and To Cherish*. The Quilt Digest Press, 1989.

Loring, John. *The Tiffany Wedding*. Doubleday, 1988.

Muzzy, Ruth, and R. Kent Hughes. *The Christian Wedding Planner*. Tyndale Publishers, Inc., 1991.

Munro, Eleanor C., ed. *Wedding Readings*. Penguin Group, 1989.

Post, Elizabeth L. *Emily Post on Second Weddings*. HarperCollins, 1991.

Smith, Lauren. *Colors for Brides*. Acropolis Books Ltd., 1989.

Sowden, Cynthia Lueck. *Wedding Occasions: 101 New Party Themes for Wedding Showers, Rehearsal Dinners, Engagement Parties, and More*. Brighton Publications, Inc., 1990.

Tober, Barbara, ed. *The Bride: A Celebration.* Longmeadow Press, 1992.

Warner, Diane. *Complete Book of Wedding Toasts.* Career Press, 1997.

Worman, Catherine. *The Classic Wedding Dress.* Chartwell Books, Inc., 1993.

Magazines

Bridal Guide

Brides and Your New Home

Elegant Bride

Modern Bride

Victoria

Wedding Cakes—Wilton Industries (www.wilton.com)

Index

X–Y–Z